Microsoft® Office 2007 For Seniors For Dummies®

Cheat Sheet

Standard Word, Excel, and PowerPoint Shortcuts

To Do This . . .	With the Mouse . . .	With the Keyboard . . .
Open file.	Office⇨Open	Ctrl+O
Print current document.	Office⇨Print	Ctrl+P
Save your work.	Office⇨Save As Save button on Quick Access toolbar	Ctrl+S
Copy selection to the Clipboard.	Home⇨Clipboard⇨Copy Right-click and choose Copy	Ctrl+C
Cut selection to Clipboard.	Home⇨Clipboard⇨Cut Right-click and choose Cut	Ctrl+X
Paste selection to Clipboard.	Home⇨Clipboard⇨Paste Right-click and choose Paste	Ctrl+V
Select all content.	*Word or PowerPoint:* Home⇨Editing⇨Select⇨Select All *Excel:* Click box at intersection of row numbers and column headers	Ctrl+A
Left-align a paragraph.	Home⇨Paragraph⇨Left Align	Ctrl+L
Center a paragraph.	Home⇨Paragraph⇨Center	Ctrl+E
Right-align a paragraph.	Home⇨Paragraph⇨Right Align	Ctrl+R
Make text bold.	Home⇨Font⇨Bold Right-click and click the Bold button	Ctrl+B
Make text italicized.	Home⇨Font⇨Italic Right-click and click the Italic button	Ctrl+I

Microsoft® Office 2007 For Seniors For Dummies®

Cheat Sheet

To Do This . . .	With the Mouse . . .	With the Keyboard . . .
Open Find dialog box.	Home⇨Editing⇨Find	Ctrl+F
Open Replace dialog box.	Home⇨Editing⇨Replace	Ctrl+H
Undo previous action.	Undo button on Quick Access toolbar	Ctrl+Z
Redo previous Undo.	Redo button on Quick Access toolbar	Ctrl+Y

Word Shortcuts

To Do This . . .	With the Mouse . . .	With the Keyboard . . .
Insert page break.	Insert⇨Pages⇨Page Break	Ctrl+Enter
Show/hide non-printing symbols.	Home⇨Font⇨¶	Ctrl+*
Clear formatting.	Home⇨Font⇨Clear Formatting	Ctrl+spacebar
Set page margins.	Page Layout⇨Page Setup⇨Margins	Alt+P, M
Number pages.	Insert⇨Header & Footer⇨Page Number	Alt+N, N, U
Indent a paragraph (all lines).	Home⇨Paragraph⇨Increase Indent	Alt+H, A, I
Indent paragraph (first line only).	n/a	Tab (at beginning of paragraph)

For Dummies: Bestselling Book Series for Beginners

Microsoft® Office 2007 For Seniors

FOR DUMMIES®

by Faithe Wempen

WILEY

Wiley Publishing, Inc.

Microsoft® Office 2007 For Seniors For Dummies®

Published by
Wiley Publishing, Inc.
111 River Street
Hoboken, NJ 07030-5774

www.wiley.com

Copyright © 2009 by Wiley Publishing, Inc., Indianapolis, Indiana

Published by Wiley Publishing, Inc., Indianapolis, Indiana

Published simultaneously in Canada

For general information on our other products and services, please contact our Customer Care Department within the U.S. at 877-762-2974, outside the U.S. at 317-572-3993, or fax 317-572-4002.

For technical support, please visit www.wiley.com/techsupport.

Wiley also publishes its books in a variety of electronic formats. Some content that appears in print may not be available in electronic books.

Library of Congress Control Number: 2009929486

ISBN: 978-0-470-49725-8

Manufactured in the United States of America

10 9 8 7 6 5 4 3 2 1

WILEY

About the Author

Faithe Wempen, MA, is a Microsoft Office Master Instructor and the author of more than 100 books on computer hardware and software, including *The PowerPoint 2007 Bible* and *A+ Certification Workbook For Dummies*. She is an adjunct instructor of Computer Information Technology at Purdue University, and her corporate training courses online have reached more than one-quarter of a million students for clients such as Hewlett-Packard, Sony, and CNET.

Dedication

To Margaret

Author's Acknowledgments

Thanks to the wonderful editorial staff at Wiley for another job well done. You guys are top notch!

Publisher's Acknowledgments

We're proud of this book; please send us your comments through our online registration form located at //dummies.custhelp.com. For other comments, please contact our Customer Care ment within the U.S. at 877-762-2974, outside the U.S. at 317-572-3993, or fax 317-572-4002.

of the people who helped bring this book to market include the following:

itions, Editorial, and Media Development

ject Editor: Pat O'Brien

Acquisitions Editor: Katie Mohr

Senior Copy Editor: Teresa Artman

Technical Editor: Vince McCune

Editorial Manager: Kevin Kirschner

Sr. Editorial Assistant: Cherie Case

Cartoons: Rich Tennant
(www.the5thwave.com)

Composition Services

Project Coordinator: Katherine Crocker

Layout and Graphics: Samantha Allen, Reuben W. Davis, Christin Swinford, Christine Williams

Proofreader: Betty Kish

Indexer: Ty Koontz

Publishing and Editorial for Technology Dummies

Richard Swadley, Vice President and Executive Group Publisher

Andy Cummings, Vice President and Publisher

Mary Bednarek, Executive Acquisitions Director

Mary C. Corder, Editorial Director

Publishing for Consumer Dummies

Diane Graves Steele, Vice President and Publisher

Composition Services

Debbie Stailey, Director of Composition Services

Contents at a Glance

Introduction 1

Part 1: Getting Started with Office 5

Chapter1: The Two-Dollar Tour 7

Chapter 2: Exploring the Common Features of Office 2007 25

Chapter 3: Opening, Saving, and Printing Files 47

Part 11: Word 67

Chapter 4: Composing Your Thoughts in Word 69

Chapter 5: Dressing Up Your Documents 89

Chapter 6: Taking Word to the Next Level 113

Part 111: Excel 133

Chapter 7: Creating Basic Spreadsheets in Excel 135

Chapter 8: Doing the Math: Formulas and Functions 155

Chapter 9: Creating Visual Interest with Formatting
  and Charts 169

Chapter 10: Using Excel as a Database 191

Part 1V: Outlook 207

Chapter 11: Managing E-Mail with Outlook 209

Chapter 12: Managing the Details: Contacts, Notes, and Tasks 231

Chapter 13: Your Busy Life: Using the Calendar 253

Part V: PowerPoint 265

Chapter 14: Getting Started with PowerPoint 267

Chapter 15: Dressing Up Your Presentations 285

Chapter 16: Adding Movement and Sound 299

Chapter 17: Presenting the Show 311

Appendix: Customizing Office Applications 323

Index 331

Contents

Introduction... 1

    About This Book 1

    Foolish Assumptions 2

    How This Book Is Organized 2

    Time to Get Started! 3

Part 1: Getting Started with Office 5

    Chapter 1: The Two-Dollar Tour 7

        Start an Office Application 8

        Explore the Office Ribbon and Tabs.................................9

        Understand the Office Button and Office Menu 13

        Create a Document 15

        Type Text 15

        Insert a Picture..16

        Move Around in a Document 18

        Select Content 20

        Zoom In and Out...21

        Change the View 22

    **Chapter 2: Exploring the Common Features
        of Office 2007** 25

        Edit Text...26

        Move and Copy Content 28

        Choose Fonts and Font Sizes 31

        Apply Text Formatting 34

        Use the Mini Toolbar..36

        Work with Themes...37

        Check Your Spelling and Grammar..................................42

Chapter 3: Opening, Saving, and Printing Files 47

Save Your Work 48
Open a Saved File 53
Change the File Listing View 55
E-Mail Your Work to Others 55
Share Your Work in Other Formats 58
Print Your Work 62
Use Print Preview Before You Print 63
Recover Lost Work 65

Part II: Word *67*

Chapter 4: Composing Your Thoughts in Word 69
Examine the Word Interface 70
Move Around and Select Text..71
Choose Paper Size and Orientation..71
Set Margins 73
Select the Right Screen View..74
Align and Indent Paragraphs 77
Change Line Spacing..82
Create Bullet and Numbered Lists 85

Chapter 5: Dressing Up Your Documents 89
Apply Styles and Style Sets 90
Insert Clip Art 96
Insert Photos.. 100
Change the Text Wrap Setting for a Picture 101
Add a Page Border.. 102
Apply a Background Color to a Page.. 105
Create Tables 107
Format a Table.. 110

Chapter 6: Taking Word to the Next Level 113
Number the Pages 114
Use Headers and Footers.. 116
Insert Cover Pages and Other Building Blocks 119

Print an Envelope... 122

Perform a Mail Merge 123

Insert the Date and Time 129

Part III: Excel 133

Chapter 7: Creating Basic Spreadsheets in Excel 135

Understand Excel's Unique Features............................. 136

Get Familiar with Spreadsheet Structure 138

Move the Cell Cursor... 138

Select a Range 139

Type and Edit Cell Contents 143

Save Your Work.. 145

Insert and Delete Rows, Columns, and Cells................. 146

Work with Worksheets.. 151

Chapter 8: Doing the Math: Formulas and Functions 155

Learn How Formulas Are Structured 155

Write Formulas That Reference Cells............................ 156

Move and Copy Cell Content 157

Reference a Cell on Another Sheet 160

Understand Functions 160

Take a Tour of Some Basic Functions............................ 163

Explore Financial Functions 165

Chapter 9: Creating Visual Interest with Formatting and Charts 169

Adjust Row Height and Column Width.......................... 170

Wrap Text in a Cell 171

Apply Gridlines or Borders... 172

Apply Fill Color... 175

Format Text in Cells... 177

Format the Spreadsheet as a Whole.............................. 180

Create a Basic Chart 181

Identify the Parts of a Chart... 184

Format a Chart 185

Chapter 10: Using Excel as a Database 191

Understand Databases 191

Prepare a List for a Mail Merge 192

Store Data in a Table 193

Sort a Table 195

Filter Data in a Table 197

Split a Column's Content 201

Merge the Contents of Columns 203

Part IV: Outlook 207

Chapter 11: Managing E-Mail with Outlook 209

Set Up Outlook 209

Set Up Additional Mail Accounts 212

Troubleshoot Mail Setup Problems 214

Take a Quick Tour of Outlook's Mail Feature 217

Receive and Read Your Mail 218

View Photos and Other Attachments 220

Reply to a Message 221

Compose a Message 223

Attach a File to a Message 225

Avoid Frauds, Scams, and Viruses 226

Chapter 12: Managing the Details: Contacts, Notes, and Tasks 231

Store Contact Information 232

Edit and Delete Contacts 235

Choose How the Contact List Appears 237

Use the Contacts List 238

Create Notes 240

Categorize Notes 243

Use Tasks and the To-Do List 245

Update the Status of a Task 249

Set a Task Reminder 250

Chapter 13: Your Busy Life: Using the Calendar.............. 253

View Your Calendar 253

Create and Delete a Calendar Event 255

Set an Event to Recur 257

Configure Event Reminders 259

Add Holidays... 261

Categorize Events 261

Print a Hard Copy of Your Calendar.............................. 263

Part V: PowerPoint.. **265**

Chapter 14: Getting Started with PowerPoint 267

Explore the PowerPoint Interface 268

Work with PowerPoint Files... 269

Understand PowerPoint Views.. 271

Create New Slides 273

Use Slide Placeholders.. 274

Turn Text AutoFit Off or On 276

Change Slide Layouts.. 278

Move or Resize Slide Content 279

Manually Place Text on a Slide 280

Navigating and Selecting Text 282

Select Content 283

Chapter 15: Dressing Up Your Presentations................... 285

Understand and Apply Themes....................................... 286

Change the Presentation Colors 288

Edit Slide Masters 289

Format Text Boxes and Placeholders 291

Insert Clip Art.. 292

Insert Pictures from Files 294

Create a Photo Album Presentation 295

Chapter 16: Adding Movement and Sound 299

    Animate Objects on a Slide 300

    Add Slide Transition Effects 305

    Set Slides to Automatically Advance 306

    Add a Musical Soundtrack 307

Chapter 17: Presenting the Show 311

    Display a Slide Show Onscreen 312

    Use the Slide Show Tools 313

    Print Copies of a Presentation 315

    Package a Presentation on a CD 317

    Save a Web Version of a Presentation 319

Appendix: Customizing Office Applications 323

    Customize the Quick Access Toolbar 324

    Customize the Status Bar 326

    Set Word, Excel, and PowerPoint Options 327

    Set Outlook Options 329

Index *331*

Microsoft Office 2007 is by far the most popular suite of productivity applications in the world, and with good reason. Its applications are powerful enough for business and professional use, and yet easy enough that a beginner can catch on to the basics with just a few simple lessons.

If you're new to Office 2007, this book can help you separate the essential features you need from the obscure and more sophisticated ones that you don't. For the four major Office applications I cover in this book — Word, Excel, PowerPoint, and Outlook — I walk you through the most important and common features, showing you how to put them to work for projects in your job, everyday life, and home.

About This Book

This book is written specifically for mature people like you, who are relatively new to using Office applications and want to master the basics. In this book, I tried to take into account the types of activities that might interest you, such as investment planning; personal finance; e-mail; and documents and presentations you might need for work, clubs, volunteer opportunities, or other organizations that you participate in.

Introduction

Conventions used in this book

This book uses certain conventions to help you find your way:

→ Wherever possible, I use labels on figures to point out what you should notice on them. These labels reinforce something I say in the text or contain extra tips and hints.

→ When you have to type something, I put it in **bold** type.

→ For menu and Ribbon commands, I use the ⇨ symbol to separate the steps. For example, if I say to choose Home⇨Copy, click the Home tab and then click the Copy button.

→ The big round button in the upper-left corner of most Office applications (Word, Excel, and PowerPoint) is the Office button. That's what I call it in commands such as Office⇨Print.

 Tip icons point out extra features, special insights and helps, or things to look out for.

Warning icons indicate potential problems to avoid that are difficult to fix or make bad things happen.

Foolish Assumptions

This book assumes that you can start your computer and use the keyboard and mouse (or whatever device moves the pointer onscreen).

 If you're using a computer for the first time, *Computers For Seniors For Dummies* shows you the essential skills that all computer applications use.

Office 2007 runs on Windows Vista (the newest version of Windows) and Windows XP computer operating systems, so I assume you're using one of these. Most of the examples in this book show Office 2007 running in Vista, but Office works the same in both systems.

How This Book Is Organized

This book is divided into several handy parts to help you find what you need and skip stuff you don't use.

Part I: Getting Started with Office

In this first part of the book, I explain some basics that apply to all the Office 2007 applications generically, such as saving, opening, and printing files. I also show you some features that all Office 2007 applications have in common, such as selecting and formatting text, using the Clipboard, and applying formatting themes.

Part II: Word

This part explores the most popular application in the Office suite, Microsoft Word. This word processing program helps you create letters, reports, envelopes, and myriad other text-based documents. You'll see how to format text, change page size and orientation, insert graphics, and more.

Part III: Excel

In this part of the book, you can read about Excel, the Office spreadsheet application. See how to enter text and numbers in a worksheet, how to write formulas and functions that perform calculations, and how to format worksheets attractively. You can also find out how to create charts and use Excel to store simple databases.

Part IV: Outlook

Outlook is the e-mail, contact management, and calendar application in Office. In this part of the book, discover how to send and receive e-mail in Outlook, and also how to use Outlook to track appointments and store your personal address book.

Part V: PowerPoint

In this part of the book, I show you the basics of PowerPoint, the Office presentation application. You can read how to create presentations that include text and graphics; create cool animation and transition effects; add a musical soundtrack; and share your presentation with others, either in a live-action show or on CD.

 The Appendix shows some simple ways to customize how Office applications work when you start them.

Time to Get Started!

This is your book; use it how you want. You can start at the beginning and read it straight through, or you can hop to whatever chapter or topic you want. For those of you who are pretty new to computers, you might want to start at the beginning. If you're new to Office, the beginning part will give you a good foundation on what features work similarly in all the programs.

 If you've used older versions of Office, Office 2007 looks and functions very differently from earlier versions. Start at the beginning for a primer of the new screens and where your favorite buttons and features are located now.

Part I
Getting Started with Office

The 5th Wave   By Rich Tennant

"No, that's not the icon for Excel, it's the icon for Excuse, the database of reasons why you haven't learned the other programs in Office."

The Two-Dollar Tour

Step right up for a tour of Microsoft Office, the most popular suite of applications in the world!

Here are some of the things you can do with Office:

➧ Write letters, reports, and newsletters.

➧ Track bank account balances and investments.

➧ Create presentations to support speeches and meetings.

➧ Send and receive e-mail.

The Office suite consists of several very powerful applications (programs), each with its own features and interface, but the applications also have a lot in common with one another. Learning about one application gives you a head start in learning the others.

In this chapter (and Chapter 2), I take you on a quick tour of some of the features that multiple Office applications have in common, including the tabbed Ribbon area. In this chapter, I show you how to insert text and graphics in the various applications, and how to move around and zoom in and out.

Get ready to . . .

➧ Start an Office Application 8

➧ Explore the Office Ribbon and Tabs 9

➧ Understand the Office Button and Office Menu 13

➧ Create a Document 15

➧ Type Text 15

➧ Insert a Picture 16

➧ Move Around in a Document 18

➧ Select Content 20

➧ Zoom In and Out 21

➧ Change the View 22

This book shows Microsoft Office in the Windows Vista operating system, not Windows XP. Office works the same way in both versions of Windows except for minor differences in the dialog boxes where files are saved and opened. Those differences are covered in Chapter 3.

Start an Office Application

All the Office applications are available from the Start menu in Windows, as shown in Figure 1-1.

Office applications are in
the Microsoft Office folder

Figure 1-1

To start any of the applications, follow these steps:

1. Click the **Start** button.

2. Click All Programs.

3. Click Microsoft Office.

4. Click the Office **application** you want to start.

Explore the Office Ribbon and Tabs

All Office 2007 applications (except Outlook) have a common system of navigation called the *Ribbon*, which is a tabbed bar across the top of the application window. Each tab is like a page of buttons. You click different tabs to access different sets of buttons and features.

Figure 1-2 shows the Ribbon in Microsoft Word, with the Home tab displayed. Within a tab, buttons are organized into groups. In Figure 1-2, the Home tab's groups are Clipboard, Font, Paragraph, Styles, and Editing.

This tab is currently active   You might not have this tab

Click a different tab to activate it   Help button

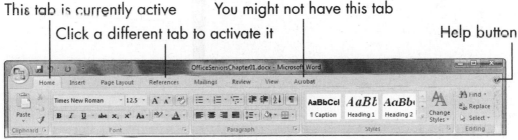

Figure 1-2

Each Office application has a set of tabs for the tasks it performs. For example, Word has a Mailings tab that holds the commands for doing mail merges. Excel has a Formulas tab that holds the commands for setting up calculations.

You might find tabs that were added by *third-party* (non-Microsoft) software. For example, Figure 1-2 has an Acrobat tab. A program called Adobe Acrobat is installed on this computer.

The buttons and controls on the tabs operate in different ways. Figure 1-3 points out some examples on the Paragraph group on Word's Home tab.

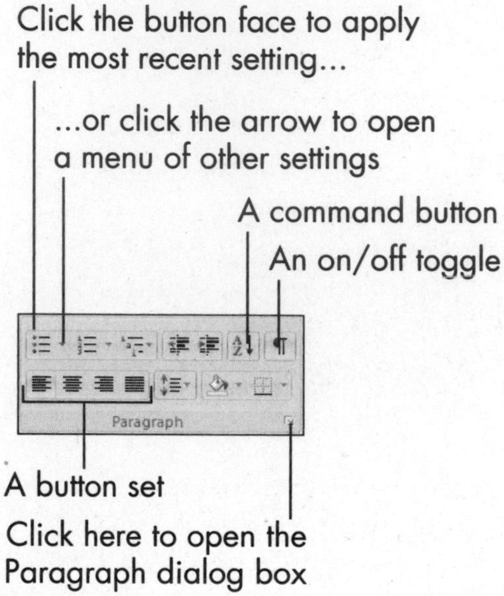

Click the button face to apply
the most recent setting...

...or click the arrow to open
a menu of other settings

A command button

An on/off toggle

A button set

Click here to open the
Paragraph dialog box

Figure 1-3

➥ **On/off toggles:** When the button is selected (it turns orange), the feature is on. Each time you click the button, it switches between on and off.

➥ **Command buttons:** When you click the button, the command executes. If you click a command button again, the command repeats.

➥ **Connected button sets:** In connected sets of buttons, selecting a button deselects (cancels) the previous selection in the set.

For example, Figure 1-3 has four buttons in the bottom row for paragraph alignment. The leftmost one is selected; if you clicked one of the others, it's automatically canceled.

➡ **Menu buttons:** Buttons with arrows on them open menus or color palettes.

 You can hover the mouse pointer over a button to see a pop-up box, called a ScreenTip, that tells the button's name and/or purpose.

With some buttons that contain arrows, you can click anywhere on the button face — directly on the arrow or not — to open the menu or *palette* (an array of colored squares from which you can choose a color). With others, the button face and the arrow are separate clickable areas. Clicking the arrow opens the menu, but clicking the button face applies whatever setting was most recently chosen from the menu.

To tell the difference between the two types of menu buttons, point the mouse at the button. If you see a thin line separating the arrow from the button face, it's the type where you have to click directly on the arrow to get the menu. If there's no separator line, you can click anywhere on the button.

In the bottom-right corner of many of the groups is a small square with an arrow. Clicking this button opens a dialog box related to that group. For example, the one for the Paragraph group in Figure 1-3 opens the Paragraph dialog box, which contains controls for every button in that group plus more options not available on the Ribbon.

At the far right of the Ribbon is a question mark button, the Help button. You can click **Help** at any time to open the Help system for the application you have open.

When you resize the application's window so the window is narrower than normal, or when you run the application on a computer that has low-resolution video settings, the controls on the Ribbon *compress* (squeeze together). Some of the groups turn into single buttons with drop-down lists for accessing the individual controls within that group. For example, in Figure 1-4, most of the groups are compressed, and one of the groups has been opened as a drop-down list.

Click the button for a collapsed group...

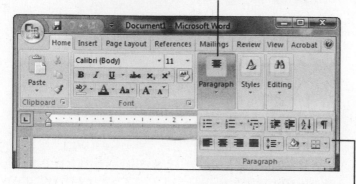

...to expand the group and
select a command from it

Figure 1-4

Above the main part of the Ribbon is a small toolbar called the Quick Access toolbar. This is the only customizable area of the Ribbon. You can add buttons for frequently used commands here (as many as you can fit). To add a button, right-click any **control** from any tab and choose **Add to Quick Access Toolbar**, as shown in Figure 1-5. To change the position of the Quick Access Toolbar, right-click it and choose **Show the Quick Access Toolbar Below the Ribbon** (or Above, if it's already below).

Quick Access Toolbar

Right-click any control on any
tab to add it to the toolbar

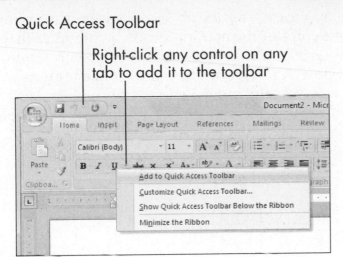

Figure 1-5

Understand the Office Button and Office Menu

The Office menu provides access to commands that have to do with
the data file you are working with—things like saving, opening, printing, mailing, and checking its properties. Open the Office menu by
clicking the big round button (the **Office button**) at the upper left.

 The Office menu is similar to the File menu in older
Office applications.

The Office menu is organized in two columns, as shown in Figure 1-6:

⟹ **Left column:** Commands you can select.

⟹ **Right column:** Shortcuts to recently used files. Click
any of these **shortcuts** to reopen that data file.

Office button   Recently used documents

Commands with arrows open submenus

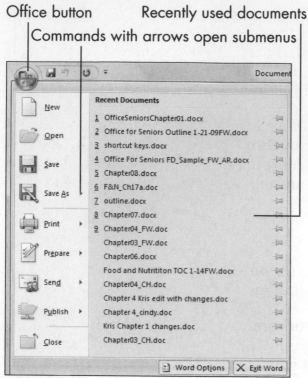

Figure 1-6

Some commands on the Office menu have arrows to their right. These open submenus with more options on them. For example, when you point to the **Send** command, a submenu of commands related to sending documents appears.

Some of the commands that have arrows next to them, such as Print and Save As, are dual function:

➡ Point to its **arrow** to open its submenu of more choices.

➡ Click directly on the **command** to choose the most common option for it.

At the bottom right of the menu is an Exit button, which you click to quit the application. Next to that is an Options button, which opens a dialog box from which you can control the settings for the application. Each of these is named for the application; in Figure 1-6, they're Exit Word and Word Options.

Create a Document

In Word, Excel, and PowerPoint, a new document (or workbook, or presentation) opens automatically when you start the program. You can just start typing or inserting content into it.

You can also create additional new documents. An easy shortcut to do so is to press Ctrl+N. You can also choose Office⇨New. That latter method has the advantage of opening up a dialog box where you can choose a template, if you don't want a totally blank document to start with.

Type Text

Putting text on the page (or onscreen) is a little different in each of the three major Office applications: Word, Excel, and PowerPoint.

➠ **Word:** The main work area of the program is a blank slate on which you can type directly. Just click in the work area and start typing! Chapter 2 explains more about typing and editing text. See Figure 1-7.

In Word, there is a single work area

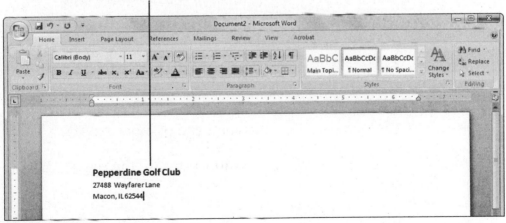

Figure 1-7

➠ **Excel:** The work area is divided into a grid of cells. Click any **cell** to make it active, and type to place text into it, as in Figure 1-8. Chapter 7 shows how to work with text in Excel cells.

In Excel, text is entered into individual cells

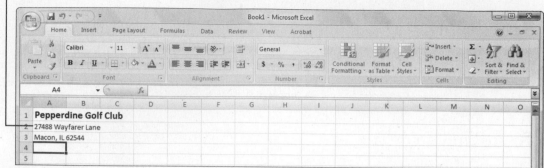

Figure 1-8

➠ **PowerPoint:** The work area is divided into three panes. The largest one, in the center, is where you insert content on a slide.

- If a slide has a text placeholder on it, you can click in the **placeholder** and type, as in Figure 1-9.

- If there isn't a placeholder on the slide, or if the placeholder doesn't meet your needs, you can place a **text box** on the slide manually. (That's covered in Chapter 11.)

Insert a Picture

All Office applications accept various types of pictures. Here's how to insert a photo (or other graphic file) into Word, Excel, or PowerPoint:

1. Click the **Insert** tab.

2. Click the **Picture** button. The Insert Picture dialog box opens. See Figure 1-10. The default location that opens is the Pictures folder for the user currently logged into Windows.

In PowerPoint, text is entered in placeholder boxes on slide layouts

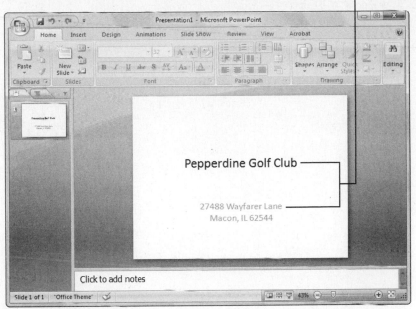

Figure 1-9

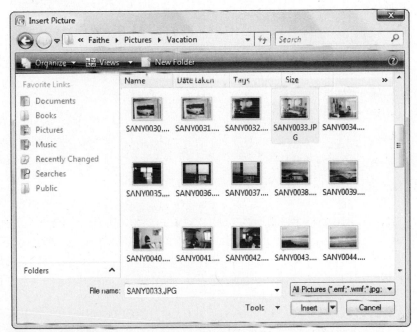

Figure 1-10

3. Select the **picture** you want to insert. (You might need to change to a different location. That's covered in Chapter 3.)

4. Click the **Insert** button.

The preceding steps apply to picture files, such as images from a digital camera or that you downloaded from the Internet. There are lots of other graphic types, such as clip art, WordArt (stylized text), and drawn lines and shapes. Each of these has its own procedure for insertion. Later chapters discuss these in more detail.

 You can drag and drop pictures directly into any document in an Office application.

Move Around in a Document

As you add content in one of the applications, there might be so much content that you can't see it all onscreen at once. You might need to scroll through the document to view different parts of it.

The simplest way to move around is by using the **scroll bars** with your mouse:

➡ In Excel, a vertical (up and down) and a horizontal (left to right) scroll bar are always available.

➡ In Word and PowerPoint, the vertical scroll bar is always available. The horizontal scroll bar disappears if there is no undisplayed text from side-to-side.

Figure 1-11 shows several ways to use a scroll bar:

➡ Click the **arrow** at the end of a scroll bar to scroll the display slowly in the direction of the arrow (a small amount each time you click).

➡ Drag the box in the **scroll bar** to scroll quickly.

⇒ Click in the empty space on the bar to one side or the other of the scroll box to move one screenful at a time in that direction.

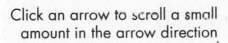

Drag the scroll box to scroll quickly

Click an arrow to scroll a small amount in the arrow direction

Click above or below the scroll box to scroll one screenful

Figure 1-11

The size of the scroll box (the blank rectangle you drag in the scroll bar) indicates how much content you can't see at the moment. For example, in Figure 1-11, the scroll bar occupies most of the scroll bar; this means that there isn't much undisplayed content. In a very large spreadsheet, the scroll bar might be very small.

You can also move around by using keyboard shortcuts. As you gain experience with the applications,
you might find using keyboard shortcuts more convenient than using than the scroll bar. Chapter 4 lists
shortcuts for Word, Chapter 7 lists shortcuts for
Excel, and Chapter 14 lists shortcuts for PowerPoint.

Select Content

Selecting content is an essential skill for any Office application. Many
commands in Office applications apply to whatever text or graphics
you select. For example, to make some text bold, select it first, and
then click the Bold button. Figure 1-12 shows some selected text.

Figure 1-12

To select text in Word or PowerPoint, you can either

➡ Drag the **mouse pointer** across it (holding down the
left mouse button).

➡ Click where you want to start and then hold down **Shift**
as you press the arrow keys to extend the selection.

When text is selected, its background changes color. The color depends
on the color scheme in use; with the default color scheme, it's light
blue.

In Excel, you usually want to select entire cells rather than individual
bits of text; when the cell is selected, any formatting or other commands that you issue applies to everything in that cell. To select a cell,

click it. You can extend the selection to multiple cells by dragging across them or by holding down **Shift** and pressing the **arrow keys**.

 You can also select text by using keyboard shortcuts. Chapter 4 lists shortcuts for Word, Chapter 7 lists shortcuts for Excel, and Chapter 14 lists shortcuts for PowerPoint.

To select a graphic, click it with the mouse. Selection handles appear around the outside of it. Depending on the graphic type, these handles are blue circles or black squares. Figure 1-13 shows a selected graphic in Word.

Selection handles

Figure 1-13

When a graphic is selected, you can do any of the following to it:

➡ **Move it.** Position the **mouse pointer** on the graphic (not on the border) and drag.

➡ **Copy it.** Hold down the **Ctrl** key while you move it.

➡ **Resize it.** Position the **mouse pointer** on one of the selection handles and drag.

➡ **Delete it.** Press the **Delete** key.

Zoom In and Out

While you're working in an Office application, you might want to zoom in to see a close-up view of part of your work, or zoom out to see a bird's-eye view of the whole project. The lower the zoom percentage, the smaller everything looks — and the more you can see onscreen at once, without scrolling.

Word, Excel, and PowerPoint all have the same Zoom controls, located in the bottom right of the window. (There are also zoom controls on the View tab in each application.) Figure 1-14 shows the Zoom controls on the status bar.

➥ Drag the **slider** to adjust the zoom (to the left to zoom out, and to the right to zoom in).

➥ Click the **minus** or **plus button** (at opposite ends of the slider) to slightly zoom out (minus) or in (plus).

➥ Clicking the **number** of the current zoom percentage opens a Zoom dialog box, which shows more zooming options.

 Zooming doesn't affect the size of printouts. It is only an onscreen adjustment.

View buttons (different in each application)

100%

Drag Zoom slider

Click here for Zoom dialog box

Figure 1-14

Change the View

Each Office application has a variety of viewing options available. Each view is suited for a certain type of activity in that application. For example, in Word, you can choose Draft view, which is speedy to work with and presents the text in a simple one-column layout. Or, you can choose a Print Layout view, where you can see any special layout formatting you applied, such as multiple columns.

Each application has shortcut buttons to the most common views. You can find these buttons to the left of the Zoom slider, as pointed out in Figure 1-14. Hover your **mouse** over a button to find out which view it selects. These views are available:

➠ **Excel**

- *Normal:* Displays a regular row-and-column grid

- *Page Layout:* Displays the content as it will appear on a printed page

➠ **Word**

- *Print Layout:* Shows the document approximately as it will be printed, including any layout features, such as multiple columns

- *Full-screen Reading:* Displays the document in a format that's easy to read onscreen

- *Web Layout:* Displays the document as it will appear if saved as a Web page and published on a Web site

- *Outline:* Displays the document as an outline, with headings as outline levels

- *Draft:* Displays the document in simple text form, in a single column

➠ PowerPoint

- *Normal:* This default view provides multiple panes for working with the content.

- *Slide Sorter:* All of the slides appear as thumbnail images, which is useful for rearranging the order of slides.

- *Slide Show:* The presentation is shown to the audience, one slide at a time.

- *Notes Page:* Each slide appears as a graphic on a page where notes are displayed.

 Notes Page view is available only from the View tab, not from the buttons.

Enjoying the tour so far? There's lots more ahead in Chapter 2, where I continue walking you through the important features that the Office apps have in common.

Exploring the Common Features of Office 2007

Text handling is quite standardized in Word, Excel, and PowerPoint. The same commands that you use to edit and format text in one program work almost exactly the same way in another. So, after you master them in one application, you'll be off and running in the others.

Some of these standardized features include

➡ **The Clipboard,** which lets you copy and move content seamlessly between applications

➡ **Text formatting,** which you use to format text with the same set of Font tools, no matter which application you're in

➡ **Themes,** which help you apply consistent formatting to documents created in different programs

➡ **The spell checker,** which you use to correct your spelling and grammar in all applications, and even maintain common custom dictionaries between them

Get ready to . . .

➡ Edit Text 26

➡ Move and Copy Content 28

➡ Choose Fonts and Font Sizes 31

➡ Apply Text Formatting 34

➡ Use the Mini Toolbar 36

➡ Work with Themes 37

➡ Check Your Spelling and Grammar 42

This chapter looks at each of these standard tools plus a few other handy standardized tools.

Edit Text

In Word, Excel, and PowerPoint, you just click where you want the text to go, and begin typing. (Chapter 1 covers the basics.)

The *insertion point* is the flashing vertical marker (cursor) that shows where the text that you type will appear. You can move the insertion point with the arrow keys, or you can click where you want to place it.

When the mouse pointer is over an area where you can place text, it turns into an I-shaped pointer called an *I-beam*. The shape of the I-beam is easy to precisely position, even between two tiny characters of text. Figure 2-1 shows the insertion point and the I-beam mouse pointer.

To insert new text, position the insertion point where you want to insert it, and then type the new text.

To remove text, you can use any of these methods:

➡ **Backspace it.** Position the insertion point and then press the Backspace key to delete text to the left of the insertion point.

➡ **Delete it.** Select the text and then press the Delete key, or position the insertion point and then press the Delete key to delete text to the right of the insertion point.

➡ **Type over it.** Select the text and then type new text to replace it. Whatever was selected is deleted.

Insertion point

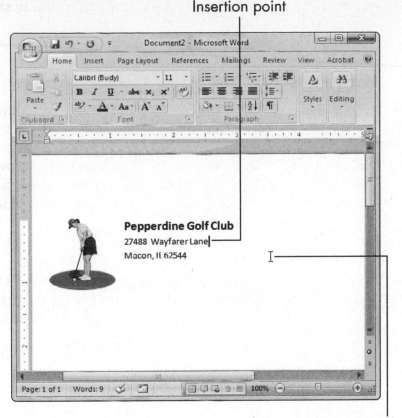

I-beam (mouse pointer)

Figure 2-1

 In Word, you can't move the insertion point past the end of the document. If you want the insertion point in the center of the document, for example, you would normally have to press Enter to create extra blank paragraphs until it arrived where you wanted it. Here's a way around that: Double-click where you want the insertion point. Even if it's beyond the end of the document, it moves there (and the end of the document moves down past the new location).

Move and Copy Content

For large-scale editing (such as whole paragraphs and pages of text), you can easily move or copy text and graphics within the same application (even different data files) or from one application to another.

For example, suppose you want to create slides for a presentation at a club meeting. You could write the outline in Word, and then copy the text over to PowerPoint for graphics and animation.

Here are two ways of moving and copying:

➡ **Drag and drop:** Use the mouse to drag selected text or graphics from one location to another.

To drag and drop between applications, both application windows must be onscreen at once. You may need to move and resize windows to make that happen. To move a window, drag its title bar. To resize a window, drag the bottom right corner of the window.

➡ **The Clipboard:** Cut or copy the content to the Clipboard (a temporary holding area in Windows), and then paste it into a different location.

To use the copy-by-dragging method, select the content to be dragged, and then hold down the left mouse button while you drag it to the new location. Then release the mouse button to drop it there.

➡ **Dragging and dropping within a document:** If you're dragging and dropping content within a document but the source and the destination locations are too far apart to see at the same time, you might want to open another window that contains the same file, and then scroll them to two different spots. To do this in Word, Excel, or PowerPoint, choose View⇨New Window. Because you need to be able to see both the starting and ending points at the same time, you might have to arrange and resize some windows onscreen.

 If you open a new window with View⇨New Window, the second window will have the same name but will have a number appended to it, such as Budget.xls:2. The second window is an alternate view of the first; any changes made in one are reflected in the other.

➡ **Dragging and dropping between documents:** Open both documents at the same time. You must be able to see both the starting and ending points at the same time, so you might have to arrange and resize some windows onscreen.

You aren't limited to copying content between documents in the same application. That is, you can copy from Word to Word, Word to PowerPoint, and so on. Figure 2-2 shows an example where I dragged content from a Word document to an Excel spreadsheet.

To make a copy of the selected text or graphic, hold down Ctrl while you drag. You'll notice as you drag that the mouse pointer shows a tiny plus sign, indicating that you're making a copy.

If setting up the display so that both the source and the destination appear onscreen at once is awkward, you're better off using the Clipboard method of moving content. This method places the source material in a hidden temporary storage area in Windows, and then pastes it from there into the destination location. Because the Clipboard is nearly universal, you can use it to move or copy data from (almost) any application to any other application, even non-Microsoft programs. For example, you could copy text from Word and paste it into a graphics program like Photoshop, and it would appear there as a graphic. Or, you could copy spreadsheet cells from Excel and paste them into a Web site–building application, such as Dreamweaver, and it would turn into a Web table.

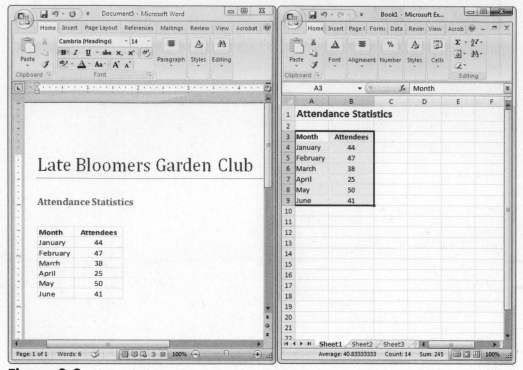

Figure 2-2

The three Clipboard operations are Cut, Copy, and Paste.

➡ **To move something:** Use Cut and then Paste.

➡ **To copy something:** Use Copy and then Paste.

 Moving or copying via the Clipboard method is always a two-step process.

Table 2-1 summarizes the ways of issuing the Cut, Copy, and Paste commands. The Home tab's Clipboard group on the Ribbon provides buttons for the commands (see Figure 2-3), but you can also use keyboard or mouse methods if you find them easier.

Figure 2-3

 If you use the Ribbon buttons often for Cut, Copy, and Paste, consider adding them to the Quick Access toolbar. Read how to do this in Chapter 1.

 First select the content you want to cut or copy.

Table 2-1	Ways to Cut, Copy, and Paste		
Command	*Keyboard Method*	*Mouse Method*	*Ribbon Method*
Cut	Ctrl+X	Right-click and choose Cut	Home⇨Clipboard⇨Cut
Copy	Ctrl+C	Right-click and choose Copy	Home⇨Clipboard⇨Copy
Paste	Ctrl+V	Right-click and choose Paste	Home⇨Clipboard⇨Paste

Choose Fonts and Font Sizes

Across all the Office programs, you can choose different fonts and font sizes for your work.

➡ A *font* is a standard way of making each letter. (It's also called a typeface.) The letters in this paragraph use the Times New Roman font.

➡ The *font size* controls the height of the letters. The letters in this paragraph are size x, which usually is a good size for documents in Microsoft Office.

The font size is based on the distance from the top of the tallest letter to the bottom of the lowest letter, measured in points. One point (pt) is $\frac{1}{72}$ of an inch.

The default font and size in Word is Calibri 11. If that isn't what you want, you can choose a different font or size.

To choose a font or resize it, follow these steps:

1. Select the text to affect.

2. Open Font or Font Size drop-down list on the Home tab (in the Font group).

3. Make your selection. See Figure 2-4.

If you don't select any text to affect before you choose a font or size, the new setting applies to the spot where the insertion point is at the moment. Any new text you type there will have that new setting.

Different computers have different size monitors, so screen size isn't a reliable indicator of how large the text will print. Also, adjusting the Zoom feature in the applications can affect how large the text looks onscreen. (Read about the Zoom tool in Chapter 1.)

Font

Font Size

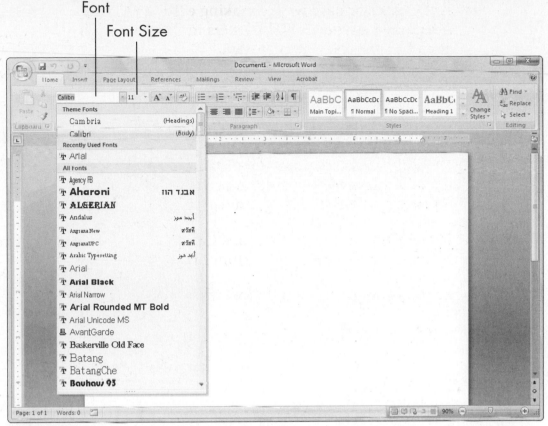

Figure 2-4

 To modify the default font and size for all new documents, open the Font dialog box (Ctrl+D), choose a different font and size, and then click the Default button. In the confirmation box that appears, click Yes.

Word, Excel, and PowerPoint all have Grow Font and Shrink Font buttons on the Home tab (Font group), immediately to the right of the Font Size drop-down list. The Grow Font button increases the font size each time you click it, and the Shrink Font button decreases the font size.

You can also specify a custom font size. Open the Font Size drop-down list box and type the size you want. See Figure 2-5.

Type a font size here if the size you
want does not appear on the list

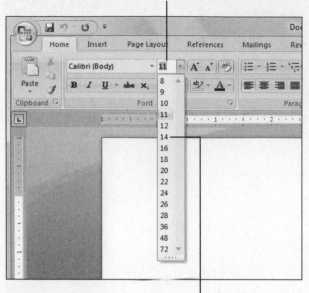

Sizes increment by 1 in the smallest sizes, and
by more in the larger sizes

Figure 2-5

Apply Text Formatting

You can modify the appearance and pick the color of text.

 The default setting for text color is Automatic, which
changes the text color so that it contrasts well with
the background. On a light background, text is black;
on a dark background, text is white.

Select text, and then use the Font Color button to change its color.
When you click the arrow to the right of the Font Color button on the
Home tab (see Figure 2-6), a palette of color choices appears. Choose
any of the following:

Click arrow to open the palette of colors

Font Color button

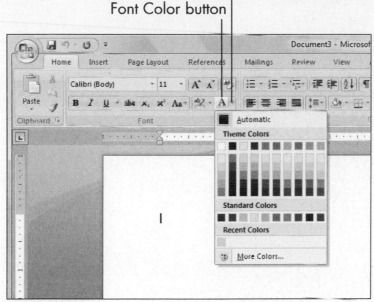

Figure 2-6

➡ **Automatic:** This resets the text color to the default.

➡ **Theme Colors:** You can choose one of the color placeholders defined by the current theme. If you later change the theme applied to the document, this color might change.

➡ **Standard Colors:** You can choose a standard fixed color that will not change even if you apply a different theme later.

➡ **More Colors:** You can choose a different fixed color than the ones in the Standard Colors section.

➡ **Recent Colors:** This section appears only if you select a color with More Colors in this document. It provides shortcuts for reselecting a color that has already been used.

Besides text color, you can also apply text attributes, such as bold (like **this**) and *italic* (like *this*).

Some text attributes can be clicked on and off from Home tab buttons (in the Font group). Figure 2-7 points out the attributes for Word.

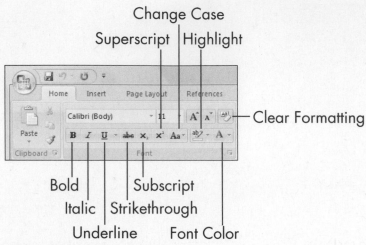

Figure 2-7

Use the Mini Toolbar

The mini toolbar appears whenever you right-click text in Word, Excel, or PowerPoint.

The mini toolbar provides a version of the Font group on the Home tab, plus a few extra buttons from other groups, as you can see in Figure 2-8. Hover your mouse over each button to find out what it does.

Right-click selected text

Mini toolbar

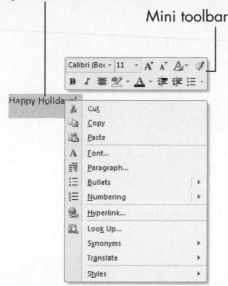

Figure 2-8

In Word and PowerPoint, the mini toolbar also is available when you select text; a faint, partly transparent version of it appears above the selected text. If you move the mouse over it, it becomes solid and usable. If you find it annoying that the mini toolbar appears for selected text (some people do), choose Office➪Word Options (or PowerPoint Options, as the case may be) and then deselect the Show Mini Toolbar on Selection check box.

Work with Themes

A theme is a set of three types of placeholders:

➠ Fonts

➠ Colors

➠ Graphic effects

Themes are useful when you want to standardize the formatting across multiple documents, or between applications. For example, you might want your resume and the cover letter that you send with it to be consistent in formatting. Applying the same theme to both would ensure that they use the same fonts and colors.

Or, bigger picture, you can use a Theme to apply consistent formatting across lots of documents, and even between applications. For example, you could have a Word document that uses the same theme as your PowerPoint presentation on the same subject, so they match.

When I use the word "theme" in a general sense in this book, you can assume that I mean a combination of those three types of placeholders: fonts, colors, and effects. However, you can also apply more specific themes that just cover one of those: font themes, color themes, and effect themes. This is great because it lets you combine the parts of different themes to create your own special look. For example, you might use the fonts from one theme and the colors from another.

Instead of choosing a specific font, color, or graphic effect for an item in one of the Office applications, you can instead choose to apply one of the theme placeholders. This formats the item with whatever definition the current theme specifies. Then if you change to a different theme later, the item changes its appearance. This is a great help in allowing you to quickly change the look of an entire document, spreadsheet, or presentation.

To apply a theme in Word or Excel, follow these steps:

1. Choose Page Layout⇨Themes.

2. Choose a theme from the menu that appears. See Figure 2-9.

Themes provided by Office 2007

Any custom themes you have created appear here

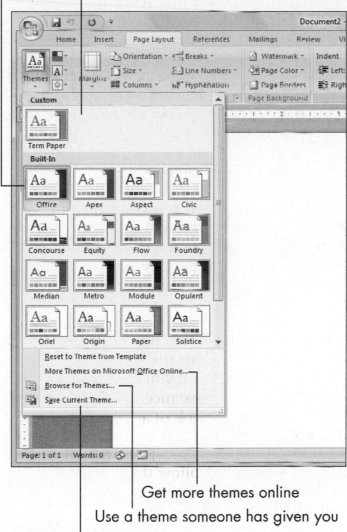

Get more themes online

Use a theme someone has given you

Save the current settings as a new custom theme

Figure 2-9

To apply a theme in PowerPoint, you have two methods:

➡ On the Design tab, click one of the samples in the Themes group.

➡ On the Design tab, click the down arrow in the Themes group and select a theme from the menu that appears. See Figure 2-10.

Click this arrow to see more themes

Click one of these themes

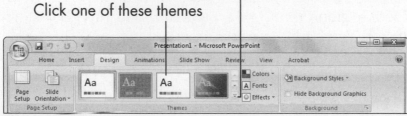

Figure 2-10

Each theme on the menu has a name, but you can't get a very good overall sense of a theme without seeing it in action. Fortunately, there's a quick way to do this. Just hover the mouse pointer over a theme, and the document behind the open menu shows a preview of how the theme will affect it.

 Make sure you have some text in the document, in an area that isn't obscured when the menu is open.

If you apply a theme (or preview one) and it doesn't seem to have any effect, you probably have specific fonts and/or colors selected that are overriding the theme choices. Earlier in the chapter, where I show you how to choose a font, I mention the Theme Fonts section at the top of the Font menu. If you choose anything other than what was in the Theme Fonts section, any theme changes you make will not affect that text.

So, say you applied various fonts to a document, but now you decide that you'd rather let a theme handle the font choice. Here are some possible ways to fix that:

1. Reselect the text.

2. On the Home tab, reopen the Font drop-down list and choose the Body font from the Theme Fonts section. Do this for all the body text.

3. Repeat this process by choosing the Heading font for any headings.

Or, reselect the text and press Ctrl+spacebar. This strips any manually applied formatting from the text. As long as you haven't applied any styles to the paragraph that specify a certain font, this allows the theme's font choices to be in effect.

You can also apply color themes, font themes, and effect themes. To the right of the Themes button in each of the applications are smaller buttons for each of those things. Figure 2-11 points them out. Each button opens a drop-down list from which you can choose a different theme of the corresponding type.

Font Themes

Color Themes

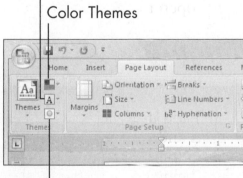

Effect Themes

Figure 2-11

 You can do a lot more with themes than the little taste I give you here in this chapter. Explore the options at the bottom of the Themes menu (refer to Figure 2-8) on your own, or check out the Help system in each application.

Check Your Spelling and Grammar

All the Office apps share a common spell-check feature that tells you what words don't appear in its dictionary. You can decide what to do with each one.

While you work in an application, your words are compared against the dictionary, and anything that doesn't appear in the dictionary is marked with a red wavy underline. See Figure 2-12.

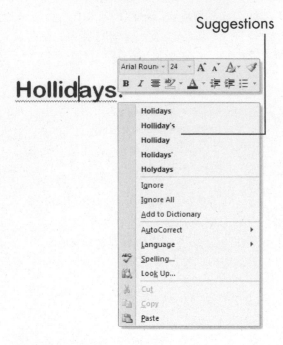

Figure 2-12

Right-click any red-underlined word to see a menu of choices. From this menu, you can

➡ Click one of the suggestions, and Word immediately changes the word to that.

➡ Click Ignore to mark this instance only as okay, and Word does nothing.

➠ Click Ignore All to mark all instances of the word as okay in this document only.

➠ Click Add to Dictionary to add this word so that it's never marked as misspelled again on your computer, in any document.

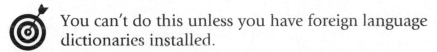 Add to Dictionary is useful when you frequently write a word that the dictionary doesn't recognize, like an unusual last name or the name of a company whose name is intentionally misspelled, like Kool Kottage. Adding the word to the dictionary helps you get it right and cuts down on the annoyance of approving it every time it pops up.

➠ Point to AutoCorrect; from the menu that opens, click one of the suggestions to always correct this misspelling with the chosen suggestion in the future, without asking.

➠ Point to Language; from the menu that opens, click a different language to mark this word as being in a foreign language so that it's checked with a different dictionary (the one for that language).

You can't do this unless you have foreign language dictionaries installed.

➠ Click Spelling to open the full-blown spell checker, covered in a bit.

➠ Click Look Up to look the word up in an online reference source. (I don't cover this feature in this book, but give it a try on your own.)

If you'd rather not check your spelling by paging through your work, looking for the red underlines, and then right-clicking each one as you find it, I have a better way. Go for full Spell Check feature instead. It asks you to choose from a similar set of options as I just listed, but it automatically moves you from one potential error to the next so you don't have to hunt for the underlines.

 One difference when you use the full Spell Check is that a Change All command is available. It enables you to change all instances of the misspelling at once in the document. But be careful, because you might accidentally make some changes you didn't intend.

To start a spell check, choose either

➡ Review➪Spelling (in Excel or PowerPoint)

➡ Review➪Spelling and Grammar (in Word)

Word also has a built-in grammar checker in addition to the spell checker.

Figure 2-13 shows the spell check in Word when a misspelling is found. (It looks nearly the same in the other applications.)

Click one of the suggestions and then
click Change or Change All

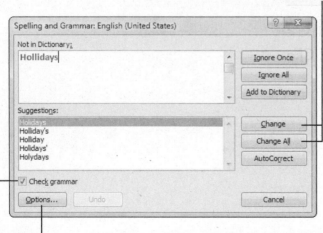

Click here to configure the spell check options
Disable grammar checking (in Word only) if desired
Figure 2-13

Word also has a grammar component. Grammar errors appear with green wavy underline. You can also work with them from the Spelling and Grammar dialog box, as shown in Figure 2-14. The Ignore Rule button suppresses further checking for the grammar rule that was broken in the notification that appears; the Explain button pops up an explanation of the grammar rule being applied.

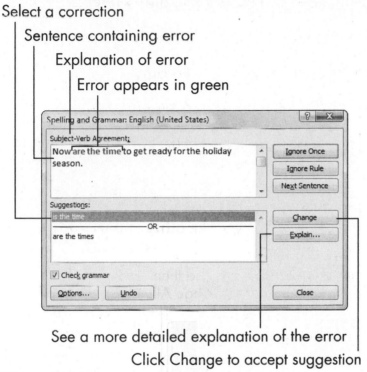

Figure 2-14

Opening, Saving, and Printing Files

All Office apps can create, open, save, and print data files. A *data file* stores your work in a particular application. If you don't save your work, whatever you have entered disappears when you close the application or turn off your computer. Not good.

Each Office 2007 application has its own data file format. For example

➤ **Word:** Document files, `.docx`

➤ **Excel:** Workbook files, `.xlsx`

➤ **PowerPoint:** Presentation files, `.pptx`

➤ **Outlook:** Personal folders files, `.pst`

Word, Excel, and PowerPoint use a separate data file for each project you work on. Every time you use one of these programs, you open and save data files.

Outlook uses just one data file for all your activities. This file is automatically saved and opened for you, so you usually don't have to think about data file management in Outlook.

Get ready to . . .

➤ Save Your Work 48

➤ Open a Saved File 53

➤ Change the File
   Listing View 55

➤ E-mail Your Work
   to Others 55

➤ Share Your Work in
   Other Formats 58

➤ Print Your Work 62

➤ Use Print Preview Before
   You Print 63

➤ Recover Lost Work 65

The steps for saving, opening, and printing data files are almost exactly the same in each application, so mastering it in one program gives you a big head start in the other programs. In this chapter, you'll see the basic skills that will serve you well for working with data files no matter which program you are using.

In this book, I'm assuming you're using Windows Vista as your operating system. I point out some differences between Vista and its predecessor — Windows XP — but the majority of what I talk about is in Vista.

Save Your Work

As you work in an application, the content you create is stored in the computer's memory. This memory is only temporary storage. When you exit the application or shut down the computer, whatever is stored in memory is flushed away forever — unless you save it.

If you want to keep what you're working on, here are some ways to save:

➡ Click the Office button and click Save.

➡ Press Ctrl+S.

➡ Click the Save button on the Quick Access toolbar.

The first time you save a file, the application prompts you to enter a name for it in the Save As dialog box. You can also change the save location if you want something other than the defaults. See Figure 3-1.

 For Windows Vista users, the default save location is a folder called Documents. For Windows XP users, look in the My Documents folder.

(Optional) Change the save location

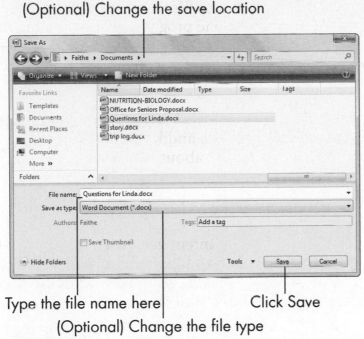

Type the file name here

(Optional) Change the file type

Click Save

Figure 3-1

When you re-save an already saved file, the Save As dialog box doesn't reappear; the file saves with the most recent settings. If you want to change the settings (such as the location or file type) or save under a different name, choose Office➪Save As to make the Save As dialog box appear.

To change the file type, open the Save as Type list and make another selection. In each of the applications, there are three important file types to know about:

➡ **Default:** The default format in each application supports all Office 2007 features except macros. The file extension ends in the letter X for each one: Word is `.docx`; Excel is `.xlsx`; PowerPoint is `.pptx`.

➡ **Macro-enabled:** This format supports all Office 2007 features, including macros. The file extension ends in the letter M for each one: `.docm`, `.xlsm`, and `.pptm`.

Macros are recorded bits of code that can automate certain activities in a program, but they can also carry viruses. The default formats don't support macros for that reason. If you need to create a file that includes macros, you can save in a macro-enabled format.

➠ **97-2003:** Each application includes a file format for backward compatibility with earlier versions of the application (versions 97 through 2003). Some minor functionality may be lost when saving in this format. The file extensions are .doc, .xls, and .ppt.

In Windows Vista, each user has his own Documents folder (based on who is logged into Windows at the moment). In Figure 3-1, the location is Faithe⇨Documents. That means that the Documents folder is located in a folder called Faithe, because Faithe is logged in right now.

To understand how to change save locations, you should first understand the concept of a file path. Files are organized into folders, and you can have folders *inside* folders. For example, you might have

➠ A folder called *Retirement*

➠ Within that folder, another folder called *Finances*

➠ Within that folder, an Excel file called BankAccounts.xlsx

The path for such a file would be

        C:\Retirement\Finances\BankAccounts.xlsx

The C at the beginning is the drive letter. The main hard disk on a computer is called C. The backslashes (\) are separators between folder levels.

At the top of the Save As dialog box, the parts of a path are separated by right-pointing triangles rather than by slashes. You can click any of the triangles to open a drop-down list containing all the *subfolders* (that is, the folders within that folder), and then click one of those folders to quickly switch to it. See Figure 3-2.

Click a folder in the path to see a list of its subfolders

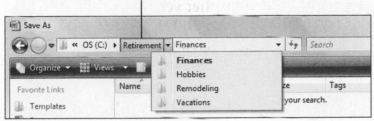

Figure 3-2

If you're using Windows XP, the Save As dialog box looks a little different than what's shown here, the regular file path (with the slashes) appears at the top of the Save As dialog box rather than the version with the triangles shown in Figure 3-2, and the folder tree (from Figure 3-3) is permanently expanded.

 If the Save As dialog box doesn't show any folders or locations, click the Browse Folders button at the bottom left of the dialog box. Conversely, if you want to hide the folders/locations (for example, if you always save in the default location and have no interest in other locations), click the Hide Folders button. (Those two commands, Browse Folders and Hide Folders, are a toggle. You'll see one or the other.)

Paths are also shown as a collapsible/expandable *tree*, with the drive on the top and all its folders and subfolders beneath. You can double-click a folder to collapse (hide) or expand (show) its contents. In Windows Vista, the folder tree can be either displayed or hidden in the lower left corner of the Save As dialog box. Figure 3-3 shows the folder tree displayed.

Folders list

Click here to hide the Folders list

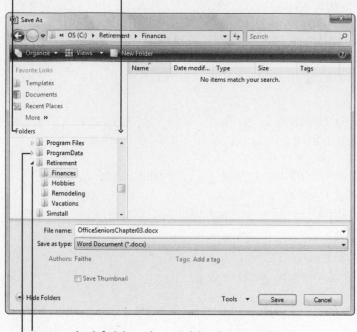

Expanded folder shows black triangle

Collapsed folder shows white triangle

Figure 3-3

You have several ways to navigate between folders:

➧ Click a shortcut in the Favorite Links list to jump to a certain folder.

➧ Click Computer in the Favorite Links list to display a list of all the drives on your PC. From there, double-click to move through the levels of folders to the area you want.

➧ Open the Folders list. Collapse or expand folders as needed to find the folder you want, and then double-click it.

➡ From the Address bar at the top, open the list for the folder level you want to see the subfolders of, and then click the one you want.

➡ Click in the Address bar. This changes its display to a traditional path (like C:\Foldername); you can manually type in a path and then press Enter.

If you find yourself changing the save location frequently, you can set a different location to be the default. Follow these steps:

➡ **In Word:** Choose Office⇨Word Options. Click Advanced, and then scroll down to the bottom of the options and click File Locations. Click Documents, click Modify, choose a different save location, and then click OK.

➡ **In Excel:** Choose Office⇨Excel Options. Click Save, and then enter a different path in the Default File Location box.

➡ **In PowerPoint:** Choose Office⇨PowerPoint Options. Click Save, and then enter a different path in the Default File Location box.

Open a Saved File

Saving your work stores it for later use. When "later" comes, you can open the file in any of a variety of ways.

In each application, links to the most recently used files appear on the Office menu, on the Recent Documents list. Click the Office button, and then click any of the Recent Documents names to quickly reopen the file. Figure 3-4 shows the list of Recent Documents on the Office menu. As you open and save more files, the list of recently used files changes. If you want to make sure that a particular file remains on the list, click the pushpin icon to its right.

Click a pushpin to keep a file on the list
Pinned files stay on the list

Recent Documents

1 outline.docx
2 Chapter 5 FW.docx
3 OfficeSeniorsChapter03.docx
4 OfficeSeniorsChapter02.docx
5 Office for Seniors Outline 1-21-09FW.docx
6 Second batch.docx
7 F&N_Ch5 Amanda Ziaer.doc
8 Chapter 5_cindy.doc
9 Chapter051COMMENTS.doc
Chapter05[1]_LQ.doc
Chapter05[1]_CH.doc
Chapter05 with my comments done e-mailed 1...
Chapter 5 Kris edit with changes.doc
Lasagna09.docx
flags answer key.docx
central america handout answers.docx
central america handout.docx

Figure 3-4

If the file you want to open doesn't appear on the Recent Documents list, click the Open command (Office⇨Open) to display the Open dialog box. From there, you can select the file you want; then click Open. See Figure 3-5.

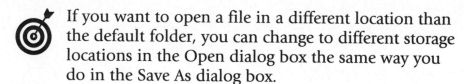

If you want to open a file in a different location than the default folder, you can change to different storage locations in the Open dialog box the same way you do in the Save As dialog box.

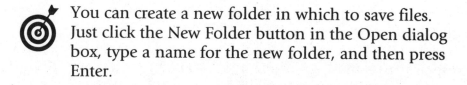

You can create a new folder in which to save files. Just click the New Folder button in the Open dialog box, type a name for the new folder, and then press Enter.

Click the file to open

Create a new folder

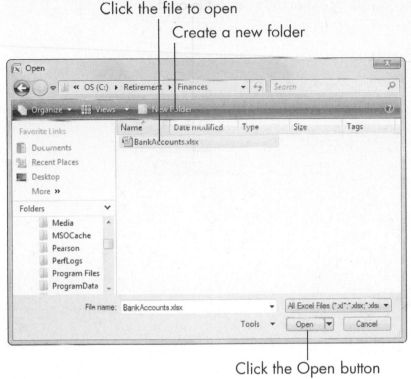

Click the Open button

Figure 3-5

Change the File Listing View

In both the Save As and the Open dialog boxes, you can change how files are displayed. Click the Views button to toggle between the available views, or click the arrow next to the View button to see a list of the available views. This list has a slider on it; drag the slider up or down to a different setting, or click directly on the choice you want. See Figure 3-6.

E-Mail Your Work to Others

One way to share your work with others is to send them a copy via e-mail. There are a couple of different ways you can send copies:

⟹ Open your e-mail application (such as Outlook), start composing a message, and then use the application's Attach command to add one or more files to the message before you send it.

Views button

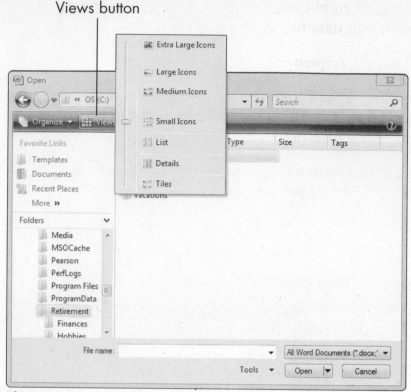

Figure 3-6

 You can attach any file — not just Office data files. For example, you can send family photos that way, or even video clips. I show you how to do this in Chapter 11, where I cover the basics of Outlook.

➠ Start composing the e-mail from within one of the Office apps. When you do that, a new message opens in your default e-mail program (which could be Outlook) and the active data file is automatically set as an attachment.

This works the same in Word, Excel, and PowerPoint:

1. Open the data file that you want to send, in whatever Office app you created it.

2. Choose Office⇨Send⇨E-mail. A new message window appears, with that data file as an attachment.

3. Fill in the e-mail recipient(s) in the To box.

4. The subject line is prefilled with the filename. Change it if you want, as I did in Figure 3-7. The file is listed as an attachment in the Attached field.

5. (Optional) If you want to type some explanation of the file, do so in the message body area.

6. Click Send.

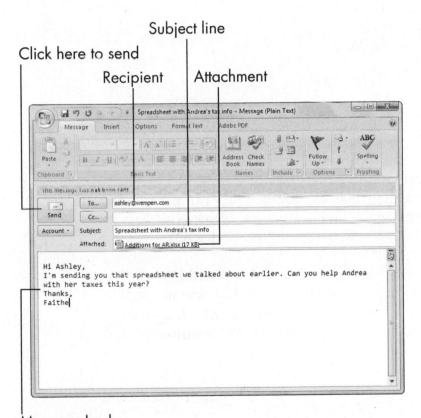

Figure 3-7

You can also copy and paste data from one of the apps directly into the body of an e-mail message that you're composing. This lets you avoid sending an attachment, which might be helpful if you're sending a document or a photo to someone who isn't very experienced with e-mail and might not understand about attachments. Chapter 2 shows how to copy and paste between applications.

Share Your Work in Other Formats

When you're sharing an electronic copy of your work, such as via e-mail attachment, there's a problem if your recipient doesn't have the same application in which to view it. For example, if you send PowerPoint presentation to a friend who doesn't have PowerPoint, he won't be able to open it.

There are some ways around this. For example, your recipient can go to the Microsoft Office Web site (`http://office.microsoft.com`), search for *Viewer*, and download a free viewer application for that file type. Viewers are available for Excel, Word, and PowerPoint there. Alternatively, as I mention earlier, you can copy and paste the content of the document directly into the body of an e-mail message, rather than sending it as an attachment.

Even though previous versions of Office don't support the new file formats in Office 2007, users of older versions of Office can download a free compatibility pack for Office 2007 that enables them to open the newer files. Go to `http://office.microsoft.com` and search for *compatibility pack*.

Another workaround is for you to save your work in another format that your intended recipient has an application for. You do this via the Save As dialog box, by selecting a different file type. For example, the Rich Text Format (`.rtf`) is a near-universal format that almost any word processing program can open, and Word users commonly save in that format when they want to exchange documents with someone who uses a very old or obscure word processing program that doesn't support Word files. Figure 3-8 shows RTF being selected as the file format.

Choose a different file type

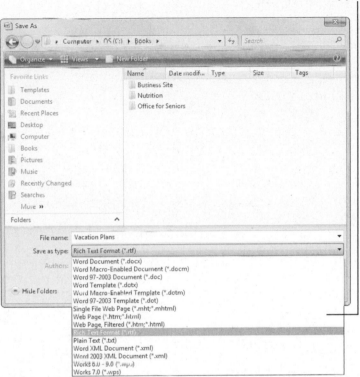

Figure 3-8

 Changing to a different file format can result in the loss of some formatting. Some features in Office 2007 applications work only when documents are saved in the native Office 2007 format, such as fill-in fields, macros, certain types of editable artwork, and formatting themes. That's why most people don't save in other formats unless it is necessary.

Perhaps a better way, though, is to create a version of your work in a special format designed for read-only sharing of laid-out pages: a *page description language*. That way, the recipient sees the page exactly as you intended it, without having to find and download a separate viewer for that specific file type.

Office 2007 supports two major page description languages:

➡ **PDF:** A format created by Adobe, widely used all over the Internet for distributing documents. It doesn't come with Windows, but a reader for this format — Adobe Reader — is free to download from www.adobe.com. Yes, the recipient does still have to download Reader, but it's just one program, and it will work for the content from all Office apps, plus many other documents.

➡ **XPS:** A format created by Microsoft, supported natively in Windows Vista and higher. Anyone who has Windows Vista already has this viewer available.

The add-ins needed to save in PDF and XPS formats don't come with Office 2007, but they're easy to download and install for free. Here's a one-time procedure for doing so:

1. Open a Web browser and navigate to http://r. office.microsoft.com/r/rlidMSAddinPDFXPS.

2. On that page, click the Download button.

3. In the File Download - Security Warning dialog box, click Run.

4. Wait for the installer to download.

5. In the Internet Explorer - Security Warning dialog box, click Run.

6. In the setup program that runs, mark the check box to accept the terms of agreement; then click Continue.

7. At the Installation Complete message, click OK.

From that point on, you can save in PDF or XPS format directly from within an application. Follow these steps:

1. Choose Office⇨Save As⇨PDF or XPS. A Publish as PDF or XPS dialog box opens. It's very similar to the Save As dialog box, as you can see in Figure 3-9.

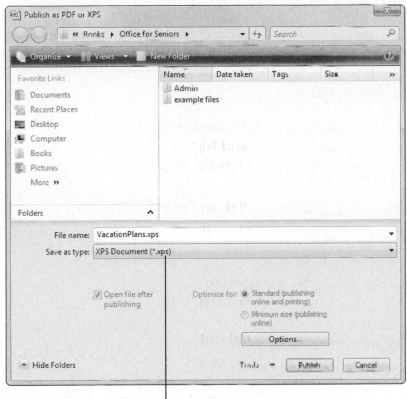

Choose between XPS and PDF

Figure 3-9

2. (Optional) Change the filename if desired. By default, it's the same name as the data file you're working with.

3. (Optional) Change the file type. The default type is what-ever type you saved as last, XPS or PDF. If you want the other type instead, open the Save as Type drop-down list and make your selection.

4. Click Publish. The saved file opens in its native program, which is either Adobe Reader (PDF format) or Internet Explorer (XPS format).

Print Your Work

To print from within any Office applications, choose Office⇨Print or press Ctrl+P. That opens the Print dialog box. Set any print options desired and then click the Print button.

The exact settings found in the Print dialog box vary slightly between the applications. Figure 3-10 shows the dialog box for Word. Later chapters of this book cover each application's printing process. The common features are

➥ **Name:** Choose from a drop-down list of the printers installed on your system. (If you have only one printer, it's used automatically.)

➥ **Page Range:** Specify which page(s) you want to print, if not the whole thing.

➥ **Copies:** Specify how many copies of each page you want.

Check out the arrow to the right of the Print command on the Office menu. Point to that arrow to open a menu of other printing choices:

➥ **Print:** This opens the Print dialog box, just like clicking the Print command directly from the menu.

➥ **Quick Print:** This option bypasses the Print dialog box and prints one copy of the entire document on the default printer. You forego the options available in the Print dialog box. What you see is what you print.

➥ **Print Preview:** This option opens a special view for examining a print job before it is actually printed, as described in the next section.

Printer

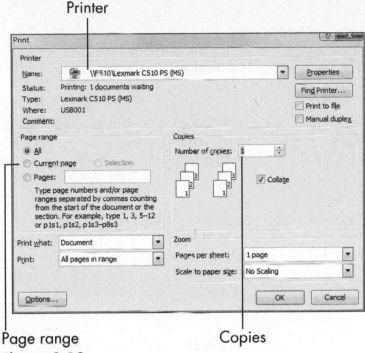

Page range   Copies

Figure 3-10

You might want to add the Quick Print command to the Quick Access toolbar to make it easier to print draft copies of your work. Chapter 1 shows you how to add buttons to this toolbar.

Use Print Preview Before You Print

Sometimes when you print something, it doesn't look exactly how you expected. The view that you work with onscreen isn't the same as the view that will be printed in many cases. (That's especially true in Excel, for example.)

Print Preview is a special view in which you can see your pages exactly as they will appear when printed. This can help you avoid needlessly printing extra copies, and wasting ink and paper.

To access Print Preview, choose Office⇨Print⇨Print Preview. The options available on the Ribbon in Print Preview are different depending on the application, but you will always see the following.

➡ **Print:** Opens the Print dialog box

➡ **Zoom:** Changes the magnification at which you see the preview

➡ **Close Print Preview:** Returns you to whatever view you were in previously

In specific applications, you can do more in Print Preview than simply look. For example, in Excel (shown in Figure 3-11), note the Show Margins check box. When you select this check box, black lines appear on the preview: one for each column divider, and one for each margin, plus more lines for header and footer boundaries. You can drag these lines to adjust the positioning of the data on the page.

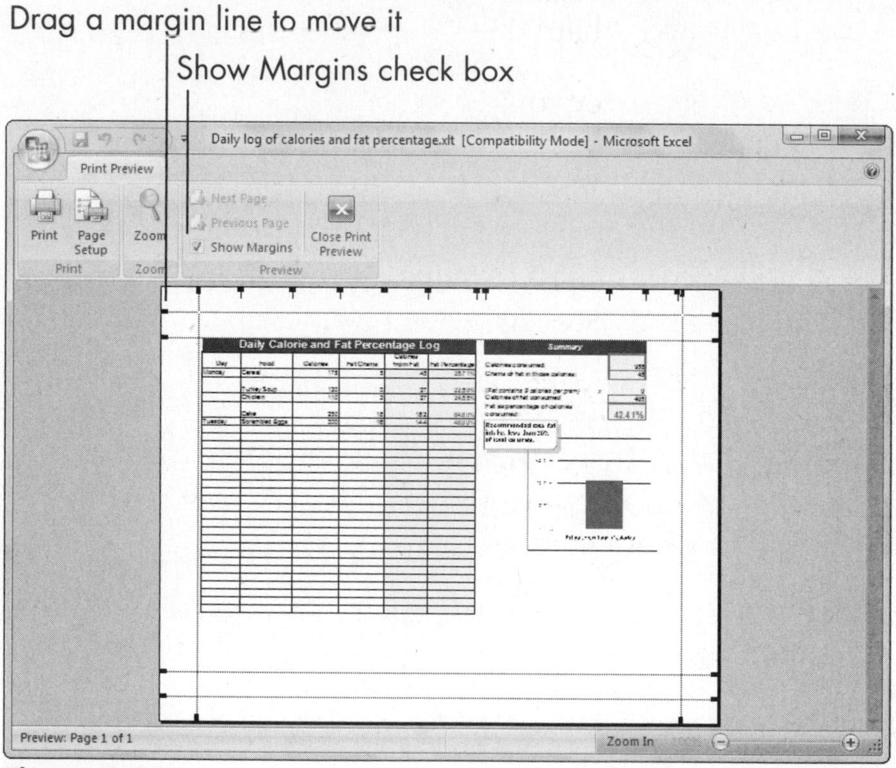

Drag a margin line to move it

Show Margins check box

Figure 3-11

Recover Lost Work

Computers lock up occasionally, and applications crash in the middle of important projects. When that happens, any work that you haven't saved is gone.

To minimize the pain of those situations, Word, Excel, and PowerPoint all have an AutoRecover feature that silently saves your drafts as you work, once every ten minutes or at some other interval you specify. These drafts are saved in temporary hidden files that are deleted when you close the application successfully (that is, not abruptly due to a lockup, crash, or power outage). If the application crashes, those temporary saves files appear for your perusal when the program starts back up. You can choose to either

➠ Save them if their versions are newer than the ones you have on your hard drive.

➠ Discard them if they contain nothing you need.

To change the interval at which AutoRecover versions are saved, follow these steps:

1. Choose Office➪Word Options (or Excel Options or PowerPoint Options). See Figure 3-12.

2. In the left column, click Save.

3. In the window that opens, make sure that the Save AutoRecover Information Every xx Minutes check box is marked.

4. If desired, change the value in the Minutes box to another number.

5. Click OK.

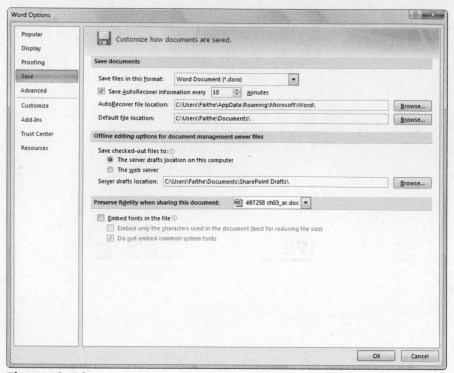

Figure 3-12

Part II
Word

"Needlepoint my foot! These are Word fonts. What I can't figure out is how you got the pillowcases into your printer."

Composing Your Thoughts in Word

*I*f you've read this book to this point, you've seen the common features across the various Office applications, in a general way. In this chapter, it's time to get down to brass tacks with one particular application: Microsoft Word.

Word is a word processing program. That's a fancy way of saying that it specializes in creating and formatting (that is, *processing*) text. Word is ideal for projects that are primarily text-based: in other words, where the text is the main attraction, and the *formatting* (how text looks) plays a supporting role. Suitable projects in Word include correspondence, club newsletters and minutes, flyers and signs, fax cover sheets, mailing labels, brochures, award certificates, and stationery.

That's a pretty broad list of projects!

Because Word is good for so many things, it's usually the first application in the Office suite that a person learns how to use. In this chapter, I show you how to get around in Word; and how to type, edit, and format text.

Get ready to . . .

➠ Examine the Word Interface ... 70

➠ Move Around and
   Select Text.......................... 71

➠ Choose Paper Size and
   Orientation......................... 71

➠ Set Margins........................ 73

➠ Select the Right
   Screen View 74

➠ Align and
   Indent Paragraphs.............. 77

➠ Change Line Spacing 82

➠ Create Bullet and
   Numbered Lists 85

Examine the Word Interface

Word differs from the other Office applications primarily in the depth of its text-handling tools. Whereas PowerPoint is all about graphics and Excel is all about numbers, Word is all about — well, words! Almost every tab on the Ribbon in Word has a text focus.

Some of Word's strongest unique features include:

➡ **A complete set of proofreading tools:** You'll find not only a spelling checker, but also a grammar checker, thesaurus, translation utility, and word counter. All these tools are on the Review tab. The spelling and grammar checkers are covered in Chapter 3.

➡ **Several features for quickly and consistently applying formatting to text:** Word offers convenient themes, styles, and style sets. Styles are on the Home tab, and themes are on the Page Layout tab. Chapter 2 discusses themes in a generic, multi-application sense, and Chapter 5 covers styles and themes specifically in Word.

 A *style* applies to an individual paragraph, or a block of selected text. A *theme* applies to the entire document.

➡ **A full-featured Mail Merge utility:** Use this feature (found on the Mailings tab)to create customized copies of letters, mailing labels, envelopes, and so on. Chapter 6 covers mail merge.

➡ **Collaboration tools:** Use these tools when working with other people, such as document sharing, change tracking, document comparison, and commenting. All of these are accessed from the Review tab.

Move Around and Select Text

In Chapter 1, I cover how to move around in a document and select blocks of text. In a nutshell, whatever you type in Word appears at the *insertion point,* which is the blinking vertical line on the page. You can move the insertion point by clicking with the **mouse** where you want it placed, or by using the arrow keys. There are also shortcut keys for moving the insertion point.

 Scrolling the document with the scroll bars moves the display (for example, from page 1 to page 2) but does not move the insertion point.

A lot of people are surprised, for example, when they scroll to another page and start typing, but the text appears back on the previous page! That's because the typing appears at the insertion point, which is still back where it was before.

To perform an action upon text — say, make it bold, or move it — you have to select the text first. To select text, drag across it with the mouse, or you can hold down the Shift key and then press the arrow keys to extend the selection. What you selected is highlighted, so that's a good sign. You can also select an entire word by double-clicking it, an entire paragraph by triple-clicking it, or the entire document by pressing Ctrl+A.

Choose Paper Size and Orientation

The default paper size in Word is 8.5 x 11 inches. That's the standard size (called Letter), which conveniently fits in most printers and copy machines in the United States. (Legal size is the other major size used in the United States: 8.5 x 14 inches.) In other countries, though, standard paper size is different. For example, in Europe, A4 paper is the standard size, at 8.27 x 11.69 inches.

Whenever Word starts a new document, it does so based on a group of settings stored in a template called Normal. A *template* is a configuration file that governs the default settings for the documents that are based on it. These settings include specifications for a paper size of 8.5 x 11 inches. If you want the document to have a different paper size — say, for a brochure — choose Page Layout⇨Size and then choose a different paper size from the drop-down list. See Figure 4-1.

Paper size is controlled from the Page Layout tab

Choose a paper size

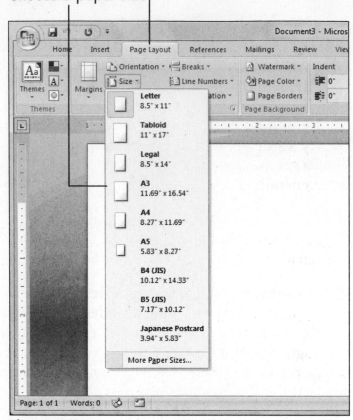

Figure 4-1

Page orientation determines whether the height or the width of the page is greater. If the text is parallel to the narrow edge, that's *Portrait*. If it's parallel to the wide edge, that's *Landscape*.

Portrait (taller than wide) is the more common orientation, used for most correspondence and reports. Landscape orientation (wider than tall) is used for brochures, certificates, and calendars, all of which fit naturally into the wider format.

To change the page orientation, choose Page Layout⇨Orientation and then click Portrait or Landscape.

Set Margins

A document's *margin* is the space between the edge of the paper and where the text begins. Ideal margins depend on many factors, including the document type, the need to limit the number of pages (for example, if you're paying by the page to fax or copy a document), and the audience's needs. Adjusting the margins can also control the perception of your document, making it look like it is longer or shorter than it actually is. Many a student who has been assigned a "three-page paper" has tried to get away with writing less by using large margins! (Of course, that generally doesn't work because teachers know that trick.)

Word offers several sets of standard margin settings. Choose Page Layout⇨Margins and then choose from the list. See Figure 4-2.

Each preset has a value assigned to the four page sides. Usually, a document uses the same margin setting for opposite sides (the same value for top and bottom, and the same value for left and right). This isn't a hard-and-fast rule, though. You might, for example, want extra space at the top of a page when you're printing on stationery with a name and address preprinted at the top. And, if you're going to bind your pages or use a three hole–punch for pages presented in a binder, you might want a larger margin.

If none of the choices on the list match what you want, choose Custom Margins from the bottom of the Margins menu (Figure 4-2) and enter precise values in the Page Setup dialog box that appears, as in Figure 4-3.

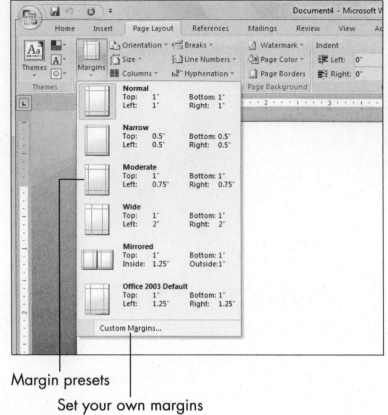

Margin presets

Set your own margins

Figure 4-2

Select the Right Screen View

Like with all the Office applications, Word gives you a variety of views to choose from. In Chapter 1, I cover views as a general concept; here, I talk about the specific views in Word.

At different points in the document creation process, you might want to see your document differently. For example, when you're hammering out the text, you might want to see your work in a very plain way, without the distraction of multiple columns and page breaks. Later, when you're fine-tuning the final look, you might want to see the document in a format closer to how it will appear when printed or published on the Web.

Enter values for each side separately here

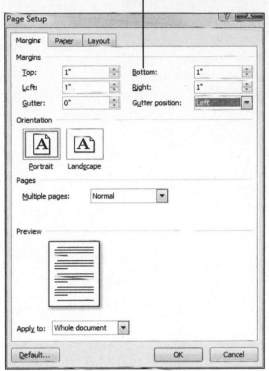

Figure 4-3

As I mention in Chapter 1, the View tab provides access to all the viewing options, and View buttons are also available in the bottom right of the Word window.

The available views in Word are

➡ **Draft:** A plain-text view. You don't see the edges of the page nor any multicolumn layouts. Page and section breaks appear as codes rather than as actual breaks. Some graphics don't appear, and others don't appear in the exact spots they will be in when the document is printed.

➡ **Print Layout:** The default view. You see each page approximately as it will look when printed, including graphics, multicolumn layouts, and breaks. This view is appropriate for most documents and work situations.

➡ **Outline:** A hierarchical view. Paragraphs are marked as headings (via the Styles feature, covered in Chapter 5) and appear in outline format. You can expand and collapse the outline to show more or fewer outline levels. Outline view is great in the early stage of a project, when you are planning the headings for a long document.

➡ **Web Layout:** A view of the document approximately as it will look when saved in Web format. Use this view when you are using Word to create content destined from the Web.

 Word isn't the most powerful tool for Web page design, but Word does enable you to create and save simple Web content.

➡ **Full Screen Reading:** A view that simulates an electronic book-reading program, laying out text in an easy-to-read, book-like format. Text can't be edited in this view. This view is good for reviewing someone else's work.

➡ **Print Preview:** Not really a view per se but an adjunct to the Print feature. Whereas Print Layout view displays the page approximately as it will look when printed, Print Preview displays it *exactly* as it will look when printed. To access Print Preview, choose Office⇨Print⇨Print Preview rather than going through the View tab.

In most cases, you will probably be happiest with Page Layout view or Draft view. I use Page Layout view most of the time, and switch to

Draft view when I need to edit a multicolumn document. I find it easier to scroll through the text when I don't have to skip from column to column onscreen.

 On some slower computers, you might notice a difference in Word's performance depending on the view you choose. For example, when you page down or move the insertion point with the arrow keys, you might experience a brief delay, especially in Print Layout view. If you find delays occurring as you edit, switching to Draft view should solve the problem.

Align and Indent Paragraphs

In Chapter 2, I cover text formatting at the individual character level: font, font size, and the like. Now take a look at some formatting that applies to entire paragraphs.

Paragraphs are the building blocks of documents. Every time you press Enter, you create a new paragraph.

You can see the paragraph markers (which never print) by clicking the **Show/Hide** (¶) button on the Home tab (Paragraph group). This button toggles on/off the display of hidden characters such as spaces, paragraph breaks, line breaks, and tabs. Figure 4-4 shows a document with the display turned on.

 Some folks find seeing these characters very distracting. However, showing them can be very helpful when you're trying to make sure you have only one space between words, or when you accidentally press the Tab key and make text skip   like   this — and then fix it.

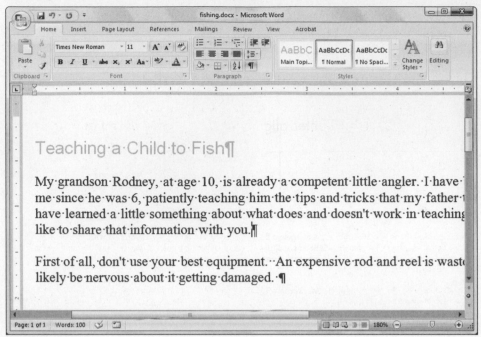

Figure 4-4

Each paragraph has a horizontal *alignment*, which determines how each line aligns between the right and left margins. The default is *left alignment*, where each line begins at the left margin. Left alignment is appropriate for most situations; the text in this book is left-aligned. The alternatives are

➡ **Right alignment:** Each line ends at the right margin. You might use this to right-align the date in some styles of business letters.

➡ **Center alignment:** Each line is centered evenly between the margins. You might want to center your name and address on stationery you create.

➡ **Justified:** Each line has additional space added to it as needed so that it begins at the left margin and ends at the right margin. With justified alignment, all lines of the paragraph except the last one are spaced that way; the final line of the paragraph is left-aligned. If the paragraph consists of only a single line, it is left-aligned.Newsletter text is often justified, making for a tidier-looking page.

Figure 4-5 shows some examples of the four types of alignment.

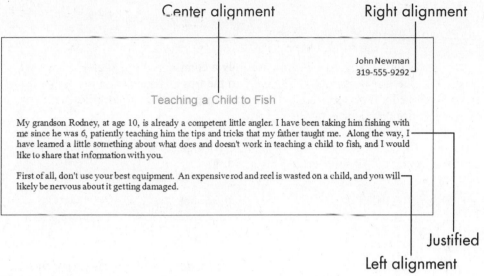

Center alignment   Right alignment

John Newman
319-555-9292

Teaching a Child to Fish

My grandson Rodney, at age 10, is already a competent little angler. I have been taking him fishing with me since he was 6, patiently teaching him the tips and tricks that my father taught me. Along the way, I have learned a little something about what does and doesn't work in teaching a child to fish, and I would like to share that information with you.

First of all, don't use your best equipment. An expensive rod and reel is wasted on a child, and you will likely be nervous about it getting damaged.

Justified

Left alignment

Figure 4-5

➠ **To change one paragraph's alignment:** Move the **insertion point** into it, or select any (or all) **text** within it. Then click the paragraph alignment button you want. See Figure 4-6.

➠ **To apply a different alignment to multiple paragraphs at once:** Select multiple paragraphs (or any part of them). Then click the paragraph alignment **button** you want.

By default, each paragraph starts in relation to the right and left margins, depending on what alignment you choose. For example, a left-aligned paragraph starts at the same position as the left margin, like this text. Sometimes you might want to *indent* one or more paragraphs, though: that is, shift their position in relation to the left and/or right margins. For example, in some styles of correspondence, it's customary to indent the first line of each paragraph by one-half inch (or five spaces). Or, when citing a quotation, it's common to indent a paragraph by one-half inch at both the right and the left.

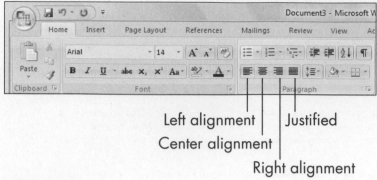

Figure 4-6

Here are the possible types of indents in Word. Each is demonstrated in Figure 4-7.

→ **First-line indent:** The starting position of the first line of the paragraph is shifted (usually inward) in relation to the left margin.

→ **Left indent:** All lines of the paragraph are shifted in relation to the left margin.

→ **Right indent:** All lines of the paragraph are shifted in relation to the right margin.

For a simple left indent, use buttons on the Home tab (Paragraph group): Increase Indent and Decrease Indent. See Figure 4-7. Each time you click one of those buttons, it changes the left indent for the selected paragraph(s) by 0.5".

If you want to specify the amount of indent or if you want to apply an indent to the right side, use the Indent controls on the Page Layout tab, as shown in Figure 4-8. You can increment the amount of indent up or down in the Left and Right text boxes.

Left indent

First line indent

Increase Indent

Decrease Indent

Right indent

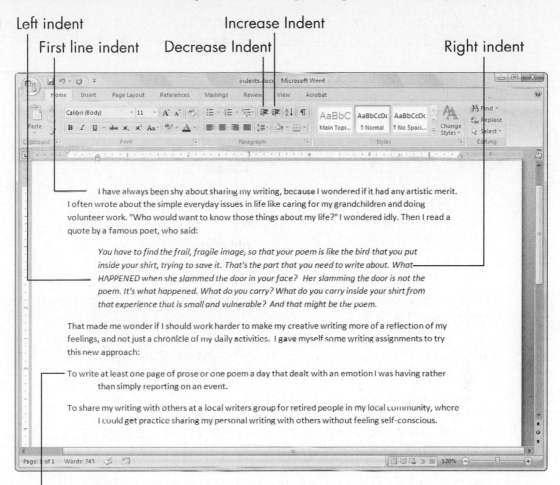

Hanging indent

Figure 4-7

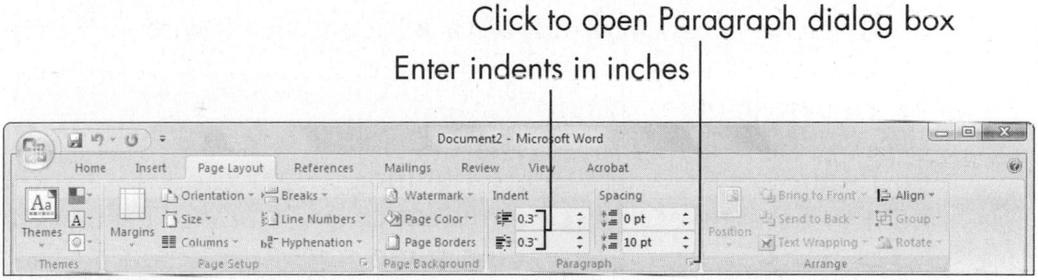

Click to open Paragraph dialog box

Enter indents in inches

Figure 4-8

If you want a special indent (hanging or first-line), use the Paragraph dialog box. To do so, follow these steps:

1. Select the paragraph(s) to which the setting should apply.

2. On the Home or the Page Layout tab, click the small **icon** in the bottom right of the Paragraph group. (It's pointed out in Figure 4-8.)

3. In the Paragraph dialog box that opens, enter values in the Left and/or Right text boxes as desired to create over-all indents for the paragraph(s). See Figure 4-9.

4. (Optional) If you want a special type of indent (such as hanging, or first-line), open the Special drop-down list and make your selection. Then enter the amount of the special indent in the text box to the right.

   In Figure 4-9, for example, a hanging indent has been set of 0.71". That means all lines *except* the first one will be left-indented by 0.71".

5. Click OK. The indent settings are applied.

Change Line Spacing

If you've used a typewriter, you're probably familiar with the terms *single spacing* and *double spacing*. You know, do you want one line of space between every line of type, or two? Most typewriters have a switch that allows you to switch between those two modes. The Spacing feature in Word is just like that but with many more choices. You can fine-tune the spacing between lines to any precise amount you want.

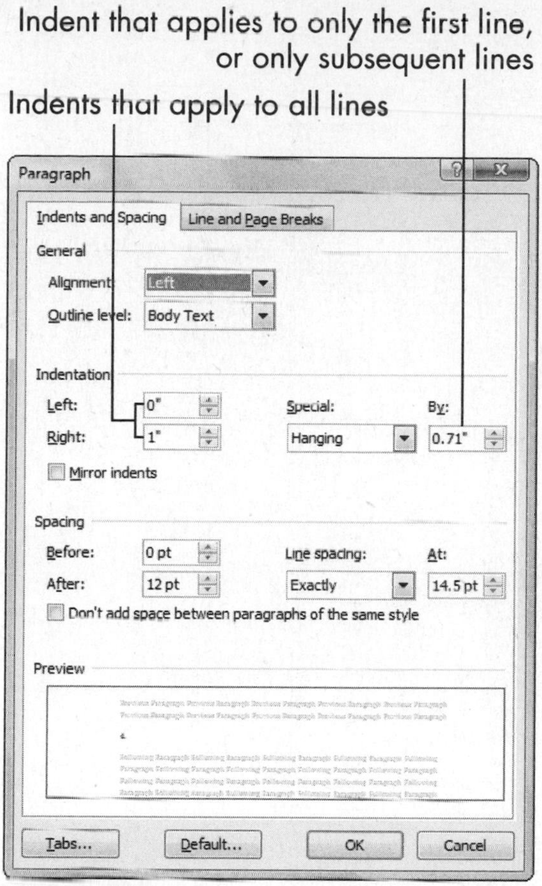

Indent that applies to only the first line,
or only subsequent lines

Indents that apply to all lines

Figure 4-9

Three settings in Word control line spacing:

➥ **Before:** The space before each paragraph

➥ **After:** The space after each paragraph

➥ **Line Spacing:** The space between the lines of each
paragraph

In Word 2007, the default settings are to include a blank line between
paragraphs and to use a line spacing value of 1.15: in other words, just
a little more vertical white space than single spacing.

If you've used earlier versions of Word, you might remember the defaults as different: single-spaced paragraphs with no extra space between them.

For basic spacing, you can use the Line Spacing button's drop-down list on the Home tab, as shown in Figure 4-10. The numbers at the top of the list refer to line spacing between the lines of paragraphs; the commands at the bottom of the list add or remove spacing before or after the paragraphs.

Line Spacing button

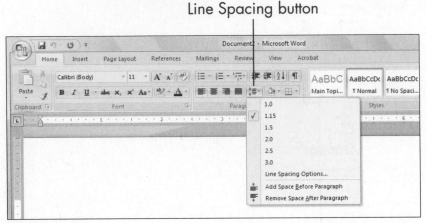

Figure 4-10

You can also set Before and After values from the Page Layout tab, as shown in Figure 4-11.

Spacing After

Spacing Before

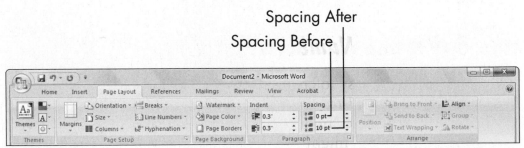

Figure 4-11

If all that still doesn't meet your spacing needs, you can open the Paragraph dialog box (click the little icon in the bottom-right corner of the Paragraph group, on either the Home or the Page Layout tab) and set specific values for spacing there. As shown in Figure 4-12, you can enter Before and After values. In the Line Spacing area, you select a unit of measurement from the drop-down list, and then enter a value.

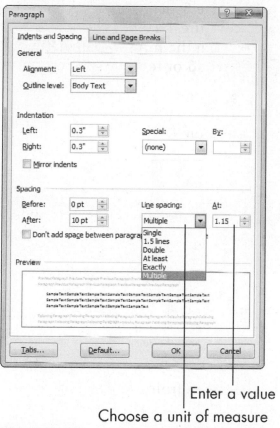

Enter a value

Choose a unit of measure

Figure 4-12

Create Bullet and Numbered Lists

Word makes it easy to create bulleted and numbered lists in your documents. Use a *bulleted list* for lists where the order of items isn't significant, and the same "bullet" character (such as • or ⇨) is used in front of each item. You might use a bulleted list for a packing list for a trip, for example, or a go-forward list. In contrast, use a *numbered list* for lists where the order of items *is* significant, and a sequential step number is used to indicate order. A numbered list might contain the steps for a recipe or a meeting agenda.

You can create a list of existing paragraphs, or you can turn on the list feature and type the list as you go. Either way, you're working with the Bullets button or the Numbering button on the Home tab.

It's just this easy:

➡ Click the Bullets or the Numbering button to apply a default bullet or number, respectively. The default bullet looks like this (•) and the default numbering treatment uses standard 1., 2., 3., and so on.

➡ Click the arrow to the right of either button to open a palette of additional choices. Figure 4-13 shows the Bullet Library and its choices.

If you go the palette route, here's the drill for bullets or numbered lists:

➡ **Bullets:** Pick one of the bullet characters on the palette (refer to Figure 4-13). If you don't find what you want, click Define New Bullet to set up a custom bullet.

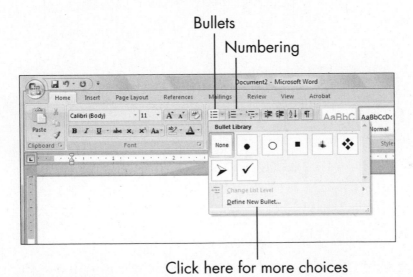

Figure 4-13

➠ **Numbered lists:** Choose from a variety of numeral styles, including Arabic (1, 2, 3) and Roman (I, II, III); or uppercase or lowercase Arabic and Roman letters (A, B, C; i, ii, iii). Clicking the Define New Number Format option opens a dialog box where you can set up your own number formats.

➠ For each numbered list, Word automatically increments the number. It isn't always perfect at guessing your wishes, though. For example, sometimes you might have a regular paragraph (not numbered) between two paragraphs that are consecutively numbered, or you might want to restart the numbering back at 1 when Word guesses that you want the numbering continued from the previous list.

To change between continuing the previous list and starting a new one, right-click the paragraph where you want the change to be made, and then choose either Restart at 1 or Continue Numbering. See Figure 4-14.

Use these commands to control the numbering

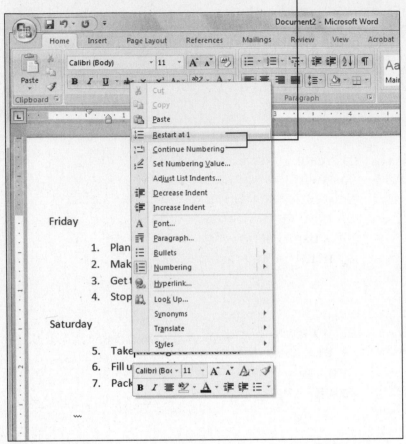

Figure 4-14

Dressing Up Your Documents

Word makes it easy to create attractive documents with consistent formatting, colorful graphics, and neatly ordered tables. In this chapter, I show you how to take advantage of some of Word 2007's user-friendly features for improving a document's appearance and readability.

In this chapter, I start with the Styles feature, which can save you a lot of time if you like to try different text formatting before deciding on a final look. With styles, you can easily switch between looks without having to worry about maintaining consistency.

Then I show you how to insert two kinds of graphics: clip art and photos.

I also explain how to make a page more colorful and attractive by adding a border around the edge of the page, and by coloring its background.

Finally, I walk you through the basics of creating tables that hold multiple columns of information in an orderly way.

Get ready to . . .

➡ Apply Styles and Style Sets ... 90

➡ Insert Clip Art 96

➡ Insert Photos 100

➡ Change the Text Wrap Setting for a Picture 101

➡ Add a Page Border 102

➡ Apply a Background Color to a Page 105

➡ Create Tables 107

➡ Format a Table 110

Apply Styles and Style Sets

Using a *style* — a named set of formatting specifications — makes it easy to apply consistent formatting throughout a document. For example, you might apply the style named Heading 1 to all headings in the document and the style named Normal to all the regular body text. Here are the advantages of this approach:

➠ **Ease:** Applying a style is easier than manually applying formatting. And, changing the formatting is a snap. If you want the headings to look different, for example, you can modify the Heading 1 style to change them all at once.

➠ **Consistency:** You don't have to worry about all the headings being formatted consistently; because they're all using the same style, they're automatically all the same.

 Of the several types of styles in Word, the most common type (by far) is a paragraph style. A *paragraph style* can contain formatting specifications, such as font, font size and color, indentation, alignment, and line spacing.

Unless you specify otherwise, each paragraph is assigned a style called Normal. In Word 2007, this default uses a Calibri 11 point (pt) font, and left-aligns your text. (Calibri is a font that comes with Office 2007.)

 Points (pt) measure how large the text is. Read more about this in Chapter 4.

In the Styles group on the Home tab (see Figure 5-1), you can find samples of several different styles: the *Quick Styles* area.

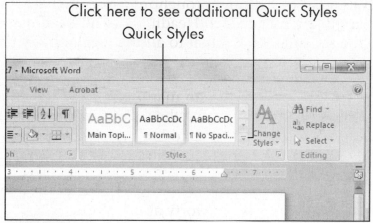

Figure 5-1

To assign a different style to a paragraph, follow these steps:

1. Click your mouse anywhere in the paragraph you want to change.

If you want to apply the style to multiple paragraphs, select them first. See Chapter 1 for how to select text.

2. Click the Home tab.

3. Click the down arrow to the right of the Quick Styles area, opening the Quick Styles Gallery (see Figure 5-2).

A few of the Quick Styles are visible without opening the Quick Styles Gallery. If the one you want to apply appears (as in Figure 5-1), you can skip Step 3.

4. Click the style you want.

Figure 5-2

Other styles are available besides the ones on the Quick Styles list. To
see them, click the small icon in the bottom right of the Styles group
to open a Styles pane that contains a larger list. See Figure 5-3. You
can select any style by clicking the style in the Styles pane.

 Mark the Show Preview check box in the Styles pane
if you want to show each style's name with the formatting the style contains.

The definitions of the styles are determined by the *style set* in use.
Different style sets can quickly change the look of an entire document
by redefining each built-in style (fonts, sizes, colors, line spacing, and
so on).

Click here to open the Styles pane

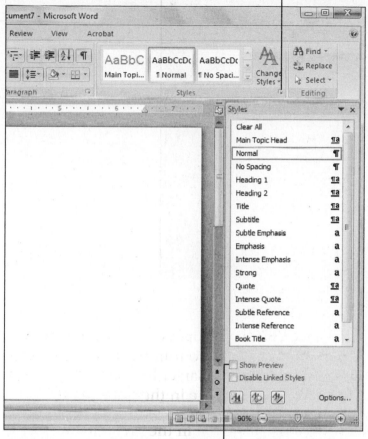

Mark this check box to preview the styles

Figure 5-3

To change to a different style set, follow these steps:

1. On the Home tab, click Change Styles.

2. In the menu that appears, point to Style Set.

3. In the menu that opens (see Figure 5-4), point to one of the style sets to see its effect previewed in the document. You can point to other styles sets to preview them as well.

4. Click the style set you want.

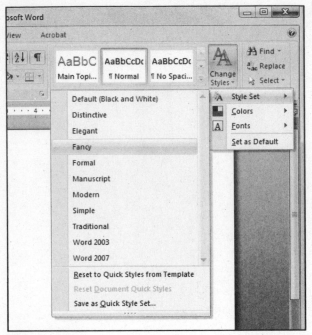

Figure 5-4

 Word 2007's default fonts and spacing are different from those in Word 2003 and earlier versions. If you're accustomed to an earlier version, you might want to use the Word 2003 style set. Just follow the preceding steps and choose Word 2003 in Step 4.

You can also manually modify any style's definition. Suppose that you want the body text in a document to be a little larger. To do this, follow these steps:

1. Open the Styles pane by clicking the small icon in the lower right of the Styles group (on the Home tab; refer to Figure 5-1).

2. In the Styles pane, point to the style you want to modify so that a down arrow appears to its right.

3. Click the down arrow to open a menu.

4. Click Modify.

5. In the Modify Style dialog box that appears, make any formatting changes as desired. This dialog box contains a variety of text and paragraph formatting settings. See Figure 5-5.

6. Click OK.

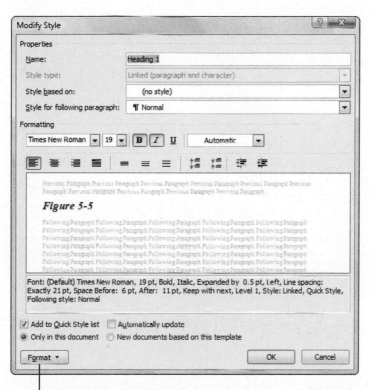

Click here for more formatting settings you can adjust

Figure 5-5

Insert Clip Art

Clip art is generic, predrawn artwork, like a simple drawing of a coffee cup or graphics related to holidays. You can use any of the free art in the Office 2007 clip art library to dress up your Word documents or any Office application.

You use the Clip Art feature to import and embed clip art proper, but you can also use it to import other types of media types of clips. Here's what you can add with this feature:

→ **Clip art:** Resizable line drawings

→ **Photos:** Pictures taken with a digital camera

→ **Sounds:** Digital clips that play sounds

→ **Movies:** Digital clips that play movies

Sounds and movies aren't used very often in Word because most Word documents are printed for distribution, and sounds and movies can't be printed. PowerPoint, on the other hand, makes great use of sounds and movies because its output is designed to be shown on a computer screen. (Read all about PowerPoint in Part V of this book.)

When you install Office 2007, a few clip art images are installed on your hard drive, but the majority of the Microsoft clip art, photo, sound, and movie collection is stored online. When you use the Clip Art feature in an Office application, it automatically connects to Microsoft's online database.

 If you don't have an Internet connection, or aren't connected to the Internet when you use the Clip Art feature, you can't access this library.

Follow these steps to insert clip art:

1. On the Insert tab, click Clip Art. The Clip Art task pane opens at the right.

2. In the Search For box, type a word that describes what you're looking for. In Figure 5-6, for example, I typed *baseball*.

Close the Clip Art task pane

Globe symbol means
clip was found online

Figure 5-6

3. Click the down arrow for the Results Should Be drop-down list and then mark or clear the check boxes to specify what media type(s) you want.

 Word remembers your settings from previous searches, so you have to do this only if you want to make a change.

4. (Optional) Open the Search In drop-down list to choose which collections to search. Most of the time, you will want to search all these locations. Your choices are

- *My Collections:* Clips you downloaded and saved via the Clip Organizer feature

- *Office Collections:* Clip art on your hard drive that came with Office

- *Web Collections:* Downloadable online clips from Microsoft

5. Click the Go button. Thumbnail images of the found clips appear in the task pane.

6. Position the insertion point in the document where you want the clip to be inserted.

> The picture will be placed wherever the insertion point is. If the insertion point is in the middle of a paragraph, the picture will split the paragraph in two, creating a possibly awkward look that you did not intend. For best results in most cases, position the insertion point on its own line, between two paragraphs.

7. Click the desired clip to place it in the document.

Right after you embed the clip art, it appears with *selection handles*, which you can click and drag to resize it. If you click anywhere in the document right after you embed the clip art, these handles disappear. To make them show again, just click the clip art.

After inserting a clip art image, you might want to resize it. To do so

1. Position the mouse pointer over one of the selection handles on the image's border. You see different directional arrows depending on what kind of handle you hover over. (Don't worry about the green circle at the top just yet.)

- *Round, corner handle:* A double-headed, diagonal arrow

- *Square, side handle:* A double-headed, horizontal arrow

2. Click the directional arrow and drag in the direction you want. The arrow turns into a crosshair, and the clip art expands or contracts as much as you make it.

You might notice some distortion when you resize the clip art. For example, when you drag a side handle, the clip art does indeed get wider, but it might look like a Silly Putty rendition. To maintain the height-to-width ratio so that the picture doesn't get distorted, hold down the Shift key while you drag one of the corner selection handles. See Figure 5-7.

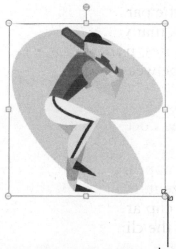

Mouse pointer turns into a double headed arrow when over a selection handle

Figure 5-7

To rotate clip art, click the graphic and then use the green circle at the top of the image.

1. Hover your mouse on the green circle until it turns into a clockwise arrow.

2. Click and hold the mouse. You get a circle of four, black clockwise arrows.

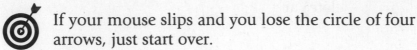 If your mouse slips and you lose the circle of four arrows, just start over.

3. Drag the circular arrow left or right to skew the image how you want.

To move an image in a document, click the image and drag it. Or, you can cut and paste it by using the Clipboard. (See how in Chapter 1.)

Insert Photos

Clip art is generic. Sometimes, you might want to insert a more personal picture, like a digital photo you took or a picture that a family member sent you via e-mail.

To insert a picture, use the Insert tab, as follows:

1. Position the insertion point where you want the picture to appear.

2. From the Insert tab, click Picture (in the Illustrations group).

3. In the Picture dialog box that opens, navigate to the folder containing the picture.

4. Click the picture you want.

5. Click Insert. The picture appears in the document.

You can resize the picture just like with a piece of clip art. See the preceding section to see how to do this.

When you click a picture in a Word document (*select* it), a Format tab appears on the Ribbon (upper right). This tab contains a variety of buttons for working with the picture, such as adding a matte or a border. Tinker with the options there. If you don't like what you've done, press Ctrl+Z to undo the last action. Or, just delete the figure (select it and then press Delete) and start over.

Change the Text Wrap Setting for a Picture

The default wrapping is In Line with Text. This type of alignment makes Word treat the picture like an individual character of text, wherever you put it. As the text floats, the picture floats, too. In this mode, the options are limited as to where you can place the picture because it has to remain associated with a paragraph.

On the Format tab is the Text Wrapping button, which opens a menu of alternative text wrap choices. Here, you can specify how the picture should interact with the adjacent text. This works on both clip art and photos. Here are the choices:

➡ **In Line with Text:** The picture is a part of the paragraph; the text doesn't wrap around it.

➡ **Square:** Text wraps around the picture's rectangular outer frame.

➡ **Tight:** If the picture is clip art that doesn't have a colored background, the text wraps around the edges of the image itself, not of its rectangular frame. Otherwise, it's the same as Square.

➡ **Behind Text:** The text appears as an overlay on top of the picture.

➡ **In Front of Text:** The image appears over the top of the text, partially obscuring it.

➡ **Top and Bottom:** The picture interrupts the text, which flows above or below it. The picture is on a line all by itself.

➡ **Through:** Mostly the same as Tight.

In Figure 5-8, the text wrapping is set to Square.

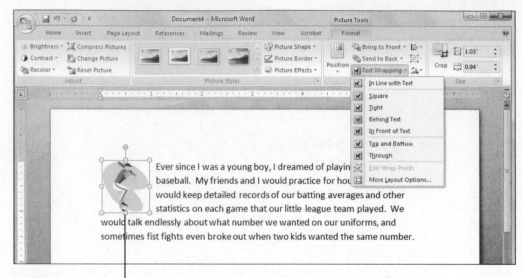

Text wraps around the picture

Figure 5-8

Add a Page Border

A *page border* can make a page look more festive and colorful; this feature is great for family newsletters, invitations, and holiday greetings. Page borders can be plain or fancy lines, or can consist of tiny pictures repeated in a pattern (Border Art).

To choose a page border, follow these steps:

1. Choose Page Layout➪Page Borders. The Borders and Shading dialog box opens with the Page Border tab displayed. See Figure 5-9.

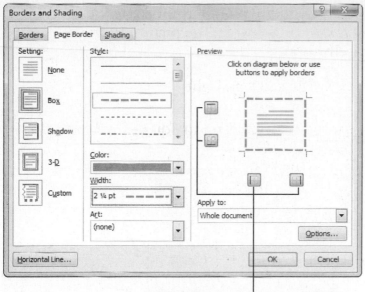

These buttons turn on/off the
border for individual sides

Figure 5-9

2. Choose one of the presets at the left side to describe the
type of border you want:

- *Box:* The border is the same on all sides.

- *Shadow:* The border is thicker at the left and
  bottom.

- *3-D:* A 3-D effect is applied to the border. (The
  effect is not always obvious, depending on other
  choices you make.)

- *Custom:* You can specify different settings for each
  side of the border individually.

3. Choose a line style from the Style list.

4. Choose a line color from the Color list.

5. Choose a width from the Width list.

6. Check the sample in the Preview area to make sure it's how you want it. Make any changes needed.

7. Click OK to apply the border.

You can also create a border by using artwork. This is where it gets really fun! For example, for a Christmas letter, you could have a border made of holly leaves or trees; for a birthday party, you could have a border made of slices of cake.

1. Choose Page Layout⇨Page Borders. The Borders and Shading dialog box opens with the Page Border tab displayed.

2. Open the Art drop-down list and select the picture you want to use.

3. In the Width box, enter the size (in points; pt) you want for the border's width. An average size border might be 30pt, for example.

4. Click OK. Figure 5-10 shows an art-based border.

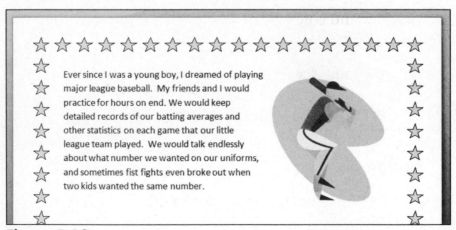

Figure 5-10

Apply a Background Color to a Page

Besides page borders, another way to dress up a page is to give it a colored background. Be aware, though, that if you print a page with a colored background, one of two things will happen:

➡ **Word will print it without the background,** and any special formatting that relies on the background might not look right. For example, if you have a black background and set the text color to yellow, you might end up with a barely readable document with yellow text on a white page.

➡ **Word will print it with the background,** meaning that you'll use a lot of ink in your printer.

 Background colors are most useful in documents that will be distributed online — such as via e-mail — rather than printed.

Background colors do not print by default. If you want to make them print, choose Office⇨Print. Then click the Options button. Mark the Print Background Colors and Images check box, and then click OK.

To set a background color (and "set" can mean to add or remove), follow these steps:

1. Choose Page Layout⇨Page Color. A color palette appears.

2. Make your choice:

- Click the color you want to use for the page background.

- Choose No Color to remove any existing background.

Like with many parts of Office, the color palette contains theme colors and fixed colors. As you can read in Chapter 2, *theme colors* are the color placeholders defined by the document's theme; they change if you choose a different theme. Comparatively, *fixed colors* don't change. See Figure 5-11.

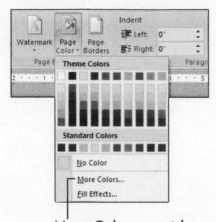

More Colors provides
additional standard color choices

Figure 5-11

You can also choose Fill Effects from the color palette. This opens the Fill Effects dialog box, where you can set up any of four types of fill effects:

➡ **Gradient:** A gradual blending between one color and another, like with a vibrant sunset

➡ **Texture:** A repeating graphic that looks like a certain type of surface, such as wood, concrete, or paper

➡ **Pattern:** A pattern of lines and/or dots in one color, with a contrasting background color

➡ **Picture:** An image (that you pick from the images stored on your hard drive) that fills the entire background

The details of using each of these fill effects is beyond the scope of this book, but you can experiment with them on your own. And don't forget, you can use the Help system in Word (press F1 or click the question mark button) to get more information about any feature.

Create Tables

A *table* is a grid of rows and columns, somewhat like a spreadsheet in Excel. Tables are useful for displaying information in multicolumn layouts, such as address lists. Figure 5-12 shows a table in a document.

Budget Committee
The following people have signed up to be on the Budget Committee.

Member	Phone Number	E-Mail	Lifetime Member?
Sally Smith	317-555-8882	sally@microsoft.com	Yes
Henry Ortega	317-555-7183	henry@sycamoreknoll.com	No
Cynthia Slater	219-555-5755	hyacinthia@wempen.com	Yes

Figure 5-12

You can create two kinds of column-based layouts in Word. One kind is a multicolumn table, which I describe here. The other kind is the *newspaper style*, where text flows all the way from the top of the page to the bottom in one column, and then loops up to the next column. I don't cover that feature in this book, but you can play with it on your own by choosing Page Layout⇨Columns.

Here's one way to insert a table:

1. Position the insertion point where you want the table to appear.

2. Choose Insert⇨Table. A menu opens that includes a grid of squares.

3. Drag your mouse across the grid until you highlight how many rows and columns you want. For example, in Figure 5-13, I'm selecting three columns and two rows.

4. Release the mouse button. The table appears in the document.

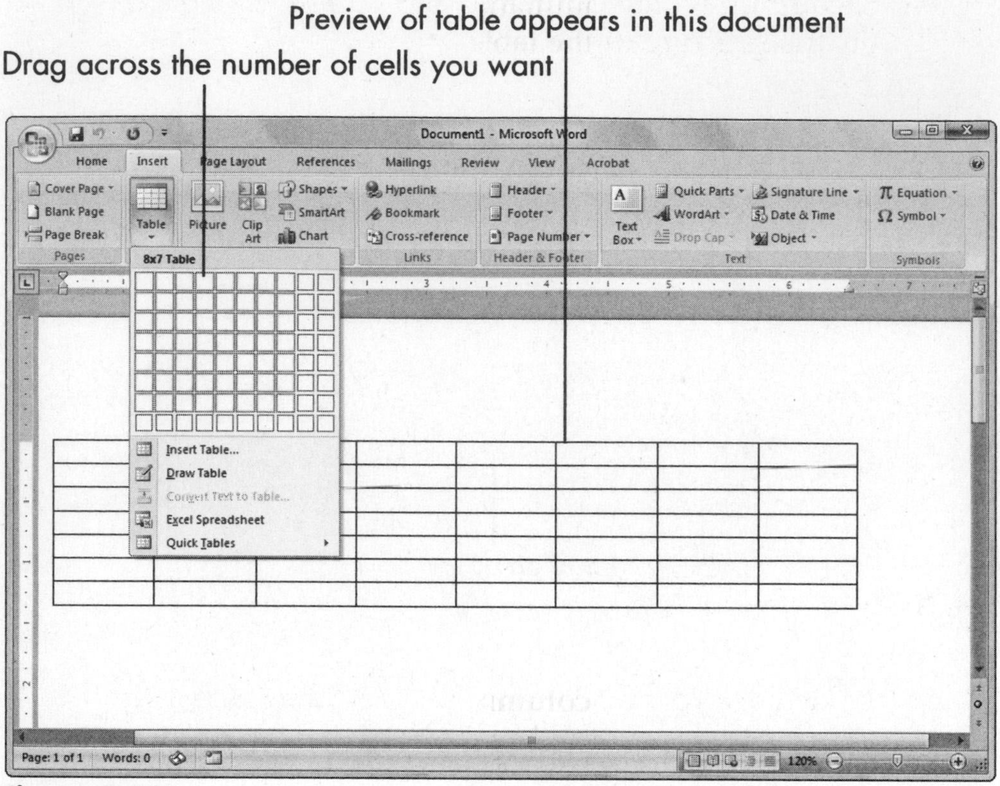

Preview of table appears in this document

Drag across the number of cells you want

Figure 5-13

If you have trouble selecting the right number of squares on the grid, choose Insert⇨Table⇨Insert Table. In the dialog box that appears, you can type a number of rows and columns you want.

To enter text into the table, just click inside the desired cell and start typing. You can move the insertion point from one cell to the next by pressing the Tab key, or move to the previous cell by pressing Shift+Tab.

When a table is *active* (that is, when the insertion point is anywhere within it), two extra tabs appear on the ribbon, under the heading Table Tools:

➡ **Design:** Contains commands and buttons for formatting the table

➡ **Layout:** Contains commands and buttons for changing the structure of the table

To change the number of rows or columns in the table, use the Layout tab, shown in Figure 5-14.

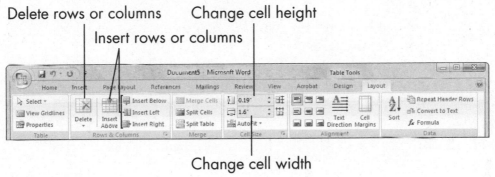

Figure 5-14

➡ **To delete a row or column:** Select it (drag across its cells) and then choose Layout⇨Delete.

➡ **To insert a row or column:** Click in a row or column that is adjacent to where you want the insertion, and then click one of the buttons on the Layout tab that describes the insertion you want: Insert Above, Insert Below, Insert Left, or Insert Right.

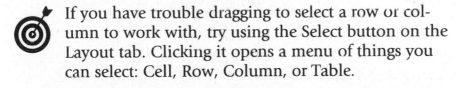 If you have trouble dragging to select a row or column to work with, try using the Select button on the Layout tab. Clicking it opens a menu of things you can select: Cell, Row, Column, or Table.

The height of each cell changes automatically depending on the cell contents. You don't have to change the size unless you want extra vertical blank space in the cell. You can specify a cell height in the Cell Size group on the Layout tab (refer to Figure 5-14).

More commonly, you'll need to change a column's width instead of a row's height. Here's how:

➡ Position the mouse pointer over one of the table's vertical gridlines. The mouse pointer turns into an I-beam with arrows on each side. Then drag to adjust the width.

➡ Click in a cell and then enter a number (in inches) in the Cell Width box on the Layout tab.

➡ Click AutoFit on the Layout tab to open a menu of AutoFit options. From there, click AutoFit Contents to automatically adjust the column width to fit the widest entry in that column.

Format a Table

You can manually format a table and its content in much the same way you format any other text: Use the formatting commands on the Home tab, for example. But the Design tab also has special formatting controls that apply specifically to tables.

For example, you can apply table styles to a table to automatically apply border and shading colors and styles, to automatically autofit the content, and to automatically apply different font formatting for the heading rows.

To apply a table style, follow these steps:

1. Click anywhere in the table. You don't have to select the whole table.

2. On the Design tab, click the down arrow to the right of the Table Style samples to open the full list of table styles.

3. While the list is open, point to a style. You can see a preview of it applied to your table, behind the open list. Figure 5-15 shows an example of that.

4. Click the style you want to apply.

Table Style Options fine-tune the way table styles are applied

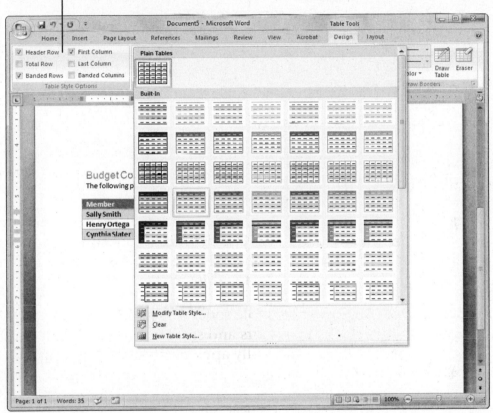

Figure 5-15

The check boxes in the Table Style Options group enable you to specify how the table style will be applied. For example, you can choose whether the header row is formatted differently than the rest of the table. If you choose Banded Rows, every other row will have a different color background, for easier reading.

Taking Word to the Next Level

Word has so many features and capabilities that most people don't even scratch the surface of what it can do. And that's okay! Word is a good tool partly because it's accessible at a variety of levels. I won't try to transform you into a Word guru, but I do want to show you some fairly simple features that you can use to make a big difference in your documents.

I start this chapter by showing you how to number the pages of a document, and also how to create headers and footers that repeat the same text at the top or bottom of each page. Then I show you how to insert cover pages and other special-purpose elements — *building blocks* — that can add style and beauty to your documents with a minimum of effort.

And when you print a letter, you also often need an envelope, so I show you how to generate envelopes in Word (and how to feed them into your printer).

Finally, I tackle *mail merge:* merging a form letter with a list of addresses. This helpful Word tool really isn't as hard as some people make it out to be.

Get ready to . . .

➡ Number the Pages 114

➡ Use Headers
and Footers 116

➡ Insert Cover Pages and
Other Building Blocks 119

➡ Print an Envelope 122

➡ Perform a Mail Merge 123

➡ Insert the Date and Time 129

Number the Pages

Have you ever dropped a stack of papers that needed to stay in a certain order? If the pages were numbered, putting them back together was fairly simple. If not, ugh: what a frustrating, time-consuming task.

Fortunately, Word makes it very easy to number your document pages. And you can choose from a variety of numbering styles and formats.

When you number pages in Word, you don't have to manually type the numbers onto each page. Instead, you place a code in the document that does the numbering for you automatically. Sweet!

Here's how it works. Each document has a header and footer area where you can place information you want repeated on every page. I explain more about headers and footers later in this chapter, but the important thing to know here is that when you use the Page Numbering feature in Word, it automatically inserts the proper code in either the header or the footer so that each page is numbered consecutively. These page numbers are visible only in Print Layout view, Full Screen Reading view, Print Preview, and on the printouts themselves. You won't see the page numbers if you are working in Draft view, even though they are there.

For simple page numbering at the bottom of each page (the *footer*), follow these steps:

1. Choose Insert⇨Page Number. (Look in the Header & Footer group.)

2. In the menu that appears, point to Bottom of Page. A submenu appears showing various samples of bottom-of-page numbering. See Figure 6-1. There are many samples; use the scroll bar on the list to see them.

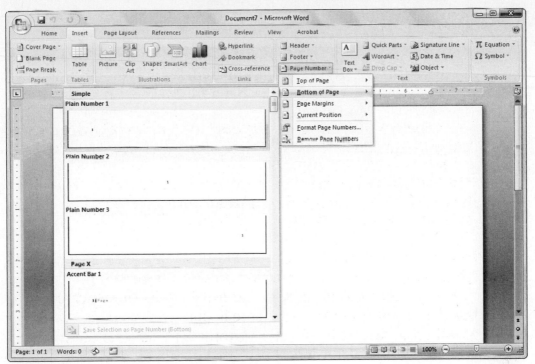

Figure 6-1

3. Click a sample to select it. The code for the page numbering is placed in the document footer, in the format you choose.

For a plain page number, select one of the first three samples: Plain Number 1, Plain Number 2, or Plain Number 3. They are all identical except for the positioning of the number (at the left, center, or right, respectively).

4. To return to editing the main document (leaving the footer), double-click anywhere within the body of your document.

Notice in Figure 6-1 the other page number position options besides Bottom of Page:

➡ **Top of Page:** Places the page number code in the *header* (top of the page). The page numbers appear on every page.

➡ **Page Margins:** Places the page number code on the side of the page. The page numbers appear on every page.

➡ **Current Position:** Places the page number code at the insertion point in the document (as a one-time thing). Because the code is not in the header or footer, it doesn't repeat on each page. It's a one-time thing. You might use this to create a cross-reference to content that's on another page, for example.

➡ **Format Page Numbers:** Opens a dialog box where you can fine-tune the formatting of the page numbering code, such as using roman numerals or letters instead of digits.

➡ **Remove Page Numbers:** Removes existing page numbering code(s).

Use Headers and Footers

In addition to a page number, you can put other content in the header and footer areas of your document. For example, if you're typing the minutes of a club meeting, you might want to put the club's name in the header so that it appears across the top of each page.

Every document has a header and footer area, which are both empty by default. The header and footer appear in Print Layout view, Full Page Reading view, and Web Layout view, and also on the printed page. (If you are in Draft view, you might want to switch to Print Layout view to follow along in this section more easily.)

Here are two ways of putting content into them:

→ **Manually:** In Print Layout view, double-click in the header or footer of the page. (Choose View➪Print Layout; see Chapter 1.) This puts you in the Header and Footer editing mode, where you can type text directly into those areas. See Figure 6-2.

 The body of the document cannot be edited while you are in this mode. To resume working within the main part of the document, double-click the main document (anywhere below the header or above the footer).

Double-click top of page to enable Header area

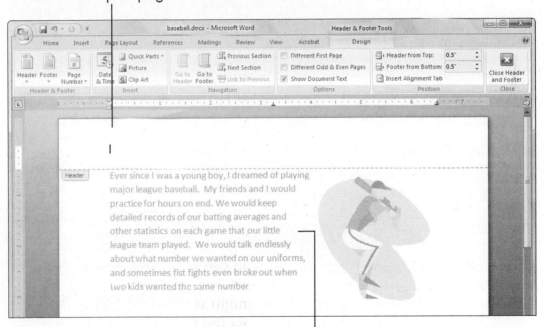

When insertion point is in Header, main document is read-only

Figure 6-2

→ **Let Word help:** Choose Insert➪Header or Insert➪Footer and then select a preformatted header or footer placeholder. This also places you in Header and Footer editing mode automatically, and you can edit the text in the placeholders that were inserted. Depending on the sample you pick, there might be not only a text placeholder but also a page-numbering code. This saves you the step of inserting the page-numbering code separately. Figure 6-3 shows the Footer menu and an inserted footer.

This footer was chosen

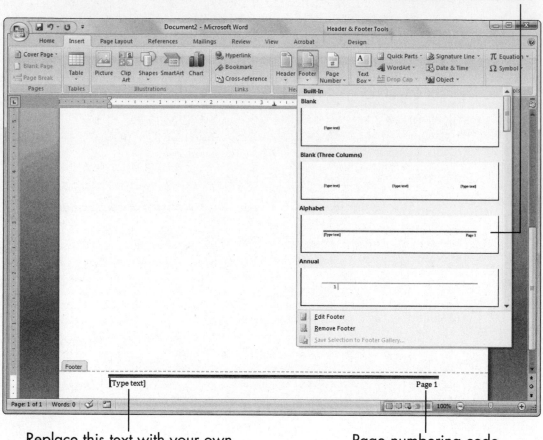

Replace this text with your own

Page numbering code

Figure 6-3

You can manually insert a page-numbering code into a header or footer as well as codes for the current date, time, and other information. When the insertion point is in the header or footer area, the Design tab appears on the Ribbon. On that tab are buttons for inserting various types of codes like that. See Figure 6-4.

Also in Figure 6-4, notice the check boxes in the Options group. Here, you can specify that you want a different header and footer for the first page (for example, so you can have a cover page without header and footer text), or that you want separate headers and footers for odd and even pages (for example, for a double-sided booklet where the page numbers should always be on the outside edge).

Finally, notice in Figure 6-4 that in the Position group, you can control the amount of space allotted to the header and footer. By default, each is one-half inch tall. You can change these values in the Header from Top and Footer from Bottom list boxes.

Page numbering code   Specify special handling for the first page

Date or time code   Adjust size of header or footer area

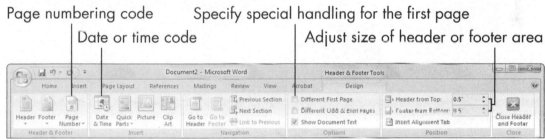

Figure 6-4

When you're done working with the header and footer, double-click the main body of the document, or click the Close Header and Footer button on the Design tab.

Insert Cover Pages and Other Building Blocks

Many different document types can benefit from a good-looking cover page: a committee report, a proposal for a home business, or a family album. Word 2007 offers a large gallery of sample cover pages that you can insert into your document and then customize.

Cover pages are automatically placed at the beginning of the document, before the current first page. You don't have to position the insertion point at the beginning of the document before you insert them.

To insert a cover page, follow these steps:

1. Choose Insert⇨Cover Page. A palette of cover page samples appears. See Figure 6-5.

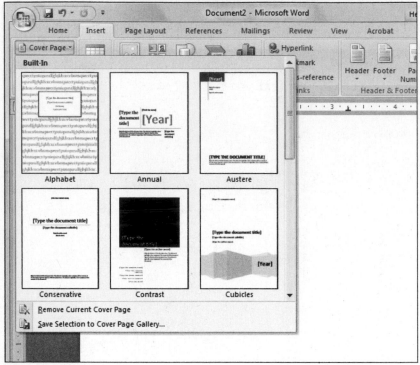

Figure 6-5

2. Click the cover page you want to insert. It is placed at the beginning of the document.

3. Fill in the placeholders on the cover page as desired.

To delete a cover page, choose Insert⇨Cover Page⇨Remove Current Cover Page.

Cover pages are just one of several types of preformatted sample content that Word collectively calls *building blocks.* The page numbering samples I show you earlier in this chapter are building blocks, as are preformatted headers and footers.

To see all the building blocks that Word offers in one convenient place, choose Insert⇨Quick Parts⇨Building Blocks Organizer. This opens the Building Blocks Organizer dialog box, shown in Figure 6-6. From here, you can browse the various types of content and insert anything you find that looks interesting. Some of the content types include equations, tables, text boxes, and watermarks.

Type of content

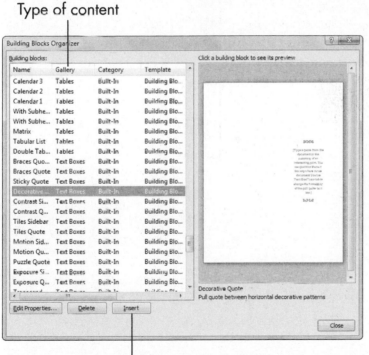

Select an item and click Insert to add it to your document

Figure 6-6

Print an Envelope

Envelopes are the natural companions of business and personal letters. Most of the time, when you print a letter, you also want an envelope for it. You can address the envelope by hand, of course, but printing an envelope is quick and easy in Word.

One nice thing about the Envelopes feature in Word is that it can automatically extract the mailing address from the letter, so you don't have to retype it. It also stores your return address, and recalls it for you each time you print an envelope.

If your letter contains the recipient's name and mailing address, follow these steps to create an envelope for it:

1. Open the letter in Word.

2. Choose Mailings⇨Envelopes. The Envelopes and Labels dialog box opens. If the letter contains a valid address, that address is automatically filled into the Delivery Address field, as shown in Figure 6-7.

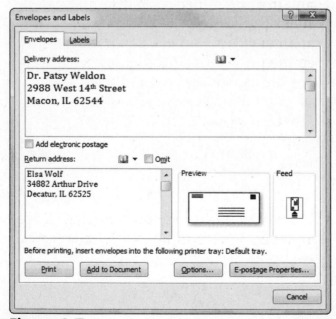

Figure 6-7

3. (Optional) Type your return address in the Return Address field if it doesn't already appear there.

 If the return address appears but you don't want to use it (this time only), mark the Omit check box. (This keeps the return address on file for later use.) You wouldn't want to use a return address if you're using envelopes with the return address preprinted, or if you're going to use stick-on return address labels.

4. Feed an envelope into your printer.

5. Click Print. The envelope prints.

If the envelope printing doesn't go as you expected — say, it prints on the wrong side, or it's not lined up correctly — you might need to try again and change the orientation at which you feed it into the printer. For example, you might need to feed it in sideways, rotated 180 degrees, or upside-down.

 To avoid wasting an envelope, do a test print using plain paper. Draw an arrow on a piece of paper, and put it into your printer's paper tray, face up, arrow facing in. Then print an envelope on that paper. The relationship between the printout and the arrow can tell you how to orient the envelopes you feed in. For example, if the arrow is on the reverse side from the printing, you know that envelopes need to be fed into the printer flap-up.

Perform a Mail Merge

A *mail merge* combines a list of names and addresses (that is, mailing information) with a form letter, a label, or an envelope template to produce customized copies of the letter for each person. Big companies use mail merge to mail customized advertisements, but it's not just for businesses. Home users can take advantage of mail merge for Christmas card mailing labels, party invitations, club newsletters, and more.

The three steps to a mail merge are

1. Create (or identify) the data source.
2. Create the main document and then insert the merge codes in it.
3. Perform the merge operation between the data source and the main document.

Start with the options for data sources. The data source must be a *delimited* file. In other words, there has to be some consistent way that it distinguishes between one column or row of data and the next.

- **Excel, Word table:** If the data source is an Excel spreadsheet, as in Figure 6-8, each type of information is in a separate column. The same goes if the data source is a Word table.

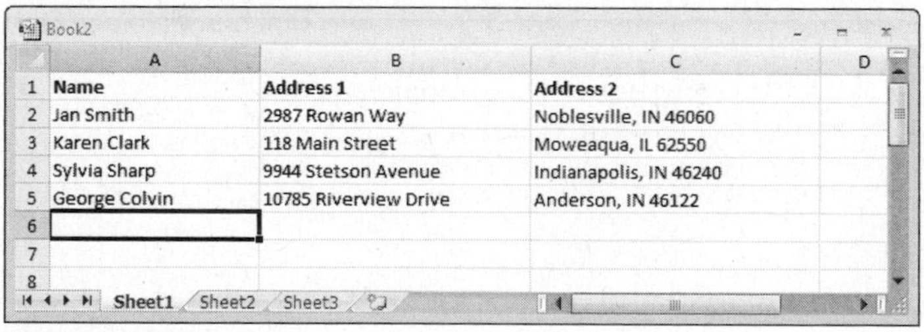

	A	B	C	D
1	**Name**	**Address 1**	**Address 2**	
2	Jan Smith	2987 Rowan Way	Noblesville, IN 46060	
3	Karen Clark	118 Main Street	Moweaqua, IL 62550	
4	Sylvia Sharp	9944 Stetson Avenue	Indianapolis, IN 46240	
5	George Colvin	10785 Riverview Drive	Anderson, IN 46122	
6				
7				
8				

Figure 6-8

- **Plain text:** If the data source is a plain text file, each column is delimited by a specific character, such as tab or a comma. In Figure 6-9, I used a comma.

(When a delimited text file uses commas, it's called a Comma Separated Values, or CSV, file.)

Commas represent the column breaks

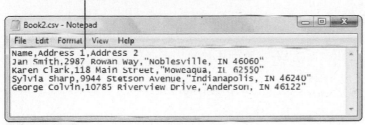

Figure 6-9

➥ **Outlook:** If the data source is an Outlook Contacts list, each type of information is in a separate field. Outlook Contacts are covered in Chapter 12.

➥ **Word list:** If you don't have a data source already, you can use the Type New List feature in Word to create one. Choose Mailings⇨Select Recipients⇨ Type New List. See upcoming Figure 6-10.

 A data file shouldn't contain anything except the data (and perhaps a single row of field labels, as in Figure 6-9 with Name, Address1, and Address2). There shouldn't be any blank rows or titles at the top of the page because that confuses the Mail Merge utility. Check your data file to remove extraneous rows before using the file as your mail merge source.

After preparing the data file, you set up the main document. You can either create the main document from scratch, or you can start with an existing document and convert it to be a mail merge main document.

Of the different kinds of main documents you can have, letters, envelopes, and labels are the most common. In this chapter, I show you how to do a letter.

Follow these steps to set up your main document:

1. Start a new document, or open an existing one that you want to use.

2. Choose Mailings⇨Start Mail Merge⇨Letters.

Next, attach the data source file to the main document.

1. Choose Mailings⇨Select Recipients.

2. Choose the type of data source:

- *Type New List:* This command opens the New Address List dialog box. Use this dialog box (see Figure 6-10) to create new address book entries. (Click the New Entry button after each one.) When you're finished, click OK. Then in the Save Address List dialog box that opens, assign a name to the new address list. You can reuse it for other mail merges.

- *Use Existing List:* This command opens the Select Data Source dialog box. Use this dialog box to select the Excel, Word, Notepad, or other file where you saved your data source. Then click Open to confirm your selection. If you choose a data source file that has multiple sheets or tables, a dialog box might prompt you to pick which one you want.

- *Select from Outlook Contacts:* This command opens the Select Contacts dialog box. Click the contact folder you want to use (there might be only one listed) and then click OK. Then in the Mail Merge Recipients dialog box that opens (see Figure 6-11), clear the check box for each record that you do *not* want to include in the merge, and then click OK.

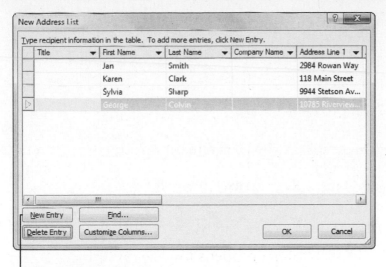

Click here to start a new row

Figure 6-10

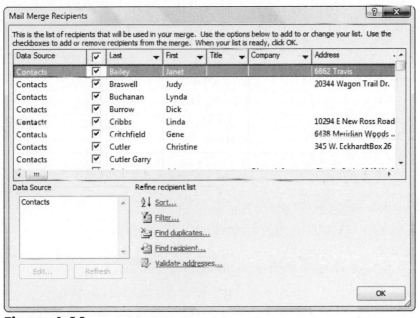

Figure 6-11

Next, insert the field codes into the main document where you want the text to be pulled in from the data source. There are several ways to do this, depending on what you want. Place the insertion point where the field should appear, and then choose from the following:

➡ If you want **the recipient's name and address to appear**

    a. Choose Mailings⇨Address Block.

    b. In the Insert Address Block dialog box that appears, check the preview in the Preview area and then click OK.

➡ If you want to **insert a greeting line (such as Dear Mr. Jones)**

    a. Choose Mailings⇨Greeting Line.

    b. Check the preview in the Preview area and then click OK.

➡ **To insert individual fields from the data source**

    a. Choose Mailings⇨Insert Merge Field.

    b. Select the field to insert.

After all the codes are inserted where you want them, check your work.

1. Choose Mailings⇨Preview Results. The first record from the data source appears filled into the main document.

2. In the Preview Results group on the Mailings tab, click the right arrow button to move to the next record. Repeat that until you have checked all the records (or at least enough to be confident that you did things right).

Finally, time to print the letters.

1. Make sure you have the right kind of paper and enough paper in your printer, and that the printer is and ready.

2. Choose Mailings➪Finish & Merge➪Print Documents.

3. In the Merge to Printer dialog box, click OK.

4. The Print dialog box that opens, check the print settings (such as printer name), and change any if needed. See Figure 6-12.

5. Click Print.

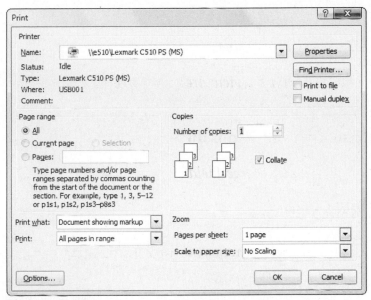

Figure 6-12

Insert the Date and Time

You can just type the current date and time into a document, such as when you are writing a letter, so you don't need a special feature for that. However, Word can insert the current date and/or time in your choice of many standard formats so that you don't have to worry about whether you've got the punctuation in the right place.

The best part is that you have the option of making the date/time a *field code*, which is a fancy way of saying that the document knows to update the date/time information. So, for example, say you start a letter one day and don't finish it until a week later. If you make the date/time a field code, the date on the letter will reflect the date when you save or print it, without you having to manually change it. This is a handy feature when you always want the document to display today's date, no matter what day you open it.

To insert a *static* (doesn't change) date or time, follow these steps:

1. Choose Insert⇨Date & Time.

2. In the Date and Time dialog box that opens, (see Figure 6-13), choose the **format** you want. The actual date or time will come from the system clock (the date/time clock in Windows).

To insert a date or time that updates automatically, follow these steps:

1. Do Steps 1 and 2 in the preceding step list.

2. In the Date and Time dialog box that opens (see Figure 6-13), select the Update Automatically check box.

3. Click OK to complete the insertion.

If you choose to insert the date/time as a code, it updates automatically whenever you save or print the file. If you want to update it any time other than that, click the date/time so that a pop-up appears with an Update button in it. Click the Update button to update the code. You can also press F9, which updates all field codes in the document.

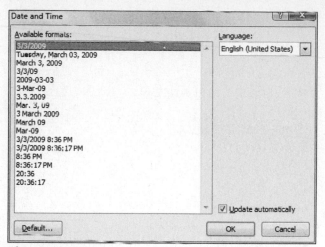

Figure 6-13

Part III
Excel

The 5th Wave   By Rich Tennant

"I started running 'what if' scenarios on my spreadsheet, like, 'What if I were sick of this dirtwad job and funneled some of the company's money into an off-shore account?'"

Creating Basic Spreadsheets in Excel

Microsoft Word works great for typing text, but sometimes you want something a little more structured for data. When you have more complex needs for column-based organizing than what Word's tables can provide, Excel is a great step up to the next level. Excel is much more than just a column organizer, though; it enables you to write formulas that perform calculations on your data. This makes Excel an ideal tool for storing financial information, such as a checkbook register and investment portfolio data.

In this chapter, I introduce you to the Excel interface and show you some of the concepts you need to know to work with a spreadsheet. Some of projects that Excel works great for include

➡ Tracking a stock portfolio

➡ Recording checkbook transactions

➡ Storing an address book list

➡ Charting progress toward a goal

Using the skills this chapter covers, you can build all these types of spreadsheets and more.

Get ready to . . .

➡ Understand Excel's Unique Features 136

➡ Get Familiar with Spreadsheet Structure 138

➡ Move the Cell Cursor 138

➡ Select a Range 139

➡ Type and Edit Cell Contents 143

➡ Save Your Work 145

➡ Insert and Delete Rows, Columns, and Cells 146

➡ Work with Worksheets 151

Understand Excel's Unique Features

Excel shares many elements with the Microsoft Office interface. Figure 7-1 and the following list, however, show you the features that are unique to the Excel program. (If you need a refresher on the Microsoft Office interface in general, including features such as the Ribbon, Quick Access toolbar, and Office button, take a few minutes to review Chapter 1.)

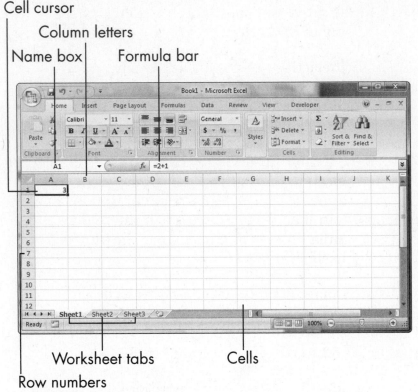

Figure 7-1

As you examine Figure 7-1, you'll see

⟶ **Row numbers:** Each *row* has a unique number. To select an entire row, click its number.

➡ **Column letters:** Each *column* has a unique letter. To select an entire column, select its letter.

➡ **Cells:** At the intersection of each row and column is a *cell*. You enter content into a cell by clicking the cell and then typing.

➡ **Active cell indicator:** This thick outline indicates which cell is the *active cell* — where your cursor is located at the moment. Whatever you type next appears in the active cell, and whatever commands you issue apply to that cell.

➡ **Name box:** The active cell's name appears here. For example, if the selected cell is at the intersection of column A and row 1, A1 appears in the Name box.

➡ **Formula bar:** The contents of the selected cell appears here. If the content is text, that text shows here as in the cell itself. If the content is a formula, the formula appears here, and the result of the formula appears in the cell. For example, if the cell contains the formula =2+1, the formula bar shows =2+1 and the cell itself shows 3.

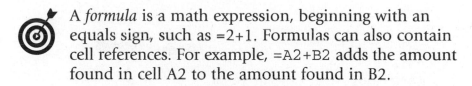 A *formula* is a math expression, beginning with an equals sign, such as =2+1. Formulas can also contain cell references. For example, =A2+B2 adds the amount found in cell A2 to the amount found in B2.

➡ **Worksheet tabs:** By default, each workbook file has three *sheets*. They're like pages in a notebook. Each sheet is shown as a tab; click a tab to switch to that sheet.

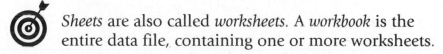 *Sheets* are also called *worksheets*. A *workbook* is the entire data file, containing one or more worksheets.

Get Familiar with Spreadsheet Structure

Each cell has a unique *cell address* consisting of its column letter and row number. In Figure 7-1, for example, the active cell is at the intersection of column A and row 1. So, its cell address is A1. See the Name box in Figure 7-1. Each cell must have its own unique address so that you can refer to it when you create a formula. For example, suppose you want to sum (add) the values in cells B3 and B4. You can write a formula like this: =B3+B4.

 When you copy a formula that refers to cells by their addresses, the references to those cells automatically adjust to take into account the new position. For example, suppose you have the formula =A1+1 in cell A2. If you copy that formula into cell B2, the copy of the formula reads =B1+1.

A *range* is a group of one or more cells. You refer to a range by the address of the upper leftmost cell in the range, followed by a colon, and then followed by the lower rightmost cell in the range. For example, the range consisting of cells A1, A2, B1, and B2 is written as A1:B2.

 Technically, a single cell can be a range, but usually it isn't called a range.

Move the Cell Cursor

As I show you in Figure 7-1, the active cell indicator is the dark outline around the active cell. To change which cell is active, you can do either of the following:

➡ **With your mouse:** Click the cell you want to be active.

➡ **From the keyboard:** Press one of the arrow keys on the keyboard to move the active cell indicator one cell at a time in the direction the arrow is pointing until you reach the cell you want to be active.

Table 7-1 provides more shortcuts for moving the active cell indicator within a worksheet.

Table 7-1	Movement Shortcuts
Press This . . .	**To Move . . .**
Arrow keys	One cell in the direction of the arrow
Tab	One cell to the right
Shift+Tab	One cell to the left
Ctrl+any arrow key	To the edge of the current data region in a worksheet (the first or last cell that isn't empty)
End	To the cell in the lower-right corner of the window (This works only when the Scroll Lock key has been pressed on your keyboard to turn on the Scroll Lock function.)
Ctrl+End	To the last cell in the worksheet, in the lowest used row of the rightmost used column
Home	To the beginning of the row containing the active cell
Ctrl+Home	To the beginning of the worksheet (cell A1)
Page Down	One screen down (The cell cursor moves, too.)
Alt+Page Down	One screen to the right
Ctrl+Page Down	To the next sheet in the workbook
Page Up	One screen up (The cell cursor moves, too.)
Alt+Page Up	One screen to the left
Ctrl+Page Up	To the previous sheet in the workbook

Select a Range

You might sometimes want to select a multicell range before you issue a command. For example, if you want to make all the text in the cell range A1:F1 bold, select that range and then issue the command for applying Bold (by clicking the B button on the Home tab or by pressing Ctrl+B). You can select a range by using either the keyboard or the mouse.

To select a range by using the mouse, follow these steps:

1. Click the upper leftmost cell in the range.

2. Click and hold down the left mouse button and drag to the lower rightmost cell in the range.

To select a range by using the keyboard, follow these steps:

1. Use the arrow keys to move the cell cursor to the upper leftmost cell in the range.

2. Press and hold down the Shift key while you press the → or ↓ keys to extend the selection until all the cells in the range are selected.

3. Release the Shift key.

 You can also select a range in reverse order: that is, starting with the lower rightmost cell and dragging upward and to the left or pressing the ← or ↑ keys.

You can also use a hybrid method involving both keyboard and mouse:

1. Select the first cell in the range using any method: either clicking it with the mouse or using the arrow keys to move the cell selector to it.

2. Hold down the Shift key and click the last cell in the range.

3. Release the Shift key.

Table 7-2 provides some shortcut keys to help you select ranges.

Table 7-2	Range Selection Shortcuts
Press This . . .	**To Extend the Selection To . . .**
Ctrl+Shift+arrow key	The last nonblank cell in the same column or row as the active cell; or if the next cell is blank, to the next nonblank cell
Ctrl+Shift+End	The last used cell on the worksheet (lower-right corner of the range containing data)
Ctrl+Shift+Home	The beginning of the worksheet (A1)
Ctrl+Shift+Page Down	The current and next sheet in the workbook
Ctrl+Shift+Page Up	The current and previous sheet in the workbook
Ctrl+spacebar	The entire column where the active cell is located
Shift+spacebar	The entire row where the active cell is located
Ctrl+Shift+spacebar or Ctrl+A	The entire worksheet

Although less common, you can also select a *noncontiguous range* (cells that don't border each other). For example, suppose you want to apply a certain type of formatting to cells A1, A5, and A9. Select those three cells before issuing your formatting command, so that the formatting is applied to the three discrete cells at once:

1. Select the first cell in the range.

2. Hold down the Ctrl key and click more individual cells to be in the range. Or, click and drag across more multi-cell blocks to be in the range. The additional selected cells appear highlighted with a very pale gray.

3. Release the Ctrl key.

An entire row or column can also be a range. Here's how to select a row or column (for example, to delete it, or to format it a certain way):

➡ **To select an entire row:** Click its row number to the left of the row.

➡ **To select an entire column:** Click its column letter at the top of the column.

➡ **To select multiple contiguous rows or columns:** Select the first row/column and then click and hold down the left mouse button while you drag to include more rows or columns.

➡ **To select multiple noncontiguous rows or columns:** Select the first row/column and then hold down Ctrl while you click more individual row numbers or column letters. A pale highlight is applied to each row or column you select.

Sometimes, you might want to apply a particular command to every cell on the entire worksheet. For example, you might want all the text in the entire worksheet to be a certain color or font. To select all cells at once, you can drag to create a range that encompasses the entire sheet; but that's somewhat cumbersome. Here are a couple of easier alternatives:

➡ Click the Select All button, which you can find in the upper-left corner of the sheet at the intersection of the row numbers and column letters (see Figure 7-2).

➡ Press Ctrl+A.

Select All

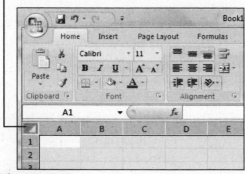

Figure 7-2

Type and Edit Cell Contents

To this point in the chapter, I've introduced you to some spreadsheet basics. Now, it's time to actually do something: enter some text and numbers into cells.

To type in a cell, you simply select the cell and begin typing. Whatever you type appears both in the cell and in the formula bar. (Refer to Figure 7-1 to see where the formula bar is located.) When you finish typing, you can leave the cell in any of these ways:

➡ Press Enter (moves you to the next cell down).

➡ Press Tab (moves you to the next cell to the right).

➡ Press Shift+Tab (moves you to the next cell to the left).

➡ Press an arrow key (moves you in the direction of the arrow).

If you need to edit what's in the cell, you have these choices:

➡ Click the cell to select it, and then click the cell again to move the insertion point into it. Edit like you would in Word or any text program.

➡ Click the cell to select it, and then type a new entry to replace the old one.

If you make a mistake when editing, you can press Esc (top left of your keyboard) to cancel the edit before you leave the cell. If you need to undo an edit after having left the cell, press Ctrl+Z or click the Undo button on the Quick Access toolbar.

Now try typing some text into your spreadsheet. I entered the text shown in Figure 7-3 to create a simple mortgage calculator. Feel free to enter your own information or type the same text I entered.

	A	B	C	D	E
1	Mortgage Calculator				
2					
3	Purchase Details				
4		Purchase Price			
5		Down Payment			
6		Amount Financed			
7					
8	Loan Details				
9		Interest Rate			
10		Loan Length (Years)			
11		Points and Fees			
12		Total Due at Signing			
13					
14	Payment Details				
15		Monthly Payment			
16					
17					
18					

Figure 7-3

If you decide you don't want the text you typed in a particular cell, you can get rid of it in several different ways:

➠ Select the cell; then right-click the cell and choose Clear Contents from the menu that appears.

➠ Select the cell; then choose Home➪Editing➪Clear➪ Clear Contents.

➠ Select the cell, press the spacebar, and then press Enter. This technically doesn't clear the cell's content, but it replaces it with a single, invisible character — a space.

 Don't confuse Clear with Delete. They are two separate things. There is a Delete command on the Home tab (Home➪Cells➪Delete), but using this doesn't *clear* the cell content; instead, it *removes* the entire cell. You find out more about deleting cells in the upcoming section, "Inserting and Deleting Individual Cells."

And while I'm on the subject, don't confuse Clear with Cut, either. The Cut command works in conjunction with the Clipboard. It moves the content to the Clipboard, from which you can then paste it some-where else. In Excel, though (unlike in other applications), using the Cut command doesn't immediately remove the content. Instead, it puts a flashing dotted box around the content and waits for you to reposition the cell cursor and issue the Paste command. If you do something else in the interim, the cut-and-paste operation is cancelled, and the content that you cut remains in its original location.

 You can also clear only the formatting from a cell by choosing Home⇨Editing⇨Clear⇨Clear Formatting. To clear both the content and the formatting, choose Home⇨Editing⇨Clear⇨Clear All.

Try clearing some content from the text you entered in your spread-sheet. Select a cell and use any of the three methods from the preced-ing bullet list to remove the contents of the cell. From the text I typed earlier, I chose to clear the text from cell A14.

Save Your Work

After you type some text in a worksheet, *save your work!* Don't wait until you type a lot of text. Always save early in the process in case something bad happens — like a power outage — that causes your computer to shut down unexpectedly.

To save your work, follow these steps:

1. Choose Office⇨Save As.

 If this is the first time saving this particular file, Office⇨Save is the same as Save As. During subse-quent saves, Save keeps your changes with the same name, type, and location, whereas Save As reopens the dialog box.

2. In the Save As dialog box that opens, type a name for the file in the File Name text box.

3. Choose the Excel Worksheet (*.xlsx) format from the Save as Type drop-down list.

4. (Optional) To change the save location, navigate to a different folder and/or drive.

5. Click Save.

 Excel 2007's native file format uses a four-letter .xlsx extension. This is different from earlier Excel versions, which use a three-letter .xls extension.

 If you save an Excel 2007 document as-is, you cannot open it (nor can anyone else) in any version of Excel prior to Excel 2007 (say, Excel 2003). This is a big deal. Unless you're sure that the document will be used only by people who have Excel 2007, consider "down-saving" the document to an earlier version so that folks not using Office 2007 can open it.

To share an Excel 2007 file with people who use an older version, you can *down-save* your file: that is, in the earlier-version format. Think of this as being "backward compatible."

To down-save your work, follow these steps:

1. Choose Office⇨Save As⇨Excel 97-2003 Workbook.

2. (Optional) To change the save location, navigate to a different folder and/or drive.

3. Click Save.

Insert and Delete Rows, Columns, and Cells

Even if you're a careful planner, you'll likely decide that you want to change your spreadsheet's layout. Maybe you want data in a different column, or certain rows turn out to be unnecessary. Excel makes it easy to insert and delete rows and columns to deal with these kinds of changes.

 Instead of inserting rows and columns, you can move the content between rows or columns. In Chapter 8, read how to move content in a worksheet.

To insert a row or column, follow these steps:

1. Select the row above or the column to the right of where the insertion should occur. Or, click in any cell in that row or column.

2. Choose Home⇨Insert to open the drop-down list for the Insert button. See Figure 7-4.

3. From the menu, choose Insert Sheet Rows or Insert Sheet Columns.

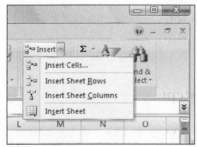

Figure 7-4

Here's another way to insert: from the right-click (contextual) menu:

1. Select a row or column adjacent to where the insertion should occur.

2. Right-click the selection and choose Insert from the menu that appears. Excel inserts either a row or a column, whichever you select in Step 1.

To insert multiple rows or columns at once, select a corresponding number of contiguous rows or columns in Step 1 in the preceding step list. For example, if you select three columns, you get three new blank columns when you choose Insert.

Deleting a row or column works in a similar way:

1. Select the row(s) or column(s) you want to delete.

2. Choose Home➪Cells➪Delete.

 The Delete button has a drop-down list, just like the Insert button does. From it, you can choose what you wanted to delete: cells, rows, or columns. However, in Step 1, you select what you want to delete, so that isn't necessary in this case; you could simply click the button to delete what was selected.

Try your hand at deleting a row from your spreadsheet. Earlier, I cleared the contents from cell A14. Now, I'm deleting rows 13 and 14. You can see how this looks in Figure 7-5.

	A	B	C	D
1	Mortgage Calculator			
2				
3	Purchase Details			
4		Purchase Price		
5		Down Payment		
6		Amount Financed		
7				
8	Loan Details			
9		Interest Rate		
10		Loan Length (Years)		
11		Points and Fees		
12		Total Due at Signing		
13		Monthly Payment		
14				
15				

Figure 7-5

You can also delete individual cells from a worksheet.

Deleting a cell is different from clearing a cell's content! When you clear only the content, the cell itself remains. When you delete the cell itself, the cells to the right or below shift to the left or up to fill in the gap.

Here's a way to envision what deletion does. Imagine that each cell is a cardboard box, stacked one on top of another in a grid. Each box opens to the front, so you can put things in it and take things out of it. When you delete a cell, you pull the box out of the stack. Gravity dictates that the boxes on top of the space fall down to fill it in. However, in Excel, gravity is backward: The cells fall *up* (or to the right if you specify that).

Excel is smart enough that it tries to guess which direction you want existing content to move when you delete cells. If you have content immediately to the right of a deleted cell, for example, it shifts it left. If you have content immediately below the deleted cell, it shifts it up. You can still override that, though, when needed.

To delete individual cells, follow these steps:

1. Select the cell(s) to delete.

2. Choose Home➪Cells➪Delete. Excel attempts to guess how you want the adjacent cells shifted, and then performs that operation.

If Excel didn't shift the other cells in the direction you expected, try again using this slightly longer, but more controllable, alternative procedure.

1. Select the cell(s) to delete.

2. Choose Home➪Cells and then click the arrow on the Delete button to open its menu.

3. Click Delete Cells. A Delete dialog box opens, as shown in Figure 7-6.

4. Select the radio button for the shift you want: Shift Cells Left or Shift Cells Up.

5. Click OK.

Figure 7-6

Inserting individual cells works in much the same way. You can choose from an easy method that guesses how you want the shift of adjacent content to occur, or a more controllable method where you get to specify how.

Here's the easy method for cell insertion:

1. Select the cell(s) above or to the left of where you want them to appear.

2. Choose Home⇨Cells⇨Insert. Excel attempts to guess how you want the adjacent content shifted and performs that action.

This method gives you direct control:

1. Select the cell(s) above or to the left of where you want them to appear.

2. Choose Home⇨Cells and click the arrow on the Insert button to open its menu.

3. Click Insert Cells. An Insert dialog box appears.

4. Select the radio button for the shift you want: Shift Cells Right or Shift Cells Down.

5. Click OK.

 Here's a shortcut for opening the Insert or the Delete dialog box. Select the cells, right-click the selection, and then choose Insert or Delete from the right-click menu.

Try deleting some individual cells from your spreadsheet. In the Mortgage file I created earlier, I deleted cells A4:A6 and A9:A13. My spreadsheet now looks like Figure 7-7.

	A	B	C	D
1	Mortgage Calculator			
2				
3	Purchase Details			
4	Purchase Price			
5	Down Payment			
6	Amount Financed			
7				
8	Loan Details			
9	Interest Rate			
10	Loan Length (Years)			
11	Points and Fees			
12	Total Due at Signing			
13	Monthly Payment			
14				
15				

Figure 7-7

Work with Worksheets

Each workbook contains three sheets by default: Sheet1, Sheet2, and Sheet3. Most people don't even notice at first that there are three sheets; they're focused solely on the spreadsheet that's in front of them. The extra sheets can come in every handy, though, for alternative versions of the same spreadsheet or for storing different spreadsheets in the same data file. For example, you could have separate sheets for your holdings at each investment firm, or separate sheets for the membership rosters of several different clubs.

To switch from one sheet to another, click the sheet's tab at the bottom of the Excel window.

With a normal Excel window size and the default three tabs, with their default names, you should have no trouble seeing all three tabs at once. However, if you add a lot more sheets to the workbook (covered shortly) or rename the tabs so that some of them have very long names (also covered shortly), and/or if you resize your Excel window so it's fairly narrow, not all the tabs may be visible at once. When this happens, you can use the tab scroll arrows to the left of the tabs to scroll the tabs to the left and right. See Figure 7-8.

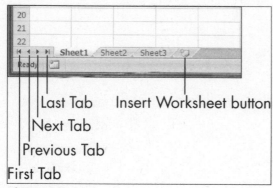

Last Tab   Insert Worksheet button
Next Tab
Previous Tab
First Tab

Figure 7-8

To create a new sheet, click the Insert Worksheet button shown in Figure 7-8, or press Shift+F11. The resulting blank sheet uses the default settings (formatting, column width, and so on).

To delete a sheet, right-click its tab and choose Delete from the right-click menu that appears. If that sheet has no data, it's deleted immediately. If the sheet does contain data, you're prompted to confirm the deletion.

 Make sure you really want to delete a sheet because this is an action you cannot undo with the Undo (Ctrl+Z) command.

You don't have to delete unused sheets in a workbook, but it also doesn't hurt anything to do so. You can always add new sheets later if you decide you need more sheets. Just click the Insert Worksheet button.

Give it a whirl. In your spreadsheet, delete all the unused sheets (Sheet2 and Sheet3). You should be left with only Sheet1, the sheet holding the text you've entered so far.

The default names for the sheets aren't particularly helpful in terms of describing what they contain. In a workbook that uses multiple sheets, you will probably want to rename each sheet's tab so that it's meaningful to you.

To rename a sheet, follow these steps:

1. Double-click the sheet's tab. The current name is selected.

2. Type a new name.

3. Press Enter.

If you want, rename the Sheet1 tab in your spreadsheet to something that's easy to remember. I renamed Sheet1 in my Mortgage spread sheet to *Mortgage*.

 You can use up to 255 characters for a sheet name, including most punctuation, but think twice before you use long, fancy names. When creating references to cells on a sheet, you must include the sheet's name in the formula, and long names can be cumbersome to type. In addition, names that include spaces and punctuation can sometimes require special handling to avoid tripping up certain Excel features. Best bet: Stick with single-word sheet names with no punctuation.

Here's a formatting trick to keep your work organized. Each worksheet tab can have a different color, or you can color several tabs all the same to indicate that they're somehow related. The coloring is all up to you!

To assign a color to a sheet tab, follow these steps:

1. Right-click the tab and hover your mouse over Tab Color on the contextual menu.

2. In the Theme Colors palette that appears, click the desired color (see Figure 7-9).

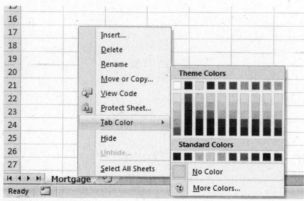

Figure 7-9

 When a colored tab is *active* (that is, when that particular sheet is displayed), the color appears slightly washed out in a soft gradient. But when you select a different tab, the inactive tab(s) appear in their full colorful glory. To remove the color, repeat the preceding steps and click No Color in Step 2.

Doing the Math: Formulas and Functions

*T*he main reason why people choose Excel is that it "excels" at storing and calculating numeric data. With Excel, you can create a grid of numbers, then insert formulas that perform math calculations on them. That capability makes it possible to build complex worksheets that calculate loan rates and payments, keep track of your bank accounts, and much more.

In this chapter, I show you how to build formulas and functions in Excel, and how to put them to work to do several types of calculation-based jobs.

Learn How Formulas Are Structured

A *formula* is a math calculation, like 2 + 2 or 3(4 + 1). In Excel, formulas are different from regular text in two ways:

➡ They begin with an equal sign, like this: =2+2

Get ready to . . .

➡ Learn How Formulas Are Structured 155

➡ Write Formulas That Reference Cells 156

➡ Move and Copy Cell Content 157

➡ Reference a Cell on Another Sheet 160

➡ Understand Functions 160

➡ Take a Tour of Some Basic Functions 163

➡ Explore Financial Functions 165

➡ They don't contain text (except for function names, covered later, and cell references). They contain only symbols that are allowed in math formulas, such as parentheses, commas, and decimal points.

Just like in basic math, formulas are calculated by using an order of precedence. Table 8-1 lists the order.

Table 8-1	Order of Precedence in a Formula	
Order	**Item**	**Example**
1	Anything in parentheses	=2*(2+1)
2	Exponentiation	=2^3
3	Multiplication and division	=1+2*2
4	Addition and subtraction	=10–4

Write Formulas That Reference Cells

One of Excel's best features is its ability to reference cells in formulas. When a cell is referenced in a formula, whatever value it contains is used in the formula. When the value changes, the result of the formula changes, too.

For example, suppose you enter 7 in cell A1 and 8 in cell A2. Then in cell A3, you put the following formula:

```
=A1+A2
```

The result of that formula appears in cell A3 as 15. See Figure 8-1. You could have just as easily entered =7+8 in cell A3 and gotten the same result. However, because you reference *the cells* — rather than the *fixed values* — you can modify the result by changing what either A1 or A2 contains. For example, if you change the value in A1 to 4, the result in A3 changes to 12.

The cell itself shows the result, not the formula

Formula in the active cell

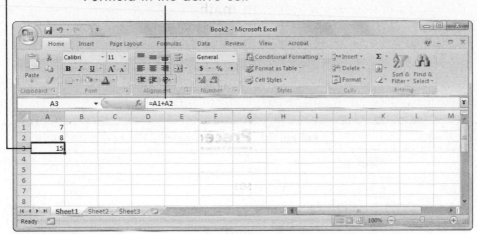

Figure 8-1

 You can use a formula to repeat a value between one cell and another. For example, the formula =A1 repeats whatever value is in cell A1 wherever you put it.

You can combine cell references with fixed numbers in cells, too. Here are some examples:

```
=A1+2
=(A1*A2)/4
=(A1+A2+B1+B2)/4
```

Move and Copy Cell Content

When you're creating a spreadsheet, it's common to not get everything in exactly the right cells to begin with. Fortunately, moving content between cells is easy.

Here are the two methods you can use to move content. Remember to first select the cell(s).

➠ **Clipboard:** Choose Home⇨Cut or press Ctrl+X. Then click the destination cell and choose Home⇨

Paste or press Ctrl+V. If you want to copy rather than move, choose Copy (Ctrl+C) rather than Cut.

 If you're moving or copying a multicell range with the Clipboard method, you can either select the same size and shape of block for the destination. Or, you can select a single cell, and the paste will occur with the selected cell in the upper-left corner.

➡ **Mouse:** Point at the dark outline around the selected range, and then drag to the new location. If you want to copy rather than move, hold down the Ctrl key while you drag. See Figure 8-2.

Drag to desired location

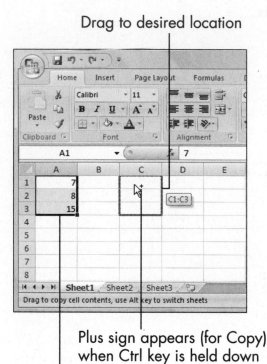

Plus sign appears (for Copy)
when Ctrl key is held down

Position mouse pointer on selection border

Figure 8-2

When you move or copy a formula, Excel automatically changes the cell references to work with the new location. For example, suppose you copy the formula in cell A3 (from Figure 8-1) into cell C3. The original formula was =A1+A2. When it arrives at C3, it changes to =C1+C2. This happens by design, as a convenience to you, because often when you copy formulas, you want them to work relative to their new locations. This is called a *relative reference.*

Sometimes, you might not want the cell references in a formula to change when you move or copy it. In other words, you want it to be an *absolute reference* to that cell. To make a reference absolute, you add dollar signs before the column letter and before the row number. So, for example, an absolute reference to C1 would be =$C$1.

You can mix relative and absolute references in the same formula. For example, in Figure 8-3, if I copy the formula from D4 to D5, the version in D5 will appear like this:

=C5*(1+$B$1)

The C4 reference changed to C5 because it didn't have any dollar signs around it, but the B1 reference stayed the same because it did have the dollar signs.

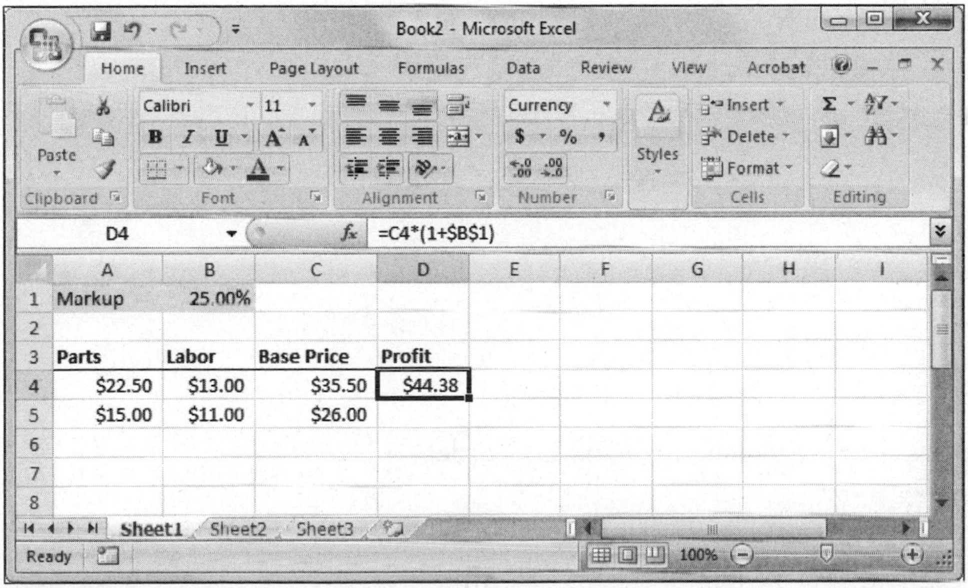

Figure 8-3

Reference a Cell on Another Sheet

In a multisheet workbook, you might want to refer to a cell on a different sheet. To do this, you put the sheet name and an exclamation point in front of the cell reference. For example, to refer to cell A1 on Sheet2, you would write it like this:

```
=Sheet2!A1
```

 The default sheet names (Sheet1, Sheet2, and Sheet3) have no spaces in the names. If you rename a sheet with a name that includes spaces, you have to put the sheet name in single quotation marks, like this:

```
='Home Budget'!A1
```

Understand Functions

Sometimes, it's awkward or lengthy to write a formula to perform a calculation. For example, suppose you want to sum the values in cells A1 through A10. You would have to write out each cell reference individually, like this:

```
=A1+A2+A3+A4+A5+A6+A7+A8+A9+A10
```

In Excel, a *function* refers to a certain math calculation. Functions can greatly shortcut the amount of typing you have to do to create a particular result. For example, instead of the using preceding formula, you could sum, using the SUM function like this:

```
=SUM(A1:A10)
```

With a function, you can represent a range with the upper-left corner's cell reference, a colon, and the lower-right corner's cell reference. In the case of A1:A10, there is only one column, so the upper left is A1 and the lower right is A10.

Each function has one or more arguments. An *argument* is a placeholder for a number, text string, or cell reference. For example, the SUM function requires at least one argument: a range of cells. So in the preceding example, A1:A10 is the argument. The arguments for a function are enclosed in a set of parentheses.

Each function has its own rules as to how many required and optional arguments it has, and what they represent. You don't have to memorize the sequence of arguments (the *syntax*) for each function; Excel asks you for them. It can even suggest a function to use for a certain situation if you aren't sure what you need.

To find a function and get help with its syntax, follow these steps:

1. Click in the cell where you want to insert the function.

2. Choose Formulas⇨Insert Function. The Insert Function dialog box opens.

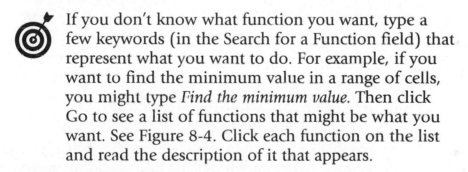

> If you don't know what function you want, type a few keywords (in the Search for a Function field) that represent what you want to do. For example, if you want to find the minimum value in a range of cells, you might type *Find the minimum value*. Then click Go to see a list of functions that might be what you want. See Figure 8-4. Click each function on the list and read the description of it that appears.

3. When you find the function you want, click OK.

4. In the Function Arguments dialog box that opens, fill in the arguments in the field provided. The arguments will be different depending on the function you choose. Figure 8-5 shows the arguments for the MIN function, for example.

Choose a function
Describe what you want

Insert Function   ? X

Search for a function:

| find the minimum value | Go |

Or select a category: Recommended ▼

Select a function:

DMIN
MIN
MINA
VALUE
FIND
DMAX
DGET

DMIN(database,field,criteria)
Returns the smallest number in the field (column) of records in the database that match the conditions you specify.

Help on this function   OK   Cancel

Read the description
Figure 8-4

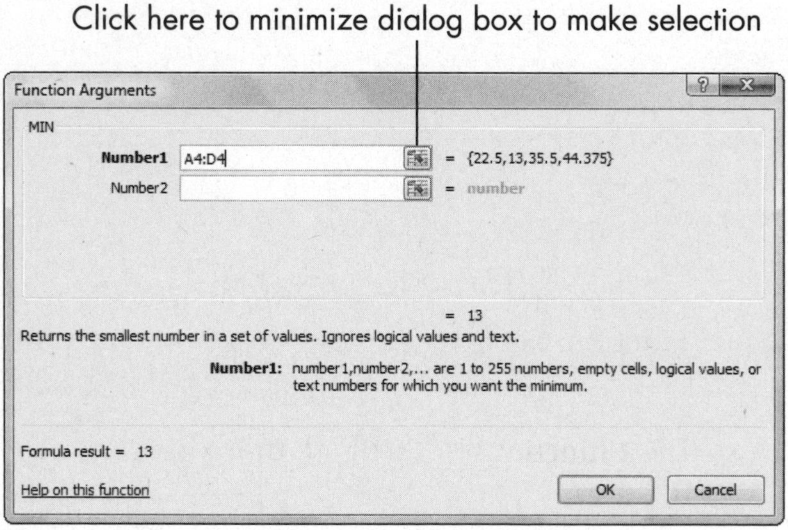

Click here to minimize dialog box to make selection

Function Arguments   ? X

MIN

| Number1 | A4:D4 | = {22.5,13,35.5,44.375} |
| Number2 | | = number |

= 13

Returns the smallest number in a set of values. Ignores logical values and text.

Number1: number1,number2,... are 1 to 255 numbers, empty cells, logical values, or text numbers for which you want the minimum.

Formula result = 13

Help on this function   OK   Cancel

Figure 8-5

Here are some ways to fill in the arguments:

• *Type a number or a cell reference (or range) directly into the box.*

Even though the argument is named Number1 in Figure 8-5, you can still enter a range for it. The Number2 argument is optional; you can tell because its name is not bold. This particular function can have an unlimited number of optional arguments; more boxes appear automatically as needed.

- *Click the Selector button to the right of the text box.* This collapses the dialog box temporarily. Select the cell or range in the worksheet, and then press Enter to return to the dialog box.

5. Click OK.

After you get comfortable with a particular function, you might prefer to type it directly into the cell rather than going through the Insert Function dialog box. As you type, Excel helps you by providing prompts for the arguments in a ScreenTip. See Figure 8-6.

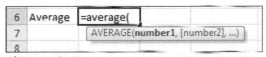

Figure 8-6

Take a Tour of Some Basic Functions

Excel has hundreds of functions, but most of them are very specialized. The basic set that the average user works with is much more manageable.

Start with the simplest functions of them all: those with no arguments. Two prime examples are

⟹ **NOW:** Reports the current date and time

⟹ **TODAY:** Reports the current date

Even though neither uses any arguments, you still have to include the parentheses, so they look like this:

```
=NOW( )
=TODAY( )
```

Another basic kind of function performs a single, simple math operation and has a single argument that specifies what cell or range it operates on. Table 8-2 summarizes some important functions that work this way.

Table 8-2	Simple One-Argument Functions	
Function	**What it Does**	**Example**
SUM	Sums the values in a range of cells	=SUM(A1:A10)
AVERAGE	Averages the values in a range of cells	=AVERAGE(A1:A10)
MIN	Provides the smallest number in a range of cells	=MIN(A1:A10)
MAX	Provides the largest number in a range of cells	=MAX(A1:A10)
COUNT	Counts the number of cells in the range that contain numeric values	=COUNT(A1:A10)
COUNTA	Counts the number of empty cells in the range	=COUNTA(A1:A10)
COUNTBLANK	Counts the number of non-empty cells in the range	=COUNTBLANK(A1:A10)

Table 8-3 shows some functions that change how numbers are presented.

Table 8-3	Functions That Change Numbers	
Function	**What It Does**	**Example**
ABS	Presents the absolute value of the number	=ABS(B1)
ROUND	Rounds the number up or down by a specified number of decimal points	=ROUND(B1,0)
EVEN	Round a positive number up, or a negative number down, to the next even whole number	=EVEN(B1)
ODD	Round a positive number up, or a negative number down, to the next odd whole number	=ODD(B1)

Here are some things to note about the items in the preceding table:

➡ **Absolute value:** This is the positive version of a number. For example, the absolute value of –15 is 15. If the number is already positive, it stays positive.

➡ **Multiple arguments:** See the entry for ROUND. There are two arguments: the cell address or number to operate on, and the number of decimal places. A value of 0 for the decimal places results in rounding to the nearest integer.

 When a function has more than one argument, the arguments are separated by commas. You can see this in the ROUND example: ROUND(B1,0).

 Two other functions, ROUNDUP and ROUNDDOWN, work just like ROUND except they specify which way the rounding will always occur.

Explore Financial Functions

Financial functions are some of the most useful tools for home and small business worksheets because they're all about the money: borrowing it, lending it, and monitoring it. Here's the basic set.

➡ **PV:** Calculates the present value or principal amount. In a loan, it's the amount you're borrowing; in a savings account, it's the initial deposit.

➡ **FV:** The future value. This is the principal plus the interest paid or received.

➡ **PMT:** The payment to be made per period. For example, for a mortgage, it's the monthly payment; in a savings account, it's the amount you save each period. A period can be any time period, but it's usually a month.

➡ **RATE:** The interest rate to be charged per period (for a loan), or the percentage of amortization or depreciation per period.

➡ **NPER:** The number of periods. For a loan, it's the total number of payments to be made, or the points in time when interest is earned if you're tracking savings or amortization.

These financial functions are related. Each is an argument in the others; if you're missing one piece of information, you can use all the pieces you *do* know to find the missing one. For example, if you know the loan amount, the rate, and the number of years, you can determine the payment.

Take a look at the PMT function as an example. The syntax for the PMT function is as follows, with the optional parts in italics:

```
PMT(RATE, NPER, PV, FV, Type)
```

 The Type argument specifies when the payment is made: 1 for the beginning of the period or 0 at the end of the period. It's not required. (I don't use it in the examples here.)

So, for example, say the rate is 0.833% per month (that's 10% per year), for 60 months, and the amount borrowed is $25,000. The Excel formula looks like this:

```
=PMT(.00833,60,25000)
```

Enter that into a worksheet cell, and you'll find that the monthly payment will be $531.13. You could also enter those values into cells, and then refer to the cells in the function arguments, like this (assuming you entered them into B1, B2, and B3):

```
=PMT(B1,B2,B3)
```

Here is the syntax for each of the above-listed functions. As you can see, they're all intertwined with one another:

```
FV(RATE, NPER, PMT, PV, Type)
PMT(RATE, NPER, PV, FV, Type)
RATE(NPER, PMT, PV, FV, Type)
NPER(RATE, PMT, PV, FV, Type)
```

Here are some common ways to use Excel functions in everyday life:

If I borrow $10,000 for 3 years at 7% yearly interest, what will my monthly payments be?

Use the PMT function. Divide the interest rate by 12 because the rate is yearly, but the payment is monthly. Here is the syntax:

```
=PMT(0.07/12,36,10000)
```

If I borrow $10,000 at 7% interest and I can afford to make payments of $300 per month, how many months will it take to pay off the loan?

Use the NPER function. Again, divide the interest rate by 12 to convert from yearly to monthly. Here's the syntax:

```
=NPER(0.07/12,300,10000)
```

If I deposit $10,000 into a bank account that pays 2% interest per year, compounded weekly, how much money will I have after 5 years?

You want the future value of the account, or FV. The period is weekly, so the interest rate should be divided by 52, and the length of the loan is 260 periods (52 weeks multiplied by 5 years). The PMT amount is 0 because no additional deposits will be made after the initial deposit. The initial deposit is expressed as a negative number because the calculation is from the perspective of the interest earner, not the interest payer. Here is the syntax:

```
=FV(0.02/52,260,0,-10000)
```

Creating Visual Interest with Formatting and Charts

Large spreadsheets with many rows and columns of numbers can be confusing or boring to look at. What do the numbers really mean? Which number goes with what descriptive text?

You can make a spreadsheet less boring and more informative by applying formatting. You can change font and text size, apply background shading, add borders, and lots more. You can also adjust the row and column sizes to create space between columns or rows of text.

To help users interpret the data, you can also add charts that summarize the data and/or show trends in the data. Excel offers a wide variety of chart types, enabling you to customize virtually every aspect of a chart's formatting.

Get ready to . . .

➡ Adjust Row Height and Column Width 170

➡ Wrap Text in a Cell 171

➡ Apply Gridlines or Borders 172

➡ Apply Fill Color 175

➡ Format Text in Cells 177

➡ Format the Spreadsheet as a Whole 180

➡ Create a Basic Chart 181

➡ Identify the Parts of a Chart 184

➡ Format a Chart 185

Adjust Row Height and Column Width

By default, each column is the same width. If you type text that exceeds the column width, one of two things happens:

➡ **If the cell to the right is blank:** The text overflows into it.

➡ **If the cell to the right is not blank:** The text appears cut off *(truncated)*. The full text is still stored there, though.

Figure 9-1 illustrates each case.

Text overflows when adjacent cells are empty

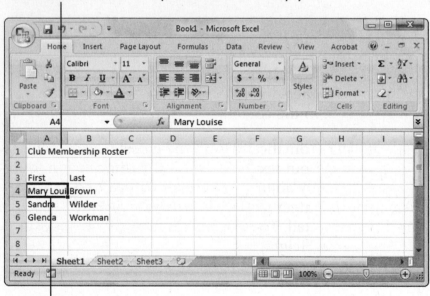

Text is truncated when adjacent cells are not empty

Figure 9-1

To fix such a problem, you must widen the column. Here are some ways how:

➡ **To widen the column exactly enough to hold the longest entry in it:** Double-click the divider between the column headers, or choose Home⇨Format⇨ AutoFit Column Width.

➡ **To widen the column manually:** Drag the divider between the column headers. See Figure 9-2.

Drag or double-click here

Figure 9-2

 You can also make a column narrower; just drag to the left, rather than to the right.

This process also works with row heights. You can drag the divider between two row numbers to change the row height, or double-click the divider to autofit to the content.

Row heights adjust automatically to fit the tallest text in them, so you don't have to worry about text being vertically truncated in rows — usually. If you manually adjust the height of a row and then put some larger text into it, the larger text might become truncated because the row height has been fixed. To make it autofit again, choose Home⇨ Format⇨AutoFit Row Height.

Wrap Text in a Cell

Sometimes, rather than making a row wider to make its content fit, you might want the content to wrap to multiple lines within the cell (like a paragraph in a Word document). To do this, select the cell and then choose Home⇨Wrap Text. (See Figure 9-3.)

Wrap Text button

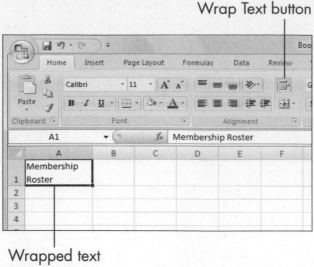

Wrapped text

Figure 9-3

 Wrapping is handy for column headings and long explanations.

Apply Gridlines or Borders

When you look at your worksheet onscreen, you see faint, gray-blue lines — *gridlines* — that separate the rows and columns.

By default, gridlines appear onscreen but not in print. To control how gridlines appear, display the Page Layout tab and then mark or clear the View and/or Print check boxes in the Gridlines group. See Figure 9-4.

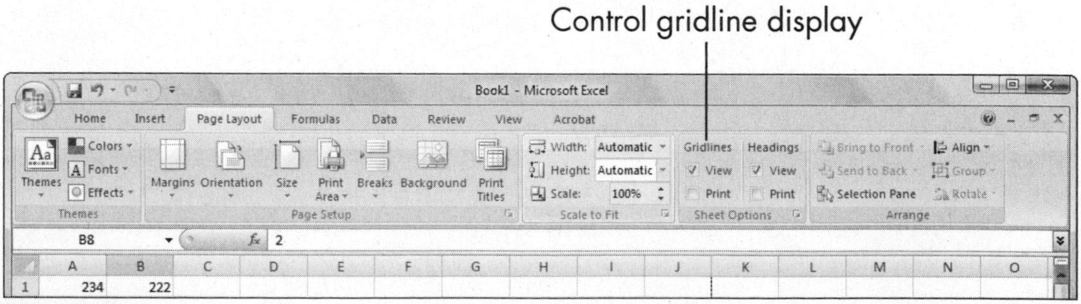

Control gridline display

Figure 9-4

You can also apply other lines around one or more sides of each cell: *borders*. These lines can be any color or thickness you want. Borders always display onscreen and always print, regardless of settings. Borders are useful for helping the reader's eyes follow the text across the printed page, and for identifying which parts of a spreadsheet go together logically.

The easiest way to apply and format borders is to use the Borders button's drop-down list on the Home tab. (It's in the Font group, as shown in Figure 9-5.) Here's how:

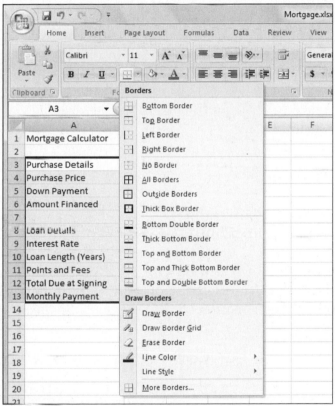

Figure 9-5

1. Select the range of cells to which you want to apply the border.

2. Choose Home⇨Borders.

3. From the list of borders that appears, choose one that best represents the side(s) to which you want to apply the border.

 The border will apply to the outside edges of the range you select. So, for example, choosing Top Border applies a top border only to the cells in the top row of the range, not to the top of every cell in that range.

- *To add a border on all sides of each cell in the range:* Choose All Borders.

- *To remove the border from all sides of all cells in the selected range:* Choose No Border.

- *To add borders on more than one side but not all sides:* Repeat the process several times, each time choosing one individual side.

If you want to choose a specific color, style, or weight for the border, follow these steps:

1. Choose Home⇨Borders⇨More Borders (the bottom command on the menu from Figure 9-5). The Format Cells dialog box appears with the Border tab displayed. See Figure 9-6.

2. In the Style area, click the desired line style.

3. In the Color area, open the drop-down list and click the desired color.

4. In the Presets area, click the preset for the sides you want to apply the border to: None, Outline, or Inside.

 If you want the border around each side of each cell, click both Outline and Inside.

OR

In the Border area, click the button(s) for individual sides, or click directly on the sample area in the desired spots, which applies the border to only certain sides.

 Step 4 is necessary. If you choose a border style and color but don't apply it to any sides of the range, that's like selecting nothing at all.

5. Click OK.

Choose a border style

Presets (optional) quickly turn on/off multiple sides

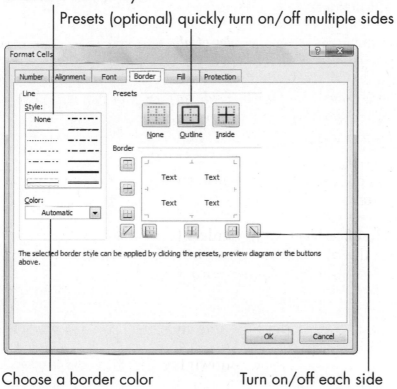

Choose a border color

Turn on/off each side individually with these buttons

Figure 9-6

Apply Fill Color

Fill color — also called *shading* — is the color or pattern that fills the background of one or more cells.

Shading can help the reader's eyes follow information across a page, and can add color and visual interest to a worksheet. In some types of spreadsheets, such as a checkbook register, it's common to shade every other line, for easier reading.

The fill color you choose can be any of the following (see Figure 9-7):

➡ **A standard color:** These colors don't change if you apply a different theme to the workbook.

➡ **A theme color, or a tint/shade of a theme color:** These colors *do* change if you apply a different theme.

➡ **No Fill:** This removes all existing fill from the selected cells.

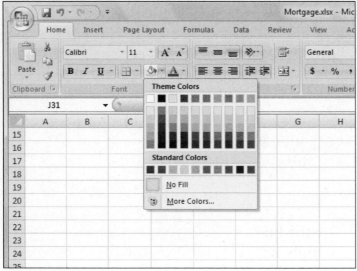

Figure 9-7

To apply fill color, follow these steps:

1. Select the cell(s) to be filled.

2. On the Home tab, click the down arrow to the right of the Fill Color button, opening its menu.

 Clicking the Fill Color button applies whatever color is selected (that is, the color that currently appears on the button's face) without opening the menu.

3. Choose your color:

- *Click one of the color swatches in the Theme Colors palette.*

- *Click one of the colors in the Standard Colors palette.*

- *Click More Colors to open a dialog box of additional stan-dard colors.* Choose one and then click OK.

 To change the workbook's theme, choose Page Layout⇨Themes. Changing themes changes the fonts and colors used. To change only the colors, choose Page Layout⇨Colors.

Format Text in Cells

Text formatting within a cell works very much like it does in Word and PowerPoint. To change the font, font size, color, or attributes (such as bold or italic) for an Excel spreadsheet cell or range

1. Select the cell(s).

2. On the Home tab, use the buttons and drop-down lists in the Font group to apply text formatting. Figure 9-8 points them out.

Text alignment controls how the text lines up within cells. Figure 9-9 points out the controls on the Home tab for working with cell align-ment, and also shows some examples. *Cell alignment* refers to how the text interacts with the available space in the cell.

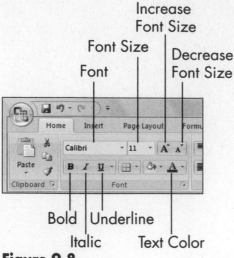

Increase
Font Size

Font Size

Decrease
Font Size

Font

Bold | Underline

Italic   Text Color

Figure 9-8

Vertical alignment (Top, Middle, Bottom)

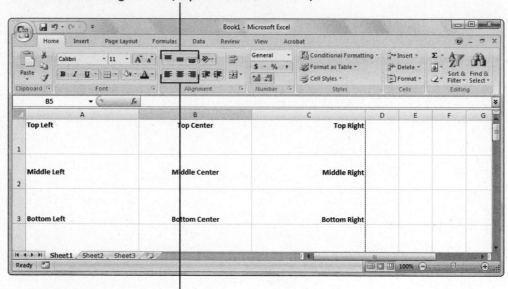

Horizontal alignment (Left, Center, Right)

Figure 9-9

➠ *Horizontal orientation* describes whether the text is left-aligned, right-aligned, or centered when the cell is wider than needed to accommodate the entry.

➡ *Vertical orientation* describes whether the text aligns with the top or bottom of the cell, or is centered vertically between the top and bottom, when the cell is taller than needed to accommodate the entry.

Orientation refers to the direction of the text. By default, text runs horizontally from left to right. You can change that with the Orientation button on the Home tab. For example, you could use vertical or slanted text so that labels in a heading row take up less space horizontally.

1. Select the cell(s).

2. Click the Orientation button.

3. Make a selection from its menu.

Figure 9-10 shows the menu but also some rotated text.

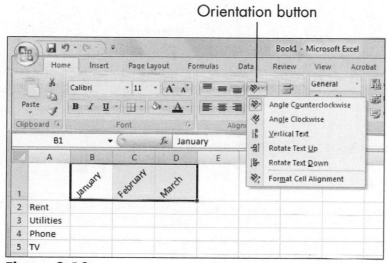

Figure 9-10

 Excel differentiates between angled and rotated text on the Orientation menu (Figure 9-10). Angled text is diagonal; rotated text is straight up-and-down.

Format the Spreadsheet as a Whole

The Page Layout tab contains various formatting controls that affect the entire worksheet. These controls affect the worksheet when it's printed (see Figure 9-11):

Figure 9-11

→ **Margins:** Here, you can set the page margins for printing your worksheet. Choose from among the presets or choose Custom Margins to set your own.

→ **Orientation:** Choose from Portrait (tall) or Landscape (wide) for printing your worksheet.

→ **Size:** Choose the paper size. The default is regular letter size (8.5" x 11").

→ **Print Area:** Use this to set only a portion of the worksheet to print. This is a handy option if you don't want everything on the sheet to print. For example, you have two tables of data on the same sheet, but you want to print only one.

→ **Background:** Use this to place a picture behind the cells of the sheet, such as a logo. (This is uncommon because pictures tend to interfere with the readability of the data.)

→ **Print Titles:** Click this button to open the Page Setup dialog box with the Sheet tab displayed. From there, you can select certain rows and columns to repeat on every page of a multipage printout (such as a row containing column headings, for example).

- **Scale to Fit group:** Options here enable you to force your printout to fit on a certain number of pages by automatically decreasing the size as needed. You can scale to a certain number of pages (with the Height and Width lists), or you can set an overall scale percentage. Refer to Figure 9-11.

Create a Basic Chart

When you have a lot of numeric data on a sheet, it can be difficult to discern its meaning. See Figure 9-12 to see what I mean. Even though this worksheet is attractively formatted, there are still a lot of numbers. Using a chart might help make more sense out of them.

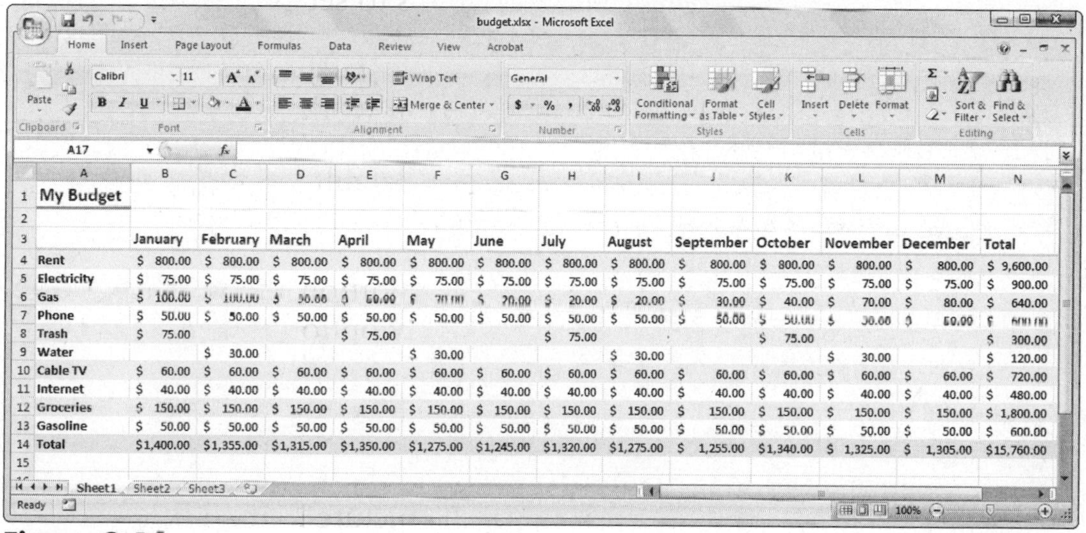

	January	February	March	April	May	June	July	August	September	October	November	December	Total
My Budget													
Rent	$ 800.00	$ 800.00	$ 800.00	$ 800.00	$ 800.00	$ 800.00	$ 800.00	$ 800.00	$ 800.00	$ 800.00	$ 800.00	$ 800.00	$ 9,600.00
Electricity	$ 75.00	$ 75.00	$ 75.00	$ 75.00	$ 75.00	$ 75.00	$ 75.00	$ 75.00	$ 75.00	$ 75.00	$ 75.00	$ 75.00	$ 900.00
Gas	$ 100.00	$ 100.00	[illegible]	[illegible]	[illegible]	$ 20.00	$ 20.00	$ 20.00	$ 30.00	$ 40.00	$ 70.00	$ 80.00	$ 640.00
Phone	$ 50.00	$ 50.00	$ 50.00	$ 50.00	$ 50.00	$ 50.00	$ 50.00	$ 50.00	$ 50.00	$ 50.00	[illegible]	$ 50.00	[illegible]
Trash	$ 75.00			$ 75.00			$ 75.00			$ 75.00			$ 300.00
Water		$ 30.00			$ 30.00			$ 30.00			$ 30.00		$ 120.00
Cable TV	$ 60.00	$ 60.00	$ 60.00	$ 60.00	$ 60.00	$ 60.00	$ 60.00	$ 60.00	$ 60.00	$ 60.00	$ 60.00	$ 60.00	$ 720.00
Internet	$ 40.00	$ 40.00	$ 40.00	$ 40.00	$ 40.00	$ 40.00	$ 40.00	$ 40.00	$ 40.00	$ 40.00	$ 40.00	$ 40.00	$ 480.00
Groceries	$ 150.00	$ 150.00	$ 150.00	$ 150.00	$ 150.00	$ 150.00	$ 150.00	$ 150.00	$ 150.00	$ 150.00	$ 150.00	$ 150.00	$ 1,800.00
Gasoline	$ 50.00	$ 50.00	$ 50.00	$ 50.00	$ 50.00	$ 50.00	$ 50.00	$ 50.00	$ 50.00	$ 50.00	$ 50.00	$ 50.00	$ 600.00
Total	$1,400.00	$1,355.00	$1,315.00	$1,350.00	$1,275.00	$1,245.00	$1,320.00	$1,275.00	$ 1,255.00	$1,340.00	$ 1,325.00	$ 1,305.00	$15,760.00

Figure 9-12

Excel offers various chart types, each suited for a different type of data analysis. For example, Figure 9-13 shows two different charts created from portions of the data from Figure 9-12.

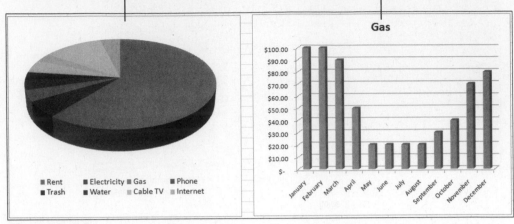

This pie chart shows how each expense contributes to the total

This column chart shows how the gas usage is less during summer months

Figure 9-13

To create a chart, follow these steps:

1. Select the data to include on the chart. Include any cells that contain text labels that should be in the chart, too.

> You might need to select a range of cells that don't touch each other *(noncontiguous)* for Step 1. If that's the case, hold down the Ctrl key while you select the cells you want.

2. On the Insert tab, click a chart type (Charts group). A menu opens showing the chart subtypes. For example, Figure 9-14 shows the subtypes of column charts available.

3. Click the subtype you want. A new chart is created and placed on the current sheet as a floating object.

After you create the chart, you can

➡ **Resize it.** Drag one of the corners of its frame, or one of the selection handles on a side (represented by several dots).

Figure 9-14

━━▶ **Move it.** Drag any part of its frame except a corner or a side selection handle.

━━▶ **Place it on its own tab.** Choose Design⇨Move Chart. Then in the Move Chart dialog box, click New Sheet and then click OK.

If the chart isn't what you expected data-wise, try one of these techniques:

━━▶ Delete the chart and try again, selecting different ranges.

━━▶ Change how the data is plotted by choosing Design⇨Switch Row/Column.

━━▶ Choose Design⇨Select Data to redefine what cells are used to make the chart.

When a chart is selected, the Ribbon has an extra set of Chart Tools tabs: Design, Layout, and Format. They disappear when you select something other than the chart, and reappear when you reselect it.

Identify the Parts of a Chart

Every part of the chart has a name. Figure 9-15 points out some of the key features of a chart.

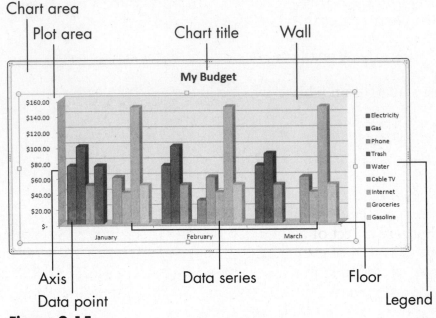

Figure 9-15

➡ **Chart area:** The entire chart, including all the labels and extras: everything in the chart frame

➡ **Plot area:** The part of the chart that contains the data bars/area/pie/points

➡ **Legend:** What each color represents

➡ **Wall:** The background of the plot area, if any

➡ **Floor:** On certain types of 3-D charts, the bottom of the plot area

➡ **Data series:** All the data points in the same data series (represented by a single color or legend key item)

➡ **Data point:** A single numeric value represented on the chart (for example, a single bar or point)

➡ **Chart title:** A text label that describes the entire chart

➡ **Axis:** A line on which data is plotted

 A column chart has both a vertical and a horizontal axis.

Format a Chart

Nearly every aspect of a chart can be formatted differently. You can change the color of every data series, for example, and change the font and size of each text item. You can adjust the rotation of a 3-D chart, move the legend to different positions, add or remove the chart title and various types of labels, and much more.

The easiest way to change the look of a chart is to apply a chart style to it. Chart styles are located on the Design tab. With the chart selected, open up the Chart Style gallery and select one of the style presets. See Figure 9-16.

 The chart style colors come from the color theme that you applied to the workbook. To choose a different color theme, choose Page Layout➪Themes or Page Layout➪Colors.

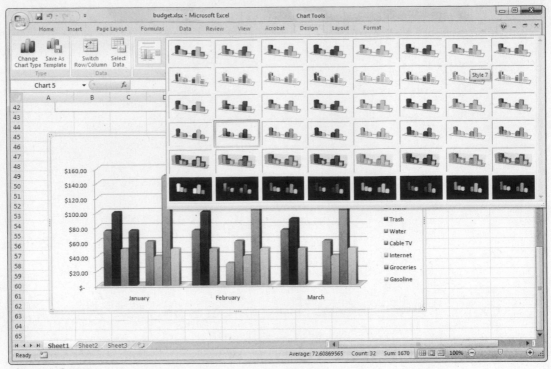

Figure 9-16

The Layout tab provides controls for many of the individual elements of a chart, such as the Chart Title, Axis Titles, Legend, and so on. Click one of those buttons, as shown in Figure 9-17, and then make a selection as to how (or if) you want that element to appear.

 If the Layout tab isn't available, make sure you have selected the chart.

Each element of the chart is also selectable for formatting. For example, you can click the legend and then apply formatting to only that.

 Sometimes it's difficult to select a tiny element of a chart so Excel offers some assistance. On the Format tab, the leftmost group is called Current Selection. It has a drop-down list from which you can select a chart element, as an alternative to clicking a chart element.

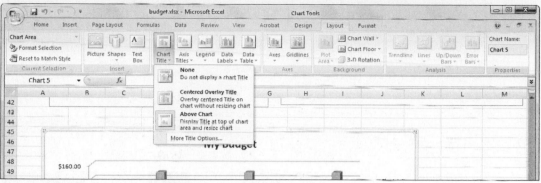

Figure 9-17

After you select a chart element, use tools on the Format tab (Figure 9-18) to apply formatting:

Figure 9-18

➠ Use any of the controls here to apply a color, border, special effect, or other formatting option to it. For example, a Shape Styles gallery provides shapes and formatting presets, and a WordArt Styles gallery provides presets for various types of text formatting.

➠ Choose Format⇨Format Selection to open a dialog box for formatting that element. See Figure 9-19.

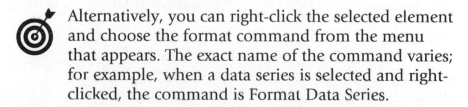

Alternatively, you can right-click the selected element and choose the format command from the menu that appears. The exact name of the command varies; for example, when a data series is selected and right-clicked, the command is Format Data Series.

When you open the Format dialog box for a particular element (select the element and then choose Format⇨Format Selection), the choices depend on the type of element. A list of categories appears at the left, as shown in Figure 9-19. Click a category to display its options, and then make your selections.

Categories vary with element
selected: Click one to see options

Dialog box name reflects selected element

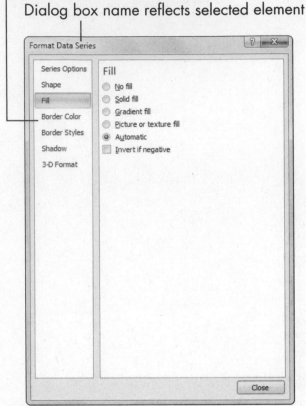

Figure 9-19

 The dialog boxes used for chart formatting are *non-modal*. That means two things:

➠ Any changes you make take effect immediately.

➠ The dialog box can remain open while you work on other parts of the worksheet.

This is different from most other dialog boxes in Windows programs, where you can't do anything else until you close them and where the changes don't take effect until you click OK or Apply.

 3-D charts can be rotated, creating some interesting effects. Choose Layout⇨3-D Rotation.

Using Excel as a Database

*B*esides calculations, the other main reason people use Excel is to store tabular data. For example, Excel works great to store the names and addresses of the people you send holiday cards to every year, or to store a home inventory that you create for insurance purposes.

Although spreadsheet programs like Excel weren't originally created for this purpose, software designers quickly figured out that a lot of people were using Excel to hold lists of data, so they built in features to help do that more effectively. In this chapter, you can read about several Excel 2007 features — such as tables and filtering — for entering and manipulating data.

Understand Databases

A *database* is an organized collection of information about a subject. Examples of databases include an address book, a telephone book, or a home inventory.

Database data is stored in *tables*, which are row-and-column grids. Although Excel isn't a full database program, the row-and-column format of its worksheets is easily adaptable to a simple database.

Chapter 10

Get ready to . . .

➡ Understand Databases....... 191

➡ Prepare a List for a Mail Merge.................. 192

➡ Store Data in a Table........ 193

➡ Sort a Table 195

➡ Filter Data in a Table......... 197

➡ Split a Column's Content............................ 201

➡ Merge the Contents of Columns...................... 203

Each row is a *record:* a set of details about a specific item. For example, a record for a friend in your address book likely contains his name, mailing address, and phone number. A record about a possession in your home could include a name, description, acquisition date, and retail value. Each piece of information you store for each record is a *field.* Field names always appear in the first row of the table. See Figure 10-1.

Each row is a record

Field names occupy the first row

Each column is a field

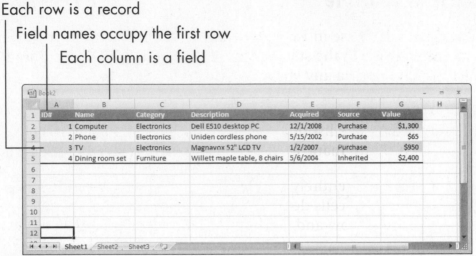

Figure 10-1

Prepare a List for a Mail Merge

One reason why you might create a database in Excel is to store names and addresses for a mail merge — perhaps with a letter you created in Word, for example. (Read all about mail merges in Chapter 6.)

Excel is a great tool for creating such a list. There are just a couple of basic rules:

➡ The first row (row 1) must contain the field names.

➡ The data must start immediately beneath the field names (row 2).

When storing lists in Excel, some people like to put a descriptive title in row 1. That's fine if you're just going to be working in Excel, but it wreaks havoc with a mail merge, so you must delete any such rows in Excel before you use the Excel file for a merge. To delete a row, select it and then choose Home⇨Delete.

Store Data in a Table

To create a database in Excel, type the field names in row 1, and then type the records in the subsequent rows. Nothing else is required. You can format the data any way you want it.

However, if you choose to turn a range of cells into a *table* (Excel's term for a database listing), you get some special benefits, such as easy-to-apply automatic formatting and easier sorting and filtering.

A table in Excel is entirely different from a table in Word. In Excel, a table is a range of cells defined as a database structure. In Word, a table is a simple row-and-column grid for holding text.

To convert a range of cells into a table and apply automatic formatting at the same time, follow these steps:

1. Select the range, including the field names in row 1.

2. Choose Home⇨Format as Table. A palette of table styles appears. See Figure 10-2.

3. Click the desired style. The Format as Table dialog box appears.

4. Confirm the range that appears in the box, and then click OK. Excel applies the formatting, and also sets up the data range as a table.

If you want just the formatting — and not the other features that a table provides in Excel — choose Design⇨ Convert to Range after performing these steps.

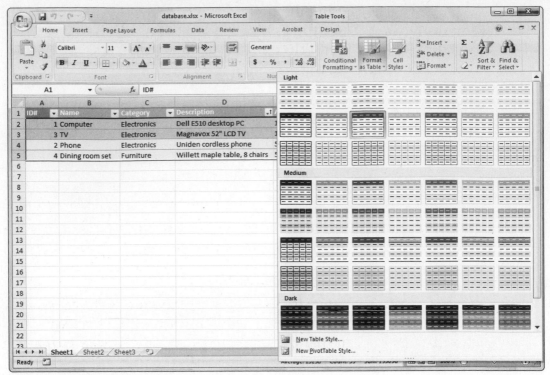

Figure 10-2

Setting up a range as a table has many benefits, including

➠ **Sorting and filtering:** Click the down arrow that appears next to each field name to open a menu from which you can sort and filter the data easily. (This is covered in more detail later in this chapter.)

➠ **Automatic table formatting:** Additional records (rows) you add to the table after its initial creation will be automatically formatted in the same way.

➠ **Other formatting options:** You can apply different formatting at any time with the Design➪Table Styles command. (The Design tab is available only when working with a table.)

The drop-down arrow buttons that appear on each field name are for your convenience; you can click one to open a menu for that column for sorting and filtering the data (described later in this chapter). If you don't want to see the arrows, you can turn off their display by choosing Data⇨Filter. (That's an on/off toggle; choose that same command again to make the arrow buttons redisplay.)

If you ever want to revert to a regular range (as opposed to a table), you can easily convert the data back to normal cells. Click anywhere in the table and choose Design⇨Convert to Range.

Sort a Table

Sorting rearranges the order of the records to meet criteria you specify. For example, you might sort an address list on the person's last name or city.

If you convert the range to a table, as in the previous section, each column heading has a drop-down arrow button on it. Click that arrow to open a menu. From that menu, you can choose to Sort A to Z or Sort Z to A on that column. See Figure 10-3.

If you don't want to use the drop-down menu on the column, you can instead click anywhere in the column and use buttons on the Ribbon:

➡ Home⇨Sort & Filter⇨Sort A to Z

➡ Home⇨Sort & Filter⇨Sort Z to A

➡ Data⇨Sort A to Z

➡ Data⇨Sort Z to A

The method I just showed you works great for single-field sorts. Sometimes, though, you might want a multifield sort:

➡ You sort the list by one field.

➡ If two or more records have the same value for that field, you choose a tie-breaker field to determine the order.

Sort ascending (A to Z) or descending (Z to A)

Click button to open menu for that column

Small arrow indicates existing sort applied

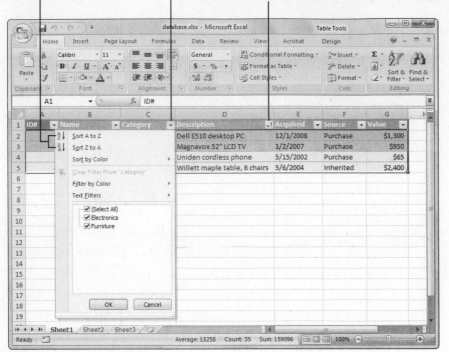

Figure 10-3

For example, you might sort by the Last Name field; and if two people have the same last name, you break the tie by sorting on the First Name field.

To do a multilevel sort, follow these steps:

1. Click anywhere inside the table.

2. Choose Data⇨Sort, or Home⇨Sort & Filter⇨Custom Sort.

3. That the Sort dialog box opens, open the Sort By list and choose the field by which to sort first. For example, you might sort an address list by Last Name.

4. Leave the Sort On box set to Values.

5. Leave the Order box set to A to Z, or change it to Z to A.

6. Click the Add Level button to add another set of controls. See Figure 10-4.

Add more sort levels   Arrow buttons rearrange the levels

Figure 10-4

7. Repeat Steps 3–5 to complete the second set of controls.

8. Add other levels if needed. When you're finished, click OK.

 You can sort a regular range of cells (that is, not a table), but you have to select the entire range before performing the sort. It's much easier if you convert the range to a table first, as I show you how to do earlier in this chapter.

Filter Data in a Table

Filtering data enables you to temporarily hide certain records so that the ones you do want to see become easier to find. Filtering is based on criteria that you specify. For example, you might want to see only items of a certain category or only people who live in a certain state.

The simplest way to filter is to choose which of the existing values for a particular column to include. Follow these steps:

1. Click the down-arrow button to the right of the column name to open its menu.

If you don't see down-arrow buttons on the column names, choose Data⇨Filter to make them appear.

2. A list of all the entries in that column appears, with check boxes for each one. Mark or clear the check boxes as needed to choose which values to include. See Figure 10-5.

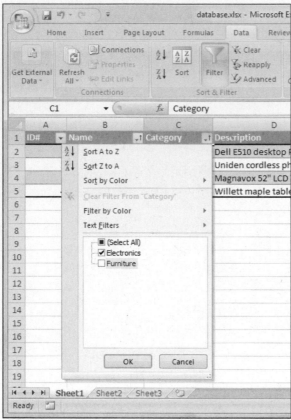

Figure 10-5

3. Click OK at the bottom of the menu. The list is filtered as you specified.

If you want to turn off the filtering, you can do any of the following:

➡️ Reopen the menu and mark the Select All check box.

➡️ Choose Data⇨Clear.

➡️ Choose Data⇨Filter to toggle off the filtering (and also the down-arrow buttons).

 Choose Data⇨Filter again to turn the button display back on.

If your filtering needs are more complex than a simple inclusion or exclusion, use one of the filters from the Text Filters submenu. Follow these steps:

1. Click the down-arrow button to the right of the column name to open its menu.

 If you don't see down-arrow buttons on the column names, choose Data⇨Filter to make them appear.

2. Depending on the field type, the command you want next will have different names. To open a submenu, point to the appropriate command:

- *Text fields:* Text filters

- *Numeric fields:* Number filters

- *Date fields:* Date filters

3. Choose the filter that most closely matches what you want to do. For example, if you're working with a Date field, after pointing to Date Filters in Step 2, you might choose Before. See Figure 10-6.

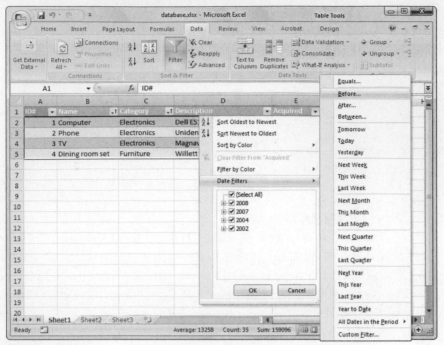

Figure 10-6

4. The Custom AutoFilter dialog box appears for you to finish filling in the desired filter information. For example,
if you choose Before in Step 2, it looks like Figure 10-7,
prompting you to specify the date that all included
records must be prior to.

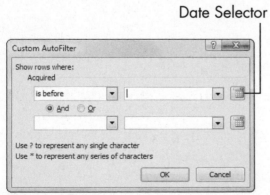

Figure 10-7

5. Type the value you want. Depending on the field type, helpers might also be available. For example, in Figure 10-7, you can click the Date Selector button to open a calendar from which you can choose a date.

6. Click OK. The filter is applied to the table.

To remove the filter, choose Data⇨Clear, or reopen the field's drop-down list and choose Clear Filter from *fieldname*.

Split a Column's Content

As you're entering data into Excel, you might not give much thought to how that data will be used later. For example, when entering people's names, perhaps you used a Name field that contained both the first and last name of each person, as in Figure 10-8.

You can't sort by last
name if the first and
last names aren't in
separate fields

	A	B
1	**Name**	**Phone**
2	Sidney Rhoades	317-555-8882
3	Pamela Sheldon	317-555-2828
4	Michelle Brick	309-555-1112
5	Roger Findlay	309-555-4422

Figure 10-8

Suppose that you then decide that you want to sort the list by the last name of the person. You can't do that with the data shown in Figure 10-8 because sorting takes place according to the first characters in the cell, and that's the *first* name.

Your best bet is to split the content into two separate cells, so that every field you want to sort or filter on is in its own separate cell. If there are only a few names, like in Figure 10-8, you could easily retype them. But what if there were hundreds?

Excel offers a feature called Text to Columns that can do a split for you automatically. It requires there to be a consistent indicator of where the split should occur, though: a *delimiter*. For example, in Figure 10-8, each first and last name are separated by a space, so the space is the consistent delimiter (separator) character.

 The Text to Columns feature doesn't work on data that's in a table in Excel. If your data is in a table (from previous work in this chapter), convert it back to a range with the Design⇨Convert to Range command before you go any further.

Have a look at the column you want to split, and decide what the delimiter character is. Then follow these steps:

1. Make sure there is an empty column to the right of the one you are going to split. Insert a new column if needed (Home⇨Insert⇨Insert Sheet Columns).

2. Select the range containing the data you want to split. In Figure 10-8, for example, the range would be A2:A5.

3. Choose Data⇨Text to Columns. The Convert Text to Columns Wizard Step 1 of 3 dialog box opens.

4. Leave the Delimited option selected and then click Next.

5. In the next page of the wizard, select the appropriate check boxes to indicate what delimiter character(s) to use. (For example, in Figure 10-9, Space is chosen as the only allowed delimiter character.) Then click Next.

6. In the final page of the wizard, leave the default choices for field types and destinations, and then click Finish. Excel splits the data into the adjacent blank column. Figure 10-10 shows the split data from Figure 10-8.

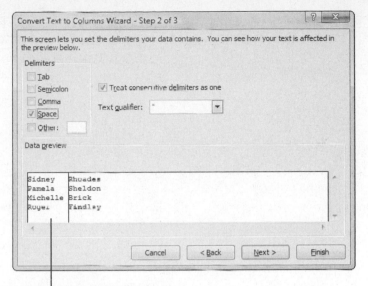

Check the preview here

Figure 10-9

Type a field name for the new column

	A	B	C
1	**Name**		**Phone**
2	Sidney	Rhoades	317-555-8882
3	Pamela	Sheldon	317-555-2828
4	Michelle	Brick	309-555-1112
5	Roger	Findlay	309-555-4422

Figure 10-10

7. Type a new field name in the first row of the new column, and change the field name for the split column if
needed. For example, in Figure 10-10, I might change the
text in cell A1 to *First*, and I might type *Last* in A2.

Merge the Contents of Columns

You can start with data in two columns (first and last names, for
example) and then combine all the data in one column. The process
of combining the columns is *merging*, or *concatenating*.

Concatenating doesn't work with data that's in a table in Excel. If your data is in a table (from previous work in this chapter), convert it back to a range with the Design⇨Convert to Range command.

Concatenating two or more columns is a four-step process:

1. Use the =CONCATENATE function to combine the values from two or more cells in the same column.

2. Copy the function to other cells so that the whole list is processed.

3. Use the Paste Values feature to paste the values from the functions into a new column.

4. Delete the original columns containing the split data, and you delete the column containing the functions.

Here's the process in detail.

In the first step, the =CONCATENATE function combines the values from two or more cells into a single cell. So, for example, if you want to combine the value from A2 with the value from B2 with a space between the two values:

    =CONCATENATE(A2," ",B2)

the commas separate the pieces to be combined. The space in quotation marks (" ") creates the space between the two values.

After creating the function, copy it into the other cells in that column. For example, in Figure 10-11, I have a CONCATENATE function in cell C2, ready to copy into C3:C5. You can use any of the standard copying methods to do this, including the Copy and Paste buttons on the Home tab, the Copy and Paste shortcut keys (Ctrl+C and Ctrl+V), or dragging the fill handle (the black square in the bottom-right corner of the selected cell).

You can drag fill handle
(black square) to copy
function to adjacent cells

CONCATENATE function combines values

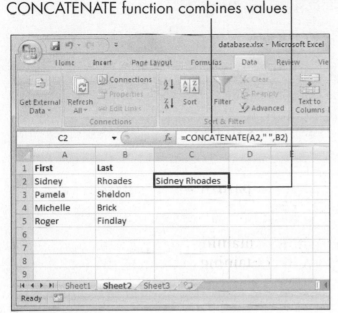

Figure 10-11

Now you have a concatenated column, but you also have a problem: You can't delete the original two columns because the functions are based on their contents. You could hide them, but that would make it awkward later when you added new records.

To work around this problem, you can use the Paste Values feature to copy the value (that is, the result) of the formula to yet another new column. Then you can delete both the original columns and the column containing the function. Follow these steps:

1. If the column to the right of the one containing the functions is not empty, insert a new blank column there.

2. Select the range of cells that contain the CONCATENATE functions.

3. Copy them (press Ctrl+C or choose Home⇨Copy).

4. Click in the first cell where you want to begin pasting the values.

5. On the Home tab, click the down arrow under the Paste button, opening a menu.

6. Click Paste Values.

7. Select and delete the columns that contained the original data and the column that contained the CONCATENATE functions. (Choose Home⇨Delete.)

Part IV
Outlook

The 5th Wave   By Rich Tennant

Managing E-Mail with Outlook

*O*utlook 2007 is a multipurpose program. It's an address book, a calendar, a to-do list, and an e-mail handling program, all in one.

The most popular Outlook feature, of course, is e-mail. Millions of people use Outlook as their primarily e-mail–handling program, and for good reason! Outlook is fast, full-featured, and easy to use and customize.

In this chapter, I show you how to set up an e-mail account in Outlook and then how to use it to send and receive e-mail. I also explain some common e-mail pitfalls and scams and tell you how you can avoid them.

Set Up Outlook

The first time you start Outlook, you're prompted to complete several setup operations. The most important of these is to set up your e-mail account. The following steps walk you through the process.

1. Start Outlook. (Choose Start⇨All Programs⇨Microsoft Office⇨Microsoft Office Outlook 2007.)

Get ready to . . .

➡ Set Up Outlook 209

➡ Set Up Additional Mail Accounts 212

➡ Troubleshoot Mail Setup Problems 214

➡ Take a Quick Tour of Outlook's Mail Feature 217

➡ Receive and Read Your Mail 218

➡ View Photos and Other Attachments 220

➡ Reply to a Message 221

➡ Compose a Message 223

➡ Attach a File to a Message 225

➡ Avoid Frauds, Scams, and Viruses 226

2. If this is the first time you started Outlook, the Outlook 2007 Setup dialog box opens. Click Next.

If you don't see that dialog box, someone might have already started Outlook on this PC before. Just skip to the next section.

3. At the E-mail Accounts screen, you're asked whether you want to configure an e-mail account. You do, so click Next.

4. In the Auto Account Setup dialog box that opens (see Figure 11-1), fill in your details and then click Next.

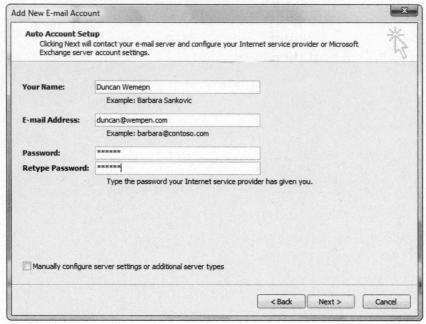

Figure 11-1

Outlook attempts to determine the name of your mail server and then contact it to set up your accounts, using an encrypted connection.

- *If the encrypted connection works,* a message appears telling you so.

- *If the encrypted connection doesn't work,* a message to
  that effect appears. Click Next, and it tries to connect
  unencrypted.

If Outlook can determine the right settings (and it does
in most cases), it logs into the mail server and sends a
test message to you. Wait while all this goes on.

 If the test message fails, see the upcoming section,
"Troubleshoot Mail Setup Problems."

5. Click Finish.

6. Next, depending on what other Office programs you have
run already, Outlook might prompt you for a User Name
(see Figure 11-2). If so, enter your name and initials in
the boxes provided and then click OK.

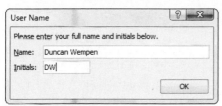

Figure 11-2

7. Outlook next offers that your RSS feeds in Outlook be
synchronized with the Common Feed List. Click Yes.

 RSS stands for really simple syndication. One of
Outlook's features is to manage messages you receive
via RSS.

8. Depending on what Office programs you've already run,
the Privacy Options window might appear with three
check boxes (see Figure 11-3). Mark or clear the check
boxes as desired. If you have an always-on connection
(like cable or broadband Internet access), mark all three;
if you use a dialup connection, you might want to clear
the check boxes so your PC doesn't try to dial up to get

the updates at inconvenient times. (You'll have to manually start the update from time to time.)

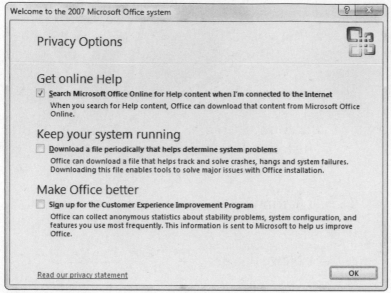

Figure 11-3

- *Get Help Online:* This enables the Help system in Outlook to get additional help from online sources.

- *Keep Your System Running:* This allows Office to download updates automatically as needed.

- *Make Office Better:* This allows Microsoft to collect non-identifiable usage information on your activities to help their future plans for updates.

9. Click OK.

Set Up Additional Mail Accounts

If you have other e-mail accounts, you can set them up in Outlook, too. If you have a separate account for a home-based business or hobby, for example, you might want to be able to get the mail for that address at the same time you retrieve the mail for your main account.

There are different kinds of e-mail servers, such as POP3, IMAP, and HTTP, but most of the differences are transparent to you as an Outlook user. A "regular" e-mail account that you get from your Internet service provider (ISP) is likely a POP3 account. A Web-based account is HTTP. IMAP accounts are uncommon for home users.

To set up another mail account (or to set up your first one, if you didn't do that when you started Outlook for the first time), follow these steps:

1. Choose Tools➪Account Settings. The Account Settings dialog box opens.

2. On the E-Mail tab, click New. The Choose E-Mail Service options appear.

- Microsoft Exchange, POP3, IMAP, or HTTP

- Other

3. Make your selection and then click Next.

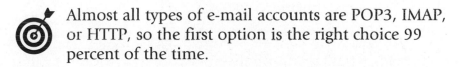 Almost all types of e-mail accounts are POP3, IMAP, or HTTP, so the first option is the right choice 99 percent of the time.

4. Fill in the information for the Auto Account Setup. (It's the same as in Figure 11-1.) Then click Next.

5. Complete the setup by following the prompts that appear. If you have any trouble with it, see the next section.

6. When you finish setting up the account, click Close to close the Account Settings dialog box.

Troubleshoot Mail Setup Problems

Each e-mail service has its own quirks in how the account has to be set up in Outlook (or any mail program) to properly send and receive. Outlook can automatically detect the settings in many cases, but it can't always detect every service correctly.

If Outlook wasn't able to successfully send a test message (see the earlier section, "Set Up Outlook"), you need to do some troubleshooting. Don't panic, though. It's not that difficult. If you get stuck, you can always call your ISP's tech support line and get help.

 If you're using a Web-based e-mail provider like Yahoo!, gmail, or Hotmail, it might not work with Outlook. This is a known issue. Some services have workarounds that you can follow to make them work in Outlook; check the tech support section at the Web site where you get your Web-based mail to see whether there is anything you can do.

To troubleshoot mail problems, make sure you have the following information handy. If you don't have it, contact your ISP. It might also be available on the ISP Web site.

➡ **Your e-mail address and password:** You probably have this already from your earlier attempt.

➡ **The incoming and outgoing mail server addresses:** They both might be the same.

 The *server address* is usually whatever comes after the @ sign in your e-mail address, preceded by the word *mail*. For example, if your e-mail address is tom@ myprovider.com, the mail server might be mail. myprovider.com. If there are separate servers for incoming and outgoing mail, the incoming one might be pop.myprovider.com, and the outgoing one might be smtp.myprovider.com. Those are just guesses, though; you will need to get that information from your ISP.

➠ **Information about whether an encrypted connection should be used**

➠ **Information about whether your outgoing mail server requires authentication:** And if so, whether the outgoing server requires a different username and password than your regular one.

Armed with all that information, do the following to troubleshoot:

1. Choose Tools⇨Account Settings. The Account Options dialog box opens.

2. Double-click the e-mail account you want to troubleshoot. The Change E-Mail Account dialog box opens.

3. Check all the information in the dialog box to make sure that it matches the information you have about your mail account. In particular, check the Account Type, Incoming Mail Server, and Outgoing Mail Server (SMTP).

4. Mark or clear the Require Login Using Secure Password Authentication (SPA) check box, whichever is different from the current setting. Then click Test Account Settings to see whether that fixed the problem. If it didn't, go back to the original setting.

5. Click More Settings. On the Outgoing Server tab, mark the My Outgoing Server Requires Authentication check box. See Figure 11-4. From here, try each of the three options. After each one, click OK and then click Test Account Settings to check whether it helped.

Figure 11-4

 If you select the Log on Using radio button, fill in your user name and password in the boxes provided. For the user name, use your complete e-mail address. If that doesn't work, try using only the part of your e-mail address before the @ sign. Try it with the Require Secure Password Authentication (SPA) check box cleared, and then try it with that check box marked.

6. Click More Settings. On the Advanced tab, drag the Server Timeouts slider closer to the word *Long* (that is, farther to the right). This can help give more time to a mail server that is slow to respond. A timeout delay of more than two minutes isn't usually needed. Then click OK, and click Test Account Settings.

7. If you got Outlook to successfully complete a test message, great. Close all dialog boxes.

If not, contact your e-mail service provider's tech support and find out what setting you need to change to make it work.

Take a Quick Tour of Outlook's Mail Feature

After you configure Outlook for e-mail, take a quick look around the Outlook interface as it pertains to e-mail. It's different from most of the other Office applications, in that it uses the older-style Office system of menus and toolbars rather than the tabbed Ribbon of Office 2007. Figure 11-5 points out the following features:

➠ **Menu bar:** Like in most Windows applications, the menu bar contains drop-down menus from which you can select commands.

➠ **Toolbar:** The toolbar is equivalent to the Ribbon in other Office 2007 applications; click a button on the toolbar to execute a command. (Point to a button to see a ScreenTip that tells its name.)

➠ **Navigation pane:** This pane shows different things, depending on the part of Outlook you're working with. When working with mail, it shows the Mail Folders list (see Figure 11-5). You can move to a different folder by clicking its name here.

➠ **Inbox:** Whatever folder is selected on the Mail Folders list appears here. In Figure 11-5, that's the Inbox. New mail arrives in the Inbox, so it's the folder you work with most of the time.

➠ **Reading pane:** Whatever e-mail message is selected in the Inbox appears here in preview. That way, you don't have to open each message (by double-clicking it) to see what it contains.

 By default, the Reading pane appears to the right of the Inbox. You can have it appear below the Inbox window, though; choose View⇨Reading Pane⇨ Bottom.

Toolbar

Menu bar   Inbox

Navigation pane   Reading pane   To-Do Bar

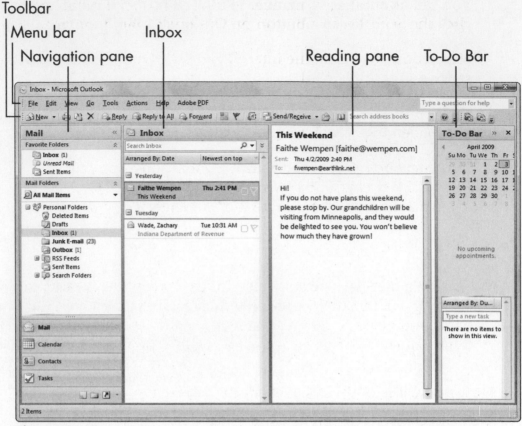

Figure 11-5

➡ **To-Do bar:** Here's where a mini-calendar appears, along with your list of to-do items (if you've created any).

 The Navigation pane, To-Do bar, and Reading pane can all be turned on or off from the View menu.

Receive and Read Your Mail

After you configure your e-mail account(s) in Outlook, receiving mail is an automatic process. Outlook automatically sends and receives mail when you start it, and also at ten-minute intervals whenever Outlook is running. Your incoming mail comes automatically into the Inbox folder.

You can also initiate a manual send/receive operation at any time. Just click the Send/Receive button on Outlook's main toolbar.

Here's how to change the interval at which Outlook automatically sends and receives mail.

1. Choose Tools⇨Send/Receive⇨Send/Receive Settings⇨ Define Send/Receive Groups; or, press Ctrl+Alt+S.

2. In the text box next to the Schedule an Automatic Send/ Receive Every check box (which should be marked), change the number of minutes for the interval.

3. Click Close.

To read a message, click it in the Inbox. Its content appears in the Reading pane. Many people read their mail exclusively in the Reading pane, and never "open" a message formally. To open a message (that is, to display it in its own window, as in Figure 11-6), double-click it.

Notice the Office 2007–style Ribbon

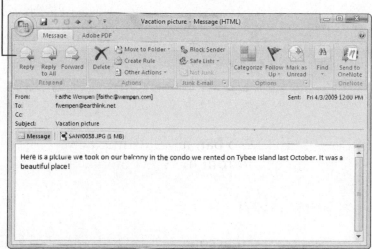

Figure 11-6

When you open a message in its own window, the toolbar changes to the Ribbon-style toolbar, like in Word 2007 and other Office 2007 applications. The main Outlook interface is a hybrid of the older menu-and-toolbar style that you see in its main window and this Office 2007–style that you see in some of the data windows like this one.

View Photos and Other Attachments

E-mail messages can contain file attachments. The most common type of attachment is a photo; family members can send you photos that they took with their digital cameras, for example. The message in Figure 11-6 has a photo attached to it.

 Some types of attachments can carry viruses. (Pictures are generally safe, though.) If you have any doubts about the safety of any file you receive, do not open it. At the end of this chapter are some tips for discerning which attachments are risky.

You can tell that a message has an attachment by the paper clip icon next to it in the Inbox, as shown in Figure 11-7. Then in the Reading pane, note the icons and text (at the top of the message) representing each attachment. Click the attachment name in the Reading pane to see a preview of it. To get back to the message itself in the Reading pane, click the Message button.

You can also open the attachment in its original program by double-clicking it.

If you want to save the attachment — *download it* — any of these ways will work:

➡ Right-click the attachment and choose Save As from the menu that appears. In the Save Attachment dialog box that opens, enter a file name and location, or accept the defaults. Then click Save.

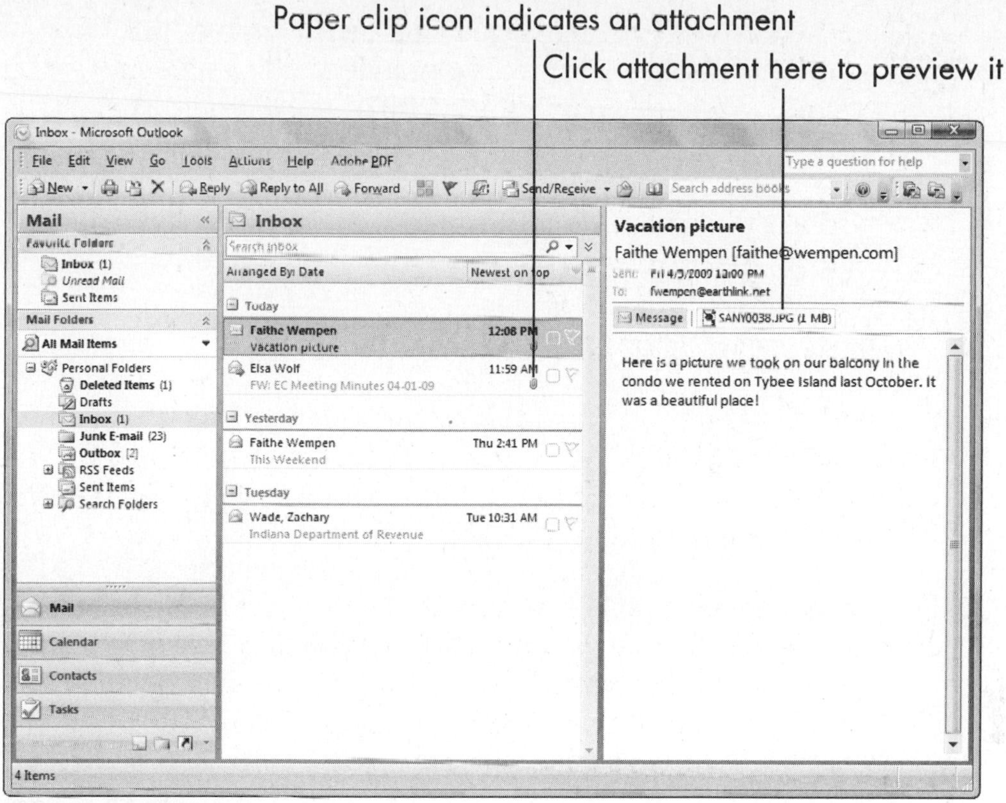

Paper clip icon indicates an attachment

Click attachment here to preview it

Figure 11-7

⟶ Choose File⇨Save Attachments and then click the attachment name. In the Save Attachment dialog box that opens, enter a file name and location, or accept the defaults. Then click Save.

⟶ Double-click the attachment to open it in its native program. Then save the file from there, using that program's Save command (probably File⇨Save As or some variation of that).

Reply to a Message

Replying to a message is quick and easy because you don't have to look up the recipient's e-mail address. It's already filled in for you.

To reply to a message, click the Reply button on the toolbar, choose Actions⇨Reply, or press Ctrl+R. A message composition window appears with the original message quoted in the body of the message and the original sender's e-mail address in the To field. See Figure 11-8. Type your reply at the top of the message box, and then click Send to send your reply.

RE: added to original subject

Original sender becomes the recipient

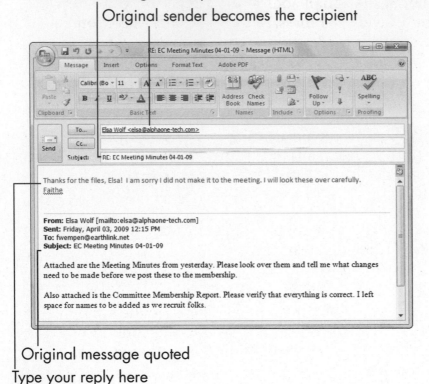

Original message quoted

Type your reply here

Figure 11-8

Clicking the Reply All button/command sends the reply to the original sender plus any other original recipients (other than you).

 Using Reply All is useful for an ongoing e-mail discussion with a group of people. Be careful, though, that you don't accidentally use Reply All and send a sensitive message to a wider audience than you intended.

Compose a Message

When you compose a new e-mail message, you (not Outlook) fill in every piece of information: the recipient(s), the subject, and the body. Unlike with replying (see the preceding section), none of that information is filled in for you automatically.

➡ **Recipient:** This is the information in the To field. You need the e-mail address of each person you want to send your message to. The Contacts section of Outlook provides storage for e-mail addresses; Chapter 12 addresses the Contacts list. For now, though, assume that you know the address and will type it in.

➡ **Subject:** You can type anything you want as the subject (or nothing at all), but your recipients will be appreciative if you keep the subject descriptive and to the point.

➡ **Body:** This is the main part of the message. It can be plain or formatted text.

 You can format the text in the message using the formatting controls on the Ribbon. These are the same as the formatting controls in Word; see upcoming Figure 11-9. Read all about Word formatting in Part II of this book.

To compose an e-mail message, follow these steps:

1. Click the New button on the toolbar, choose Actions➪ New Mail Message, or press Ctrl+N.

2. In the new message window that appears, type the e-mail address(es) for the recipient(s) in the To field.

 If you have more than one recipient, separate the addresses with a comma.

3. (Optional) To send a courtesy copy to someone other than a main recipient, type the e-mail address in the Cc (carbon copy) field.

 You can also send a blind carbon copy (Bcc) to someone. A Bcc differs from a regular Cc in that none of the other recipients see the Bcc person's name listed. To send a Bcc, click the To or Cc button, opening a Select Names box. At the bottom of that box is a Bcc line. Type the cloaked recipient's address there.

4. (Optional) If you have more than one e-mail account set up in Outlook, click the Account button and select the account from which you want to send.

5. Type a subject in the Subject line.

6. Type the message body in the body area (below the Subject line). Figure 11-9 shows a message ready to send.

Use these formatting tools, the same as in Word

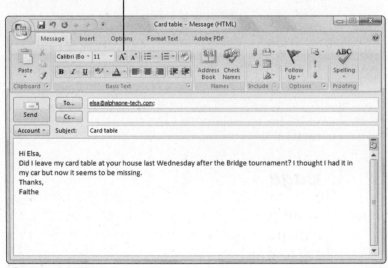

Figure 11-9

7. Click Send to send the message.

When you send a message, it's immediately moved to your Outbox folder. There it waits until the next Send/Receive operation. You can send it immediately by clicking Send/Receive on the toolbar, or let it go out during the next scheduled Send/Receive.

If you click Send and then immediately realize you made a mistake and want to call back the message, here's the fix:

1. Double-click the Outbox folder in the folder list at the left.

2. Immediately double-click the unsent message to open it. As long you have the unsent message open, it won't be sent. With the unsent message open, you can edit it or delete it.

If Outlook won't let you open it because it already started transmitting, do the following:

1. Click the Send/Receive indicator in the bottom right-corner of the Outlook window to open a menu.

2. From that menu, choose Cancel Send/Receive as quickly as you can.

 Another workaround is to quickly exit from Outlook. A prompt will appear that you still have messages in your Outbox; click Yes to exit anyway. Then disable your Internet connection before you reopen Outlook.

Attach a File to a Message

You might sometimes want to send pictures from your own computer to other people via e-mail attachment, such as a photo, a document, or a spreadsheet. It's easy to do!

After you compose the e-mail message (or reply to a message), click the Attach File button.

The Attach File button doesn't have a name on it, like Send or To. Instead, it's an icon of a paper clip; see Figure 11-10.

This opens the Insert File dialog box. From here, you can navigate to the file you want and then click Insert. The attachment appears on the Attached field in the message composition window. See Figure 11-10.

Attach File button

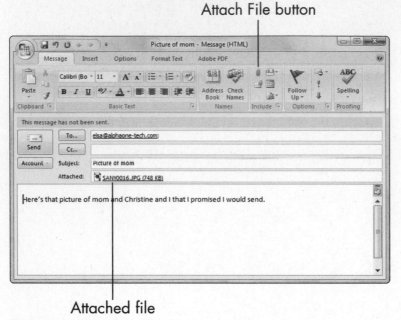

Attached file

Figure 11-10

If you change your mind about sending that attachment, you can delete it from the message by selecting it and pressing the Delete key.

Avoid Frauds, Scams, and Viruses

You might have heard horror stories about people whose computers became infected with viruses, worms, and all sorts of other nasty things, and who had to pay a lot of money to get it cleaned up – if they could. These stories are real, and so is the threat. However, you can do some very basic things to minimize your exposure to such risks.

First, look at what the threats are:

➡ **Spoofing/phishing:** These legitimate-looking e-mail messages contain bogus links to Web sites that can trick you into providing confidential information, such as passwords and bank account data. Thieves then use this information to steal your identity and empty your bank accounts.

➡ **Viruses:** These *executable* files (that is, program files) do destructive things to your computer, such as delete files or corrupt a disk. Watch out for files with an EXE extension.

➡ **Worms:** These program files or scripts use your computer to send out mass-mailings of spam without your knowledge or consent.

➡ **Exploits:** These program files or scripts target weaknesses in your computer's security to use it to send out spam or do other harmful things. These usually come from hidden utilities built into some Web sites.

➡ **Spyware:** These hidden programs spy on your usage habits (including passwords you type, in some cases) and report them back to their owner via the Internet.

➡ **Adware:** These hidden programs pop up ads on your screen, or change the behavior of your Web browser to display its own ads.

➡ **Unwanted search toolbars:** These add-on toolbars replace your default search tools with the search database sponsored by a certain company, so that the results of your searches bring up their sponsored sites.

Those are the threats you face. Now, look at how to face them down. Here are my top ten tips:

1. Because Windows XP and Vista don't come with an anti-virus program, you need one. Two of the most popular are Symantec (Norton) Antivirus and McAfee VirusScan. Install one, and keep it updated.

2. Most good-quality antivirus programs include incoming and outgoing e-mail scanning. Keep that feature turned on. It will protect you from most viruses and worms attached to e-mails.

3. Use the built-in, free Windows Vista program called Windows Defender, which protects against most spyware and adware. It is enabled by default. Do not turn it off.

4. If you get an e-mail with an attachment, be suspicious of it. Do not open the attachment until you verify the following:

➡ Is the attachment from someone you know?

➡ Were you expecting a file from that person?

If the answer to either question is No, contact the person who sent it to you and find out what it is before you open it.

5. Never open any attachments that have any of these extensions (file types): EXE, COM, BAT, VBS.

6. If you get an e-mail with an attachment with a ZIP extension, be extra suspicious. (A ZIP file contains other files.) One common worm infection distributes itself in a ZIP file that's marked as an online greeting card, for example.

7. If you get an e-mail message that appears to be from your bank, be very suspicious. Most banks don't do important business via e-mail. Instead, go directly to the bank's

Web site directly, by typing its address into your Web browser. Whatever you do, *do not click the link in the message.*

8. If you get an e-mail message that appears to be from PayPal or eBay, be suspicious. These companies do send out legitimate e-mails, but phishing sites often impersonate those sites. Go directly to PayPal or eBay those sites via your Web browser; *do not click the links in the e-mails.*

   If a message from PayPal or eBay doesn't address you by name, it's more likely to be a fake. However, this isn't a reliable way to tell.

9. If you're not sure about a link in an e-mail, point the mouse pointer to the link. A ScreenTip appears showing the actual address that the link is pointing to. If it doesn't match the text on the link, it's probably a fake.

10. Some unwanted search toolbars trick you into installing them as you install other software. You can usually get rid of them via Control Panel in Windows. (Choose Start➪Control Panel➪Programs➪Uninstall a Program.) Scroll through the list of installed programs there and look for anything with *toolbar* in the name — and remove it.

    The Yahoo! and Google toolbars are okay to keep; these are legitimate.

Managing the Details: Contacts, Notes, and Tasks

Outlook has a lot more to offer than just e-mail! Outlook is a full-fledged, personal information management program. It does a great job as an address book, a to-do list, and a storage cache for all the miscellaneous info that you might have "organized" on sticky notes all over your desk. Whatever information you need to organize, Outlook can help.

In this chapter, I show you how to use the Contacts part of Outlook to store and look up names and addresses, both e-mail and postal mailing addresses, which is a handy substitute for a standard paper address book. I also introduce you to the Tasks list (which helps you prioritize and manage your responsibilities) and the Notes database (where you can store everything from confirmation numbers for your next vacation to passwords for the Web sites you visit).

Chapter 12

Get ready to . . .

➡ Store Contact Information 232

➡ Edit and Delete Contacts 235

➡ Choose How the Contact List Appears 237

➡ Use the Contacts List 238

➡ Create Notes 240

➡ Categorize Notes 243

➡ Use Tasks and the To-Do List 245

➡ Update the Status of a Task 249

➡ Set a Task Reminder 250

Store Contact Information

Outlook refers to the information you store about people and organizations as *contact information,* which stores it in a folder called Contacts. To access the Contacts folder, click Contacts in the lower part of the navigation pane, on the left side of the Outlook window.

The Contacts folder, shown in Figure 12-1, shows each contact that you've entered.

 Although Figure 12-1 shows a lot of contacts, you don't have any when you start out. You must enter each one individually.

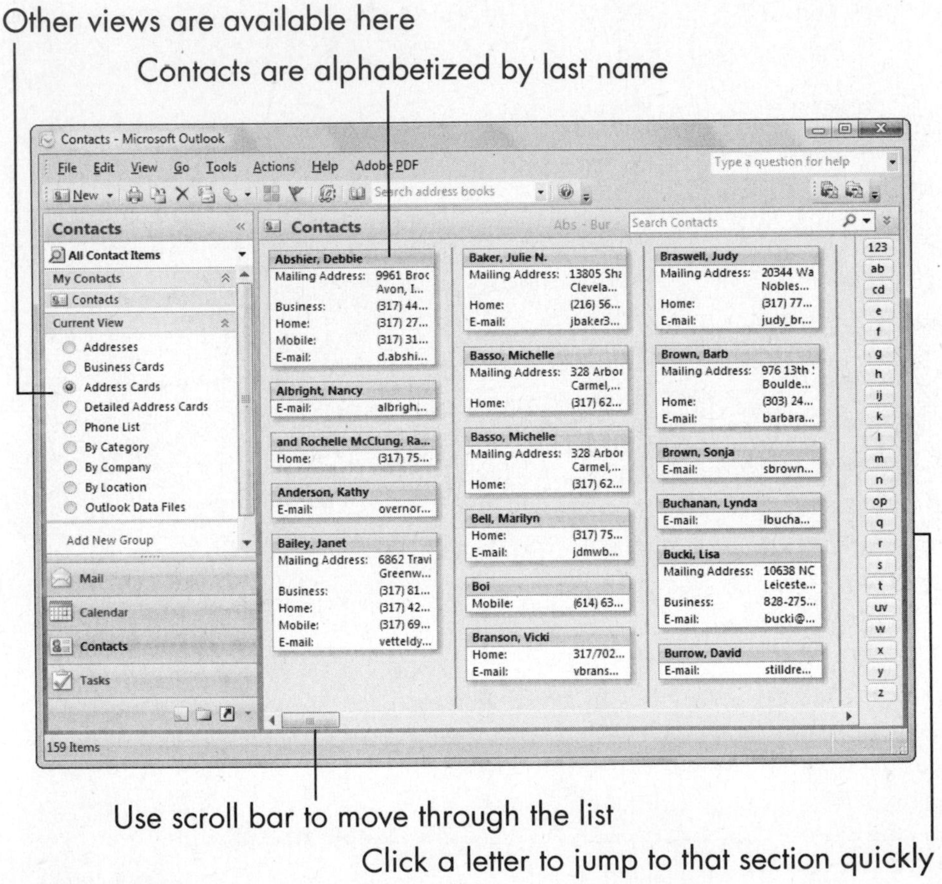

Other views are available here

Contacts are alphabetized by last name

Use scroll bar to move through the list

Click a letter to jump to that section quickly

Figure 12-1

To store someone's contact information, follow these steps:

1. From the Contacts folder, do any of the following to open an Untitled - Contact window:

- Click the New button on the toolbar.

- Choose File⇨New⇨Contact.

- Press Ctrl+N.

2. In the Untitled - Contact window that appears, fill in the information you want to store for the person or organization. You can fill in as much or as little as you like. For example, you can omit the Company if it's not a business contact. Figure 12-2 shows an example.

File As determines how it will be alphabetized

Click Details for more fields

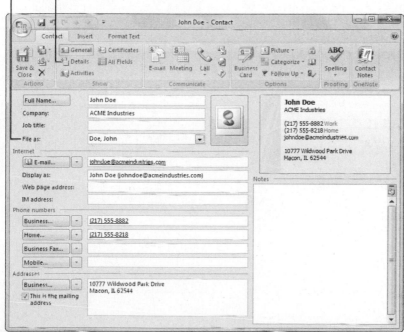

Figure 12-2

None of the fields are mandatory, but if the File As field is blank, Outlook displays a warning when you save, asking whether you intended that.

 The more complete you make an entry for a person, the more helpful Outlook can be. However, it takes more time to enter all the details required for a complete record than to just enter a name and e-mail address.

3. Click the Save & Close button on the Ribbon. The contact is added to your Contacts list.

Here are some tips when entering contact information.

➡ Whatever you type in the Full Name field replaces *Untitled* in the dialog box's title bar immediately.

➡ In the File As field, specify how this entry is alphabetized. The default is by last name, so it reverses whatever you put in the Full Name field. For example, if you enter **John Doe** in the Full Name field, the File As appears as *Doe, John*. For people's names, this is usually the best way to go. For a company name, though (such as ACME Industries), you probably don't want it alphabetized as Industries, ACME. To fix that, open the File As drop-down list and choose *ACME Industries*.

➡ If you enter a company name (in the Company field), even more choices are available from the File As list. For example, you can choose to alphabetize by the company name rather than the individual, and to put the individual or company name in parentheses, like these:

• ACME Industries (Joe, John)

• Doe, John (ACME Industries)

➥ You can store multiple e-mail addresses for the same person. Notice that E-mail isn't just a field label, but also a drop-down list. Open the list and choose E-mail 2, E-mail 3, and so on for additional addresses.

➥ All Phone Numbers fields also have drop down lists associated with their labels. You can store four phone numbers for a person, and you can choose which labels each of those will carry. For example, you could assign the label Mobile to one of the phone numbers.

➥ You can have three addresses for a person: Business, Home, and Other. Switch between them with the drop-down list in the Addresses section.

➥ When you enter an address but don't enter it in proper mailing format (address, city, state, and zip code), a dialog box will prompt you to fill those in. This is for your own protection: to make sure every address you enter is usable.

➥ Use the Notes pane to store any additional information about the person that doesn't match up with any of the fields.

➥ To customize how your Contacts appear, choose from sets of fields other than the defaults. The ones in Figure 12-1 are the General fields. On the Ribbon, click the Details button for additional fields.

Edit and Delete Contacts

People move, get new phone numbers, and change e-mail providers. In a paper address book, you have to cross out the old address and write new information. (That sloppy look is a big part of what I hate about paper address books!) With Outlook, though, you can simply edit the stored information onscreen.

Editing a contact is a snap.

1. Double-click the Contact.

2. When that Contact's dialog box opens (refer to Figure 12-2), make any changes, and then click the Save & Close button.

To delete a contact from the list, do the following:

1. Select the contact.

2. Press the Delete key on the keyboard, or right-click it and choose Delete, or click the Delete button on the toolbar.

If you delete a Contact by mistake, you can retrieve it from the Deleted Items folder.

To restore an accidentally deleted Contact

1. In the navigation pane, click Mail. (No, it's not really mail you're after, but the Mail area provides easy access to the Deleted Items folder.)

2. In the navigation pane, under Mail Folders, click Deleted Items.

3. Locate the deleted contact in the list of items. See Figure 12-3.

4. Drag and drop the deleted contact onto Contacts in the lower part of the navigation pane. It's restored.

 If you want to completely delete a contact, so it is irretrievable, delete it from the Deleted Items folder.

Deleted Items folder Deleted contact

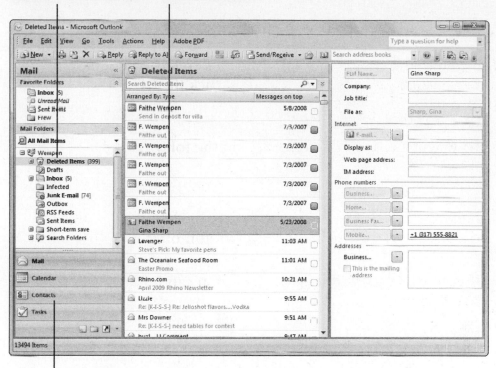

Drag the deleted contact here to restore it

Figure 12-3

Choose How the Contact List Appears

Usually, the default view of the Contacts list is Address Cards; refer to Figure 12-1. You can easily switch to other views whenever you like, such as Business Cards view, as shown in Figure 12-4.

To switch to a different view, just click one of the buttons in the navigation pane under Current View.

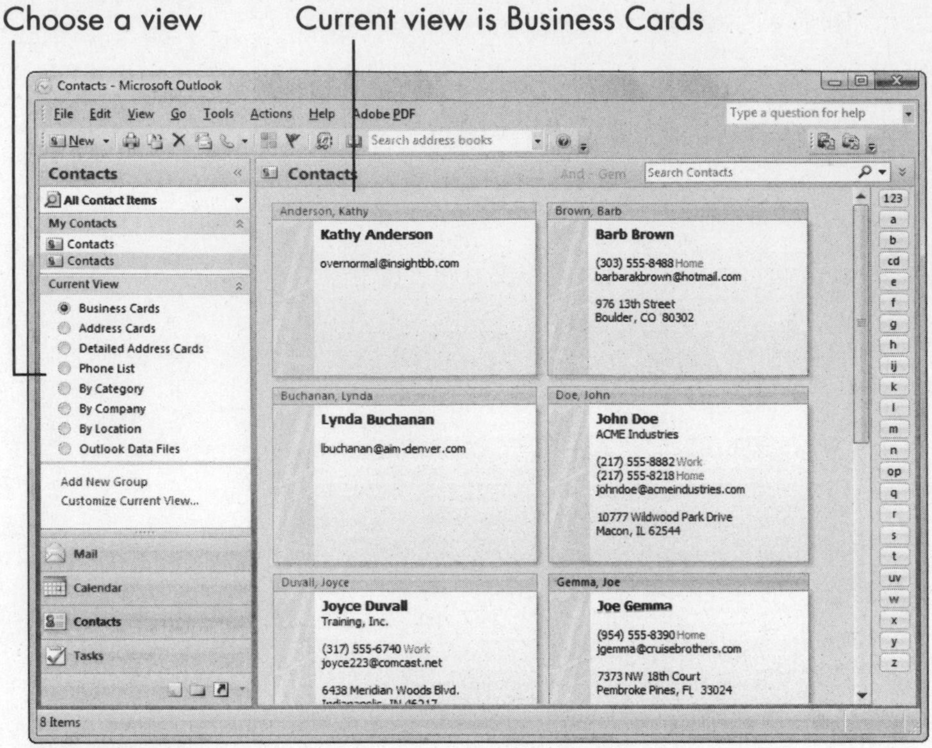

Choose a view   Current view is Business Cards

Figure 12-4

Use the Contacts List

After you get your Contacts list set up, it's good for lots of things other than a substitute for your paper address book.

To quickly locate a specific contact by filtering

1. Click in the Search Contacts field (upper-right corner).

2. Type a word that the contact information contains. (It doesn't need to be the person's name. For example, you could enter a town to find everyone who lives there.) The Contacts list is temporarily filtered to show only entries that contain that word.

To clear the filter, click the Clear Search (X) button to the right of the Search Contacts field.

To address e-mail messages

1. When composing an e-mail message, click the To button, opening the Select Names: Contacts dialog box.

2. Click in the To field at the bottom of the dialog box.

3. Double-click a contact to add that person as a recipient.

You can do the same thing with the Cc and Bcc fields.

4. Click OK when finished. See Figure 12-5.

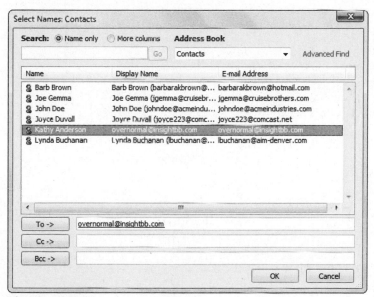

Figure 12-5

To start an e-mail from the Contacts folder

1. With the Contacts folder displayed, select a contact.

2. Click the New Message to Contact button on the toolbar. See Figure 12-6. A new message composition window opens with that person's e-mail address pre-filled in the To field.

New Message to Contact

Dial

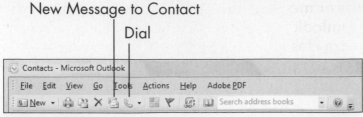

Figure 12-6

If your PC uses a dialup modem connected to a live phone line, you can use Outlook to dial the phone for you.

To place a phone call

1. Select the contact and then click the Dial button on the toolbar. Refer to Figure 12-6.

2. In the New Call dialog box that opens, confirm the contact name and address and then click Start Call.

3. Lift the phone receiver, click Talk, and begin your call.

 Dialing a telephone isn't a big chore, so why use Outlook to dial? For one thing, Outlook doesn't make any dialing mistakes. That can be a great help if you have a disability. Another reason is that if you let Outlook manage the call, it adds a record of the call (and its length) to the Journal area of Outlook. The Journal is a tool for tracking your activities in Outlook. It's used frequently by people who bill customers by the hour.

Create Notes

Lots of people use sticky notes to create reminders for themselves of bits of information: everything from Web site passwords to memorable quotations. Outlook includes *Notes*, which are the electronic equivalent of these sticky notes. You can store anything you want on a note, but they are best used for small bits of data, like reservation confirmation codes or membership ID numbers. You can leave a note open (as long as Outlook is open) so you will be reminded every time you see it, or you can close the note so that it isn't in your way. Figure 12-7 shows a couple of open notes, with the rest of them closed.

Choose a different view

Change the icon size

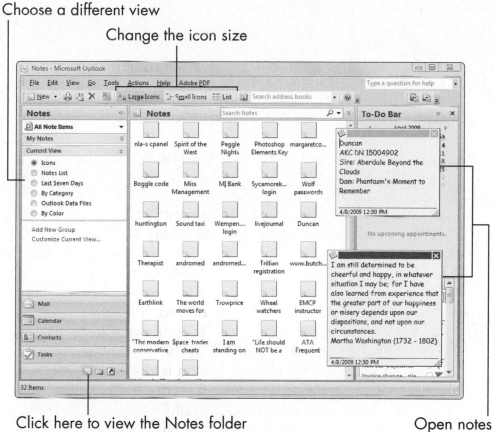

Click here to view the Notes folder

Open notes

Figure 12-7

To create a note, follow these steps:

1. Display the Notes folder. Depending on the height of the Outlook window, Notes might show as a large button near the bottom of the navigation pane (like Contacts), or it might show as a small icon of a yellow sticky note, as in Figure 12-7.

2. Do any of the following to start a new note:

- Click the New Note button on the toolbar.

- Press Ctrl+N.

- Choose File➪New➪Note.

A new blank note appears.

3. In the new, blank note that appears, type whatever you want.

The first few words of the first line will appear as an icon title, so try to be descriptive there. Unless, of course, you're trying to camouflage information, like a password; then you might want some misleading text as the first line. I have a friend who keeps her passwords note that is titled Family Birthdays, thinking that someone snooping to steal her passwords would not care about family birthdays and would pass that by.

4. Close the note by clicking the X button in its upper-right corner. It's saved automatically.

Here are some handy Note tips:

➡ **To reopen a note:** Double-click it. It remains open until you close it, or until you exit Outlook.

➡ **To move a note:** Drag it around by its title bar (the colored bar at the top of it), placing it anywhere onscreen, even outside boundaries of the Outlook window. It stays there until you close Outlook.

➡ **To edit a note:** Open it and edit away.

➠ **To change the size of the note:** Click on and drag its lower-right corner.

➠ **To delete a note:** Select it and do one of the following: Click Delete on the toolbar, press the Delete key on the keyboard, or right-click the note and choose Delete from the menu that opens.

 Just like with a deleted contact, a deleted note is moved to the Deleted Items folder.

To retrieve a deleted note, open the Mail section of Outlook, display the contents of the Deleted Items folder, find the note, and drag it back to the Notes area. You can also right-click it, choose Move to Folder, and then specify where you want to move it.

Categorize Notes

Because a note is such a multipurpose item, you might find it useful to create categories to differentiate one type of note from another.

Outlook provides six color categories: Blue, Green, Orange, Purple, Red, and Yellow. By assigning a color to a note, you can indicate what type of information it contains. For example, you might choose to make financial notes green and make family notes blue.

To assign a color category to a note

1. Select the note.

2. On the toolbar, click the Categorize button. A menu of color choices appears.

3. Click the desired color. See Figure 12-8. The note's icon and background turn that color.

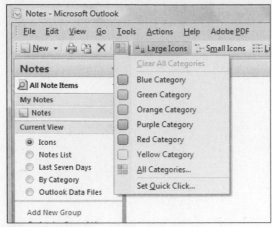

Figure 12-8

Outlook doesn't affix any special meaning to a color; you do that on your own. Here's how to assign text descriptions to each color:

1. Select a note.

2. On the toolbar, click the Categorize button.

3. Click All Categories. The Color Categories dialog box opens.

4. Click a category and then click the Rename button.

5. Type the new name for the category and then press Enter. See Figure 12-9, where I renamed the Blue Category as Registrations.

6. Repeat for each category; then click OK.

 You can also add more colors/categories. Click the New button. In the Add New Category dialog box that appears, give the category a name, choose an unused color, and (optional) create a shortcut key. See Figure 12-10.

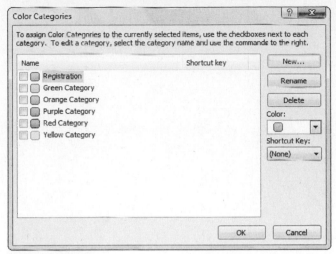

Figure 12-9

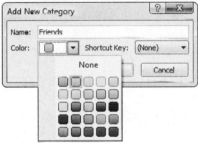

Figure 12-10

Use Tasks and the To-Do List

The Tasks feature in Outlook helps you create and manage action items for yourself and others. Not only can Outlook keep track of what you need to do, but it can remind you of upcoming deadlines, record what percentage of a large job you've completed, and even send e-mails out that assign certain tasks to other people.

To view the Tasks area of Outlook, click Tasks in the lower-left part of the navigation pane. See Figure 12-11.

Crossed-out items are completed

Only items with the Task icon are tasks

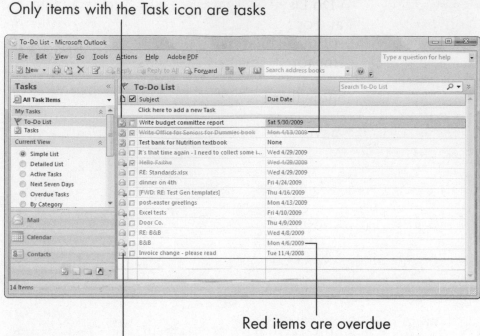

These are all to-do items (flagged mail messages, in this case)

Red items are overdue

Figure 12-11

Pay attention to the subtle difference in Outlook between Tasks and the To-Do List:

⟶ **Tasks** are specific items you created in the Tasks section of Outlook. Something isn't technically a *task* unless it was created in the Tasks section.

⟶ **The To-Do List** contains everything from the Tasks list, plus other items you have marked for action, such as e-mail messages you flag for follow-up.

 In the Inbox section of Outlook, you can flag a message for follow-up by selecting it and then clicking the red flag button on the toolbar.

In the upper part of the navigation pane, in the My Tasks section, you can click either To-Do List or Tasks to specify which set of activities you want to look at. For the purposes of this book, I assume that you chose Tasks. I describe how to work only with to-do items that are true tasks, not other items for follow-up.

To create a task, follow these steps:

1. Click Tasks in the navigation pane to display the Tasks area of Outlook.

2. Start a new task by doing any of the following:

- Click the New button on the toolbar.

- Choose File⇨New⇨Task.

- Press Ctrl+N.

3. Fill in the fields in the Task dialog box that appears. See Figure 12-12 for an example.

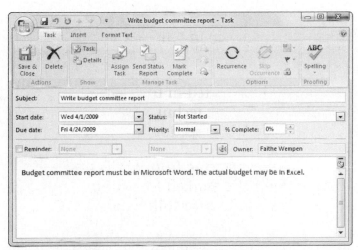

Figure 12-12

4. Click the Save & Close button. The task appears on the task list.

Tasks might appear differently on the list, depending on their statuses and due dates. For example, overdue tasks appear in red. Tasks that are 100-percent complete appear in gray with strikethrough in some views, and do not appear at all in other views (because they're no longer active).

To reopen a task, double-click it. The list of tasks looks different depending on which you chose (from the navigation bar). Figure 12-13 shows the Detailed List view.

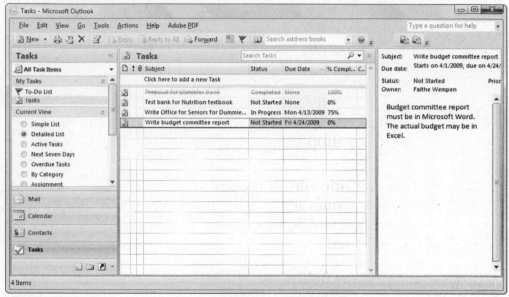

Figure 12-13

 Any notes you typed when you created the task appear in the preview pane at the right.

 Completing a task does not automatically delete it. Depending on the view, a completed task might disappear from the task list, but it's not gone. Switch to another view, such as Detailed List, and it will reappear.

To delete a task — say, one that you completed — select the task and press Delete. (Or, click the Delete button on the toolbar, or right-click the task and choose Delete from the menu that appears.)

Update the Status of a Task

As you make progress on a task, you can update its status in Outlook to reflect that.

➡ **If the view you're using contains a Status field (column), as in Figure 12-13:** Click the task's current status to open a drop-down list, and then select a new status from there. Your choices are Not Started, In Progress, Waiting on Someone Else, Deferred, or Completed.

➡ **If the view doesn't contain a Status field:** Double-click the task to open it in its own window, and then use the Status drop-down list there.

You can also provide additional information about an in-progress task by entering a number in the % Complete field. If you set the % Complete value to 100%, Outlook automatically changes the Status to Completed.

 Use the Priority field to prioritize tasks. All tasks have Normal priority by default. The other choices are Low and High. You can then sort or filter the task list according to task priority if the view you are using includes the Priority field. (Switch to another view if it doesn't.) The Priority field's symbol is an exclamation point. High-priority tasks appear with a red exclamation point in that column; low-priority tasks show a blue down-pointing arrow there.

Set a Task Reminder

To help you remember to work on a task, you can set an alarm for it: a *reminder*. A reminder pops up onscreen at a certain date and time you specify.

To set a reminder for a task, follow these steps:

1. Double-click the task to open it.

2. Mark the Reminder check box.

3. Set the date and time for the reminder.

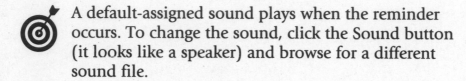 A default-assigned sound plays when the reminder occurs. To change the sound, click the Sound button (it looks like a speaker) and browse for a different sound file.

4. Click the Save & Close button.

Figure 12-14 shows a reminder being set for 8:00 a.m. on the task's Due Date, for example.

 Set your reminder to occur before the task's actual due date to give yourself some time to work on it. For example, set a budget's reminder for two weeks prior to the date.

When the date and time come for the reminder, it pops up in a box within Outlook (if Outlook is running), and a sound plays, if assigned. If Outlook isn't running at that date/time, it pops up the next time Outlook starts.

Enable the reminder

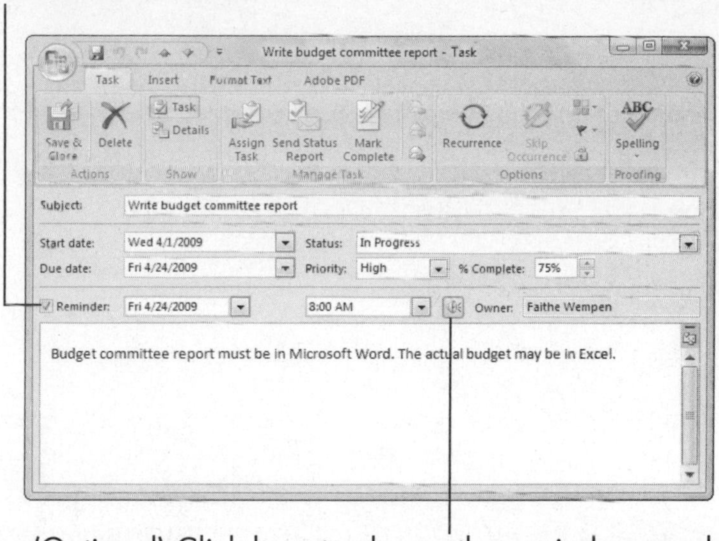

(Optional) Click here to choose the reminder sound

Figure 12-14

In the Reminder box that appears (see Figure 12-15), click the Dismiss button to dismiss the reminder, or click the Snooze button to temporarily turn off the reminder but have it pop up again later. (You get to define "later" by specifying that from the drop-down list to the left of the Snooze button.)

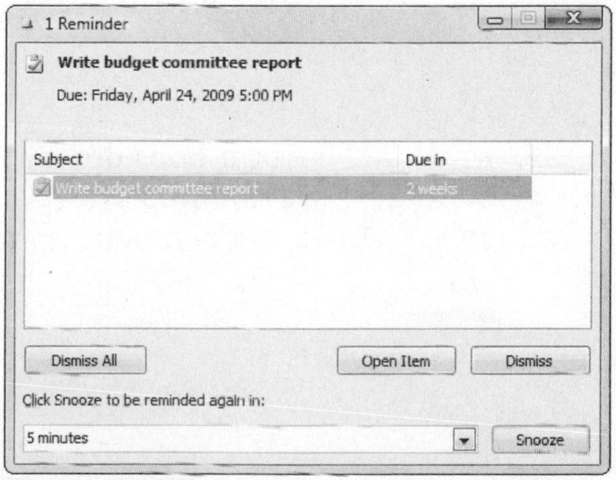

Figure 12-15

Your Busy Life: Using the Calendar

*Y*ou probably have a paper calendar you use to keep track of your appointments, meetings, and events. The problem with a paper calendar, though, is that it's, well, *paper*. It's limited.

The Calendar in Outlook offers everything a paper calendar does, and much more. You can easily switch between different views (daily, weekly, or monthly), and you can edit and delete calendar items without any messy pencil edits. You can even set up Outlook to remind you of an event shortly before it occurs. This chapter covers all that and more.

View Your Calendar

To view Calendar in Outlook, click Calendar at the bottom of the navigation bar.

The default view of the calendar is Month view, as shown in Figure 13-1.

Get ready to . . .

➠ View Your Calendar.......... 253

➠ Create and Delete
    a Calendar Event.............. 255

➠ Set an Event to Recur......... 257

➠ Configure Event Reminders. 259

➠ Add Holidays 261

➠ Categorize Events 261

➠ Print a Hard Copy
    of Your Calendar.............. 263

Switch between views · Today's date appears highlighted

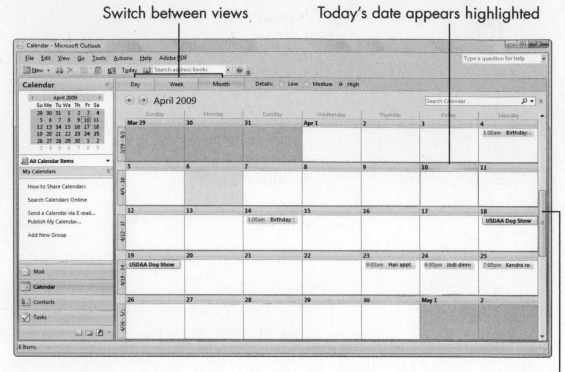

Use scroll bar to see past or future dates

Figure 13-1

 To switch to a different calendar view, click the Day, Week, or Month button, located across the top of the calendar.

➠ **Month view** shows the entire month at a glance. Only the titles of the appointments/events are shown, and sometimes these are truncated.

➠ **Week view** shows one week at a time. Each day is represented by a large box, with all its appointments and events in it. Your Tasks list appears at the bottom.

➠ **Day view** shows one day at a time. An hour-by-hour grid appears, with the appointments and events slotted at their appointed times. Your Tasks list appears at the bottom.

By default, Outlook's Month and Week calendars show the first day of the week as Sunday. If you want Monday to be the first day of the week in those views, do the following:

1. Choose Tools⇨Options.

2. Click Calendar Options.

3. Set the First Day of Week value to Monday.

To change the color scheme of the calendar

1. Choose Tools⇨Options.

2. Click Calendar Options.

3. Open the Default Color list and select a different color.

Create and Delete a Calendar Event

Outlook calls all calendar items *events*. In reality, events can be anything date-related: meetings, birthdays, parties, and even reminders of things to be done on a certain date. For example, if there's a show that you want to buy tickets for, you could put an event on your calendar to buy them on the day they go on sale.

To create an event, follow these steps:

1. Display the calendar (any view).

2. Double-click a blank spot on the date you want. An Event dialog box opens.

3. Fill in the boxes provided to describe the event, as shown in Figure 13-2.

Clear check box to enter a time

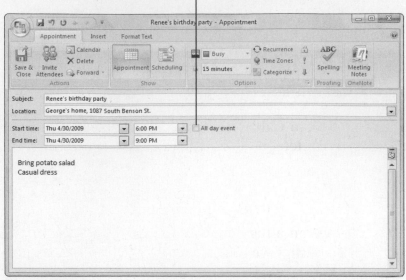

Figure 13-2

- *Subject:* Type a brief title for the event. Whatever you enter here will appear on the calendar and in the title bar when the event is open in its own window.

- *Location:* This is optional. Indicate where the event will occur, if relevant.

- *All Day Event:* This check box is marked by default. Clear it if you want to enter a start time and/or end time. See the following bullet.

- *Start Time, End Time:* Enter start and end times for the event if applicable. If not applicable, mark the All Day Event check box (if it's not already marked).

- *Notes:* This is optional. Enter any additional information you want to record about the event. This might include meeting attendees, a list of things you need to bring, or information about the type of dress expected.

4. Click the Save & Close button to add the event to the calendar.

 If you want to edit the event's settings, double-click it in Calendar to reopen this same dialog box. Then make your changes and click Save & Close.

To delete an event from Calendar, select it and press Delete, or right-click it and choose Delete, or click Delete on the toolbar.

Set an Event to Recur

Some events happen on a regular schedule. For example, birthdays come every year (whether we like it or not!), organizations have monthly meetings, and religious services happen the same day and time every week.

Rather than setting up each occurrence as a separate event, you can create a *recurring event*. Outlook then puts all the occurrences on the calendar for you automatically.

To set up recurrence for an event, follow these steps:

1. Open the event, if it's not already open, by double-clicking it in Calendar. The Event window opens (refer to Figure 13-2).

2. On the toolbar, click Recurrence. The Appointment Recurrence dialog box opens.

3. In the Recurrence Pattern area, select a radio button that best represents the type of recurrence you want. For example, in Figure 13-3, I chose Weekly.

4. Use the controls to the right of the option you just chose to specify the details of the pattern. For example, in Figure 13-3, the event recurs every week on Thursday.

These options change if you make a different selection at the left

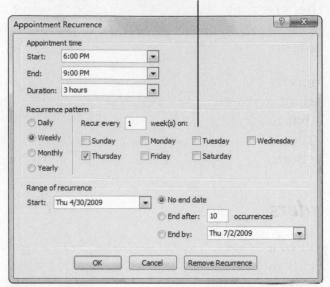

Figure 13-3

Notice in Figure 13-3 that a Weekly event can actually occur on multiple days of the week, and does not have to occur every week. If you set it to occur every four weeks, that's basically once per month, but it's different from choosing Monthly because it determines the next occurrence by counting weeks, not by counting months. In some months that have five weeks, an event that occurs every four weeks would happen twice, for example.

5. In the Range of Recurrence area, specify how many times, or for how long, the recurrence will continue. In Figure 13-3, there is no end date specified, so the recurrence will continue indefinitely.

6. Click OK to accept the recurrence settings.

7. Click the Save & Close button to save your changes to the event.

From this point on, when you double-click the event on the calendar, a dialog box asks whether you want to open that one occurrence or the series. If you choose to open the series, the changes you make to the event affect all occurrences.

If you want to edit or remove the recurrence, reopen the event, and then click the Recurrence button again. In the Appointment Recurrence dialog box that reopens (refer to Figure 13-3), you can make any changes you like. To remove the recurrence entirely, click the Remove Recurrence button.

Configure Event Reminders

Outlook can remind you of an event by popping up a Reminder box. The default lead time is 15 minutes, but you can set any amount of lead time you want. For example, if it takes you 45 minutes to drive to the meeting place, you might set the reminder for one hour prior to the meeting time.

To set a reminder for an event, follow these steps:

1. If the event isn't already open, double-click to open it.

2. In the Options section of the event dialog box, open the drop-down list for the Reminder box and choose a time interval. See Figure 13-4. Or, to turn off the Reminder feature, choose None.

 At the bottom of the drop-down list is a Sound command, which you can use to change the sound that plays when the reminder occurs. The default sound is reminder.wav, which is a simple chime.

3. Click the Save & Close button to save the changes to the event.

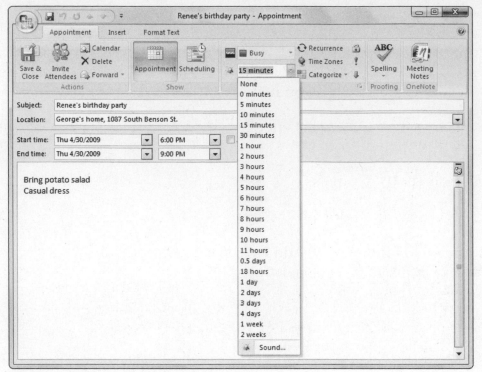

Figure 13-4

Here's how to change the default reminder time, or to set it to None so that no reminders are used:

1. Choose Tools⇨Options.

2. On the Preferences tab, in the Calendar section, make your choice:

- Clear the Default Reminder check box if you don't want to use reminders by default.

- Enter a different amount of time to use as the default.

Add Holidays

One of the nice things about a paper calendar is that the major national holidays are already printed on it. When is Easter this year? When is Thanksgiving? You never have to wonder.

You can achieve this same effect by adding holidays to the Outlook Calendar. Here's how:

1. Choose Tools⇨Options.

2. Click Calendar Options.

3. Click Add Holidays. The Add Holidays to Calendar dialog box opens.

4. Mark the check boxes for each country's holidays that you want. By default, only the United States is marked.

5. Click OK. Outlook adds holidays to your calendar.

6. Click OK three times to close all open dialog boxes.

Categorize Events

Just like with tasks (covered in Chapter 12), you can categorize calendar events, and assign a different color to each category. That way, you can tell at a glance which events go together. You might assign a different category to each person in your household, for example, or you might have different categories for home, family, and hobbies.

To assign a category to an event

1. Select the event on the calendar.

2. On the toolbar, click the Categorize button. A menu of color choices appears.

3. Click the desired color. The event's bar on the calendar turns that color. See Figure 13-5.

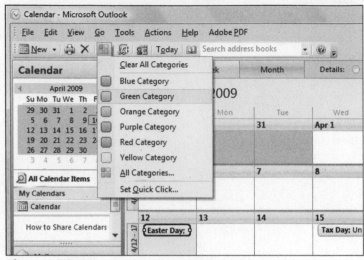

Figure 13-5

As I mention in Chapter 12, Outlook doesn't affix any special meaning to a color, but you can do so on your own. Here's how to assign text descriptions to each color:

1. Select an event.

2. On the toolbar, click the Categorize button.

3. Click All Categories. The Color Categories dialog box opens.

4. Click a category and then click Rename.

5. Type the new name for the category and then press Enter.

6. Repeat for each category; then click OK.

Print a Hard Copy of Your Calendar

With an Outlook calendar, you can have your cake and eat it, too. You can not only have an electronic calendar, but also a paper one. Just print it yourself! You can print your calendar in Day, Week, or Month view, for whatever date ranges you like.

To print your calendar, follow these steps:

1. Display the calendar.

2. Do any of the following to open the Print dialog box (see Figure 13-6):

• Click the Print button on the toolbar.

• Choose File➪Print.

• Press Ctrl+P.

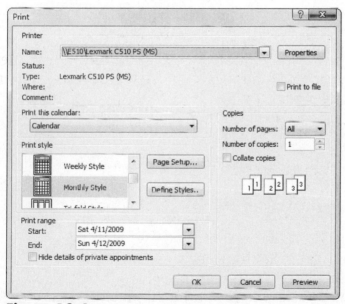

Figure 13-6

3. Check the printer name in the Name box. If it's not correct, open the drop-down list and choose a different printer.

4. In the Print Style area, click the style you want. Not only can you choose Daily, Weekly, or Monthly styles, but you can choose from a couple of other views that are for printing only.

- *Tri-fold Style:* Creates a compact calendar that shows your daily calendar, your Tasks list, and your weekly calendar, all in a format that you can easily fold for carrying in a pocket or envelope.

- *Calendar Details Style:* Creates a listing of all the events on your calendar for the day, including all details stored about each one.

After selecting a style, you can click the Page Setup button to customize how the calendar appears. The options available depend on the style you choose. For example, you can specify how many pages are shown per day, month, or week, and what fonts are used.

5. In the Number of Copies field, enter the number of copies you want. (1 is the default.)

6. In the Print Range area, enter the starting and ending dates for the printout.

If you specify that you want to print only a few days, but you choose Month view to print, Outlook prints the entire month (or months, if the chosen dates span two months). The same goes for weeks. If you specify only one day to print but print Week view, Outlook prints the entire week.

7. Click OK. The calendar prints.

Part V
PowerPoint

So old Dave's presentations are boring? They're dull, huh? "Add some dynamic content," they said. I'll give you dynamic content...

CAUTION LIVE SNAKES

Getting Started with PowerPoint

PowerPoint is best known for creating business presentations — slide shows, if you will — but it's actually a much more versatile tool. PowerPoint is great tool for almost any situation where you need to convey a visual message. For example

➡ An overview of an organization or club for new members

➡ Posters and signs with large lettering, such as *Please Help Yourself* or *Sign In Here*

➡ A photo tribute for an anniversary celebration or memorial service

➡ Lyrics for a group sing-along

➡ Information about meeting rooms and activities at a seminar

This chapter offers you some basics for working with PowerPoint, including how to use slide layouts and content placeholders that make it easy to create all these types of materials and more.

Get ready to . . .

➡ Explore the PowerPoint Interface 268

➡ Work with PowerPoint Files 269

➡ Understand PowerPoint Views 271

➡ Create New Slides............ 273

➡ Use Slide Placeholders 274

➡ Turn Text AutoFit Off or On 276

➡ Change Slide Layouts 278

➡ Move or Resize Slide Content.................... 279

➡ Manually Place Text on a Slide 280

➡ Navigating and Selecting Text 282

Explore the PowerPoint Interface

In PowerPoint, you work with slides and presentations rather than documents (as in Word) or worksheets (as in Excel). A *slide* is an individual page of the presentation. The term *page* isn't a perfect descriptor, though, because PowerPoint slides are designed to be displayed on a computer screen or with a projector rather than printed. A *presentation* is a collection of one or more slides saved in a single data file.

At a big-picture level, PowerPoint's interface is very similar to that in Word and Excel: It has a Ribbon, an Office button, and a status bar. The default view of the presentation, called *Normal view*, consists of three panes, as shown in Figure 14-1.

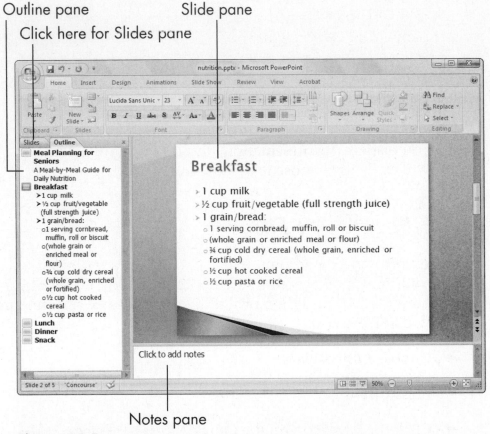

Figure 14-1

➡ The **Outline/Slides pane** is the bar along the left side. It has two tabs: Outline and Slides. When the Outline tab is selected, a text-based outline of the text from the slides appears here. When the Slides tab is selected, thumbnail images of the slides appear here.

🎯 The Outline tab doesn't always show all text on all slides. It only shows text that has been entered using the text placeholders in the slide layouts. (More about this shortly.) If you add text to a graphic, or add a manually placed text box to a slide, that text is not included in the Outline tab.

➡ The **Slide pane** (that's singular, not plural) in the middle shows the active slide in a large, editable pane. Here's where you will do most of your work on each slide.

➡ The **Notes pane** runs along the bottom of the screen. Here you can type any notes to yourself about the active slide. These notes don't show onscreen when you display the presentation, and don't print (unless you explicitly choose to print them).

Work with PowerPoint Files

When you start PowerPoint, it automatically starts a new blank presentation for you, with a single slide in it. You can work with this presentation, and then save it in any of these ways, the same as in Word and Excel:

➡ Choose Office⇨Save.

➡ Press Ctrl+S.

➡ Click the Save icon on the Quick Access toolbar.

Or, if you prefer, you can open an existing presentation file, just like in other Office applications:

➡ Choose Office➪Open.

➡ Press Ctrl+O.

➡ Click the Office button and then choose one of the recently opened files on the right side of the Office menu.

Figure 14-2 points out these controls.

Office button

Save button   Recently used files

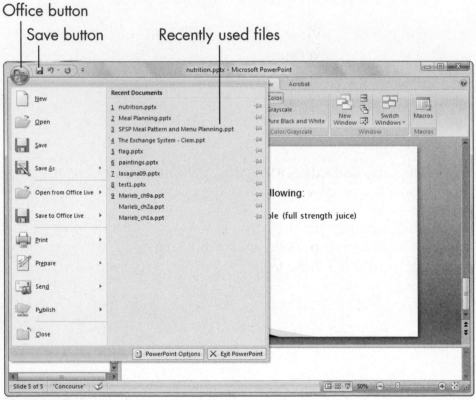

Figure 14-2

You can also start PowerPoint and open an existing file at the same time by double-clicking the filename from any file management window (such as Computer or Documents) in Windows Vista.

Understand PowerPoint Views

Like other Office applications, PowerPoint provides several different views for you to work with. Each view is useful for a different set of activities. Normal view (see Figure 14-1) — the default — is the most commonly used view. You can choose between the other views in either of these ways:

➡ Click one of the View buttons in the bottom-right corner of the PowerPoint window. (Not all the views are represented there.)

➡ On the View tab, click a button for the view you want.

Figure 14-3 shows Slide Sorter view, and also points out the two places where you can switch views.

Table 14-1 summarizes the available views and tells what each view is good for. I show you many of these views in more detail later, when I discuss how to do activities that these views are well suited for.

Select views here

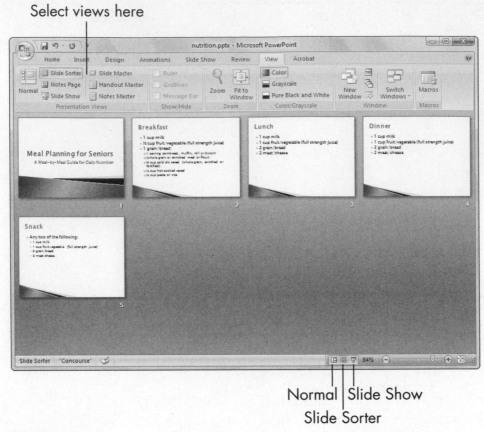

Normal | Slide Show

Slide Sorter

Figure 14-3

Table 14-1	PowerPoint Views	
View	**How to Select**	**Useful For**
Normal	Click button in bottom-right corner; or, choose View⇨Normal	Editing the content of a slide
Slide Sorter	Click button in bottom-right corner; or, choose View⇨Slide Sorter	Viewing all slides in the presentation at a glance, rearranging slide order
Slide Show	Click button in bottom-right corner; or, choose View⇨Slide Show	Showing the presentation on a computer screen
Notes Page	Choose View⇨Notes Page	Editing the speaker notes for each slide

View	How to Select	Useful For
Slide Master	Choose View⇨Slide Master	Making global changes that affect all slides in the presentation
Handout Master	Choose View⇨Handout Master	Making changes that affect the design of the handouts you print
Notes Master	Choose View⇨Notes Master	Making changes that affect the design of the speaker note pages you print

Create New Slides

Each new presentation begins with one slide in it: a title slide. You can easily add more slides to the presentation in any of these ways:

➡ Select the slide that the new slide should come *after* and then choose Home⇨New Slide.

➡ In the Outline/Slides pane, click the Slides tab. Then click the slide that the new slide should come *after*, and then press Enter.

➡ In the Outline/Slides pane, click the Outline tab. Click at the beginning of the title of the slide that the new one should come *before*, and then press Enter.

When you add a new slide in any of these ways, you get the Title and Content layout. This is the default slide layout for all slides in the presentation except the first one. (The first slide's default layout is Title Slide.) The next section covers slide layouts in more detail.

If you want a different slide layout when inserting a new slide, click the down arrow under the Home⇨New Slide button. A palette appears showing various layouts. Click the one you want. See Figure 14-4.

To duplicate an existing slide, including all its content, select it and then choose Duplicate Selected Slides from the New Slide button's menu.

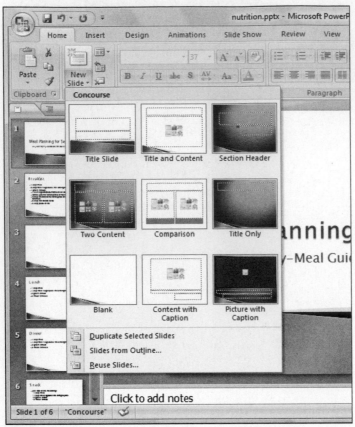

Figure 14-4

Use Slide Placeholders

A *slide layout* is a combination of one or more content placeholders. For example, the default slide layout — Title and Content — has two boxes: a text box at the top for the slide's title, and one multipurpose content placeholder in the middle that can be used for text, a graphic, or any of several other content types. See Figure 14-5.

Title placeholder

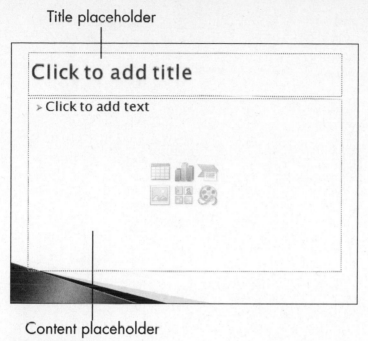

Content placeholder

Figure 14-5

Some placeholders are specifically for text. For example, the place-holder for each slide's title is text-only. Click in such a placeholder and type the text you want. A content placeholder, such as the large place-holder on the default layout, can hold any *one* type of content: text, table, chart, SmartArt graphic, picture, clip art, or media clip (video or sound). Later chapters explain some of these other types of content in more detail.

To add text to a content placeholder, click the Click to Add Text area and type what you want. To add any other type of content, click the icon in the placeholder for the type you want. These are identified in Figure 14-6.

 Use placeholders whenever possible rather than man-ually placing content on a slide. If you change the presentation's design (covered in Chapter 15), any content in placeholders is automatically shifted and reformatted to match the new design.

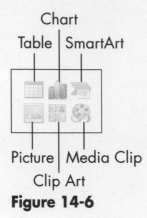

Chart

Table | SmartArt

Picture | Media Clip

Clip Art

Figure 14-6

Turn Text AutoFit Off or On

If you type more text than will fit in that text box (especially common for a slide title, for example), the text automatically shrinks itself as much as is needed to allow it to fit. This feature — *AutoFit* — is turned on by default. AutoFit is very useful because it prevents text from being truncated.

Sometimes, however, you might not want text to AutoFit. For example, it might be important to you that all the titles on your slides be exactly the same font size, for consistency.

To control whether AutoFit is in effect in a particular text placeholder, follow these steps:

1. Right-click the text box and choose Format Shape from the menu that appears.

2. In Format Shape dialog box that appears, click Text Box (on the left).

3. In the AutoFit section of the dialog box (Figure 14-7), select the Do Not AutoFit radio button.

4. Click the Close button.

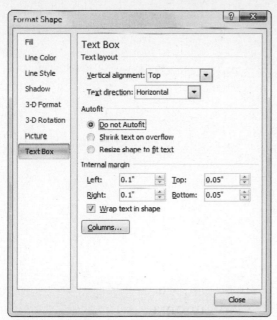

Figure 14-7

If you don't want to use AutoFit at all, you can turn it off at a global level. To do so, do the following:

1. Choose Office➪PowerPoint Options.

2. Click Proofing (on the left).

3. Click the AutoCorrect Options button. The AutoCorrect dialog box opens.

4. Click the AutoFormat As You Type tab.

5. In the Apply as You type section (see Figure 14-8), clear the following check boxes:

- AutoFit Title Text to Placeholder

- AutoFit Body Text to Placeholder

6. Click OK.

Figure 14-8

Change Slide Layouts

The Title and Content layout is very versatile. You can place any one type of content on the slide, in addition to a text title. Sometimes, though, you might want something different: for example, two different content types on the same slide (like a bulleted list on one half and a picture on the other) or just a title with an empty space underneath it (for manually inserted content).

To change a slide's layout, follow these steps:

1. Select the slide for which you want to change the layout.

2. Choose Home⇨Layout. A palette of the available layouts appears, as shown in Figure 14-9.

3. Click the layout you want.

Layout button

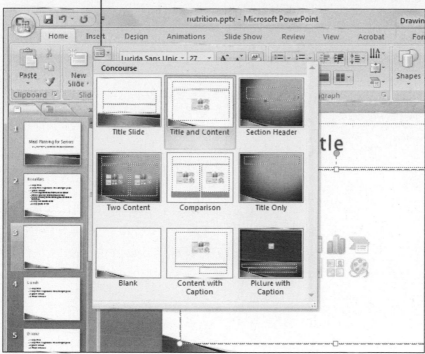

Figure 14-9

Move or Resize Slide Content

Each placeholder box on a slide is a separate object. It can be moved or resized freely.

To resize a box, select it and then drag a selection handle. A *selection handle* is a circle or square on the border of the box. Each box has eight selection handles: one in each corner, and one on each side. (The green circle handle at the top of the selected box rotates it when dragged.) To maintain the height-width proportion for the box — its *aspect ratio* — hold down the Shift key while you drag one of the corner selection handles. See Figure 4-10.

Side selection handles resize only one dimension

Corner selection handles resize both height and width at once

A Meal–by–Meal Guide for Daily Nutrition

Figure 14-10

To move a placeholder box, position the mouse pointer over the border of the box, but not over a selection handle. The mouse pointer changes to a four-headed arrow. Click and drag the box to a new location.

 If you resize the placeholder(s) on a slide and then apply a different layout or design to the slide, everything snaps back to the default size and location. So make sure you have the right layout and design chosen before you spend a lot of time resizing or moving placeholders.

 If you want to move or resize a certain placeholder on every slide in your presentation, do so from Slide Master view (covered in Chapter 15). That way, you can make the change to the layout's template, and the change is applied automatically to every slide that uses that layout.

Manually Place Text on a Slide

Whenever possible, you should use the layout placeholders to insert slide content. However, sometimes you might not be able to find a layout that's exactly what you want. For example, maybe you want to add a caption or note next to a picture, or you want to create a collage of text snippets arranged randomly on a slide.

The text in such a text box doesn't appear in the Outline, so use this type of text box sparingly.

Here's how to create a manual text box on a slide:

1. Display the slide.

2. Choose Insert➪Text Box. The mouse pointer turns into a vertical line.

3. Click where you want the text to appear, and then start typing.

Manually placed text boxes behave somewhat differently from place-holder text boxes.

➡ **The text box widens as you type.** The text doesn't automatically wrap to the next line. You can press Enter to create a new paragraph, or press Shift+Enter for a line break within the same paragraph.

➡ **Manually placed text boxes aren't resizable.** The box resizes itself to fit whatever text is inside it.

If you want a manual text box to behave more like a placeholder, adjust its AutoFit setting:

1. Right-click the text box and choose Format Shape from the menu that appears.

2. Click Text Box.

3. In the AutoFit section, select one of these options:

• *Do Not AutoFit:* Turns off all AutoFit properties, which allows you to manually resize the text box. Text doesn't resize if it doesn't fit in the box.

- *Shrink Text on Overflow:* Turns on AutoFit. You can manually resize the text box. Text resizes if it doesn't all fit in the box.

Navigating and Selecting Text

As in Word and Excel, you might find using keyboard shortcuts more convenient than using the scroll bar (shown in Chapter 1).

 The function of some PowerPoint keyboard shortcuts depends on whether you're editing in a text box or navigating in a presentation.

Table 14-2 lists the most common navigation shortcuts in PowerPoint.

Table 14-2	Navigation Keyboard Shortcuts	
Press This	**PowerPoint Text Box**	**PowerPoint Presentation**
Up arrow (↑)	One line up	Previous slide
Down arrow (↓)	One line down	Previous slide
Right arrow (→)	One character to the right	Next slide
Left arrow (←)	One character to the left	Previous slide
Tab	Next tab stop	Next placeholder box on this slide
Shift+Tab	Next tab stop	Previous placeholder box on this slide
Ctrl+arrow key	→ or ←: one word to the left or right; ↑ or ↓: one paragraph up or down	→ or ←: one word to the left or right; ↑ or ↓: one paragraph up or down
Home	Beginning of the line	First slide
End	End of the line	Last slide
Ctrl+Home	Beginning of the text box	First slide
Ctrl+End	End of the text box	Last slide

Press This	PowerPoint Text Box	PowerPoint Presentation
Page Down	Next slide	Next slide
Ctrl+Page Down	Next slide	Next slide
Ctrl+Page Up	Previous slide	Previous slide

Select Content

To select text in PowerPoint, you can either

➡ Drag the mouse pointer across it (holding down the left mouse button).

➡ Click where you want to start and then hold down Shift as you press the arrow keys to extend the selection.

When text is selected, its background changes color. The color depends on the color scheme in use; with the default color scheme, it's light blue.

Table 14-3 shows keyboard shortcuts to help you select text.

Table 14-3	Keyboard Text Selection Shortcuts
Press This.	**PowerPoint Extends Selection This Much**
Shift+← or →	One character in arrow direction
Shift+↑ or ↓	One line in arrow direction
Ctrl+Shift+←	The end of the word
Ctrl+Shift+→	The beginning of the word
Ctrl+Shift+↓	The end of the current paragraph (if in a text box)
Ctrl+Shift+↑	The beginning of the current paragraph (if in a text box)
Ctrl+Shift+End	The end of the current text box (if in a text box)
Ctrl+Shift+Home	The beginning of the current text box (if in a text box)
Ctrl+A	All slides

Dressing Up Your Presentations

*I*n this chapter, I show you a variety of techniques for adding attractive and interesting formatting to your PowerPoint presentation slides. You see how to apply consistent formatting across multiple slides, and also how to format individual objects on individual slides.

In this chapter, I also show you how to insert clip art and digital photos in a presentation. Finally, stay tuned to see how to create photo albums in PowerPoint.

Chapter 15

Get ready to . . .

➨ Understand and Apply Themes 286

➨ Change the Presentation Colors 288

➨ Edit Slide Masters 289

➨ Format Text Boxes and Placeholders 291

➨ Insert Clip Art 292

➨ Insert Pictures from Files 294

➨ Create a Photo Album Presentation...................... 295

Understand and Apply Themes

A *theme* is a design set that you apply to a PowerPoint presentation to change several elements at once, including background, color scheme, fonts, and the positions of the placeholders on the various layouts. Word and Excel also use themes, but in PowerPoint, the theme feature is exceptionally strong and full featured.

All presentations have a theme, but the default theme — literally named Blank — is so plain that it's almost like it's not there at all. Blank uses a white background, black Calibri text, and no background or design graphics.

To switch to a different theme, display the Design tab and then do one of the following:

➡ Click one of the themes in the Themes group. See Figure 15-1.

➡ Open the Themes menu (by clicking the arrow pointed out in Figure 15-1) and then click the one you want.

Click here to see more themes

Click a theme

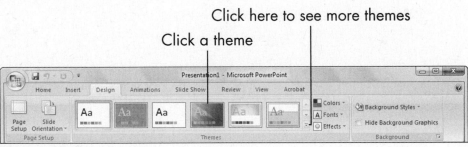

Figure 15-1

Notice the several categories on the Themes menu (see Figure 15-2). The Built-In themes — the ones that come with PowerPoint — are always available. The theme under This Presentation is the one in use. The Custom section contains any themes you created yourself.

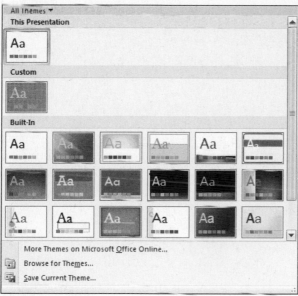

Figure 15-2

For even more themes, click More Themes on Microsoft Office Online (bottom of the Themes menu). Browsing additional themes requires an Internet connection.

To create your own theme, set up a presentation's formatting how you want by formatting the Slide Master (covered later in this chapter), and then use the Save Current Theme command on the Themes menu (see Figure 15-2) to save it.

Change the Presentation Colors

Each theme can be applied in a variety of color combinations, so you don't have to choose between a theme that has the right style and one that has the right colors.

When you apply a theme, it appears with its default colors. Here's how to choose different colors for it:

1. Choose Design⇨Colors.

2. Click the color combination you want. See Figure 15-3.

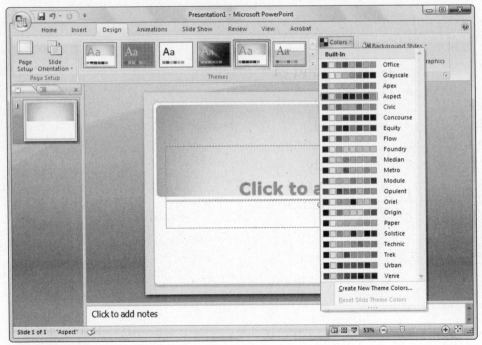

Figure 15-3

If none of these color combinations appeal to you, create your own combination. At the bottom of the Colors menu, click Create New Theme Colors, and then choose the exact colors you want from the Create New Theme Colors dialog box that appears.

Edit Slide Masters

When you choose a theme, the theme is applied to the *Slide Master*, which is a template that affects the look of all slides in the presentation. Formatting the Slide Master automatically formats every slide, and that's a big bonus because a presentation looks more professional when all the slides match.

After applying a theme, if the appearance isn't exactly the way you want it, you could change the formatting on each individual slide, but it's much more consistent and easy to simply make the change once to the Slide Master and let that change trickle down to the individual slides.

To edit the Slide Master, choose View➪Slide Master. The slide that appears isn't an actual slide in your presentation, but rather a template. Or, more precisely, a series of templates: one for each of the different layouts. You can make changes in two ways, depending on the scope of change you want to make:

➥ **To make a change that affects every slide, regardless of its layout:** Click the top left slide in the left pane. This top slide is the master for the entire presentation.

➥ **To make a change that affects only a certain layout:** Select that layout's thumbnail image from the left pane. See Figure 15-4.

Select the topmost slide to affect all slides

Change the fonts and sizes of the sample text to change the text on all slides

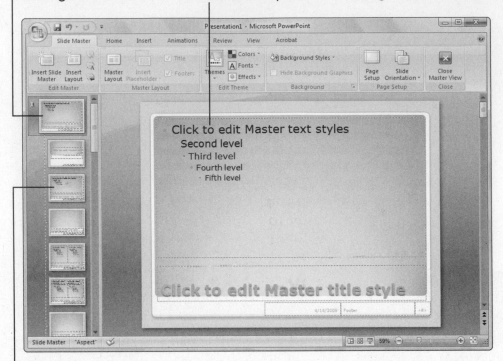

Select one of the individual layouts to affect only slides with that layout

Figure 15-4

Here are some of the edits you might want to make:

➠ **Select a different set of fonts** from the Slide Master➪Fonts list.

➠ **Change the font used for an individual bullet level** by selecting the text sample representing that level and then choosing a different font from the Home tab's Font drop-down list.

➠ **Apply a different bullet type to each line of sample text** (from the Home tab) to change the bullet characters used at each level.

➠ **Move a placeholder** on the slide by dragging its border.

 To move a placeholder, drag its border — not the selection handle. See the next bullet.

➠ **Resize a placeholder** by dragging one of its selection handles.

➠ **Delete, resize, or recolor the background graphic** provided by the theme (if any).

When you're finished working with the slide master, choose Slide Master➪Close Slide Master to return to Normal view. (I talk about the different views in PowerPoint in the preceding chapter.)

Format Text Boxes and Placeholders

In most cases, presentations look best when they're consistently formatted. That means that usually your best bet is to apply formatting to the Slide Master, as I discuss in the preceding section.

Sometimes, however, you might want to format an individual text box or object differently from the rest, to make it stand out.

The easiest way to apply formatting to an object is with the Shape Styles command. *Shape Styles* are formatting presets that use the theme colors in the presentation. Depending on the style you choose, a Shape Style can include a border, a fill color, and special effects that make the shape look shiny, matte, or raised.

To apply a Shape Style to an object

1. Select the object. If it's a text box, click its outer border to select the box itself (not text inside it).

2. Click the Format tab.

If you don't see a Format tab, you don't have an object selected.

3. Open the Shape Styles palette by clicking the down arrow in the Shape Styles group. See Figure 15-5.

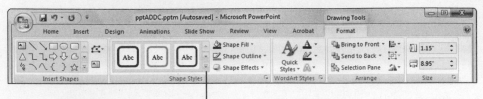

Click here to open palette of Shape Styles

Figure 15-5

4. Click the desired shape style.

If none of the Shape Styles is what you want, you can also choose the background and an outline for an object separately. Use the Shape Fill, Shape Outline, and Shape Effects button menus on the Format tab (see Figure 15-5).

 To quickly change text formatting within a text box, use the WordArt Styles button, also on the Format tab. It works just like the Shape Styles feature except that it applies to text.

Insert Clip Art

Clip art is predrawn generic artwork, and Microsoft provides many clip art files for free with its Office products.

The easiest way to insert clip art is by using one of the placeholders on a slide layout. (I talk about placeholders in Chapter 14.) Follow these steps:

1. Display a slide that contains a Clip Art icon on one of its placeholders. You can see this icon in Figure 15-6.

 If the current layout doesn't contain a Clip Art icon as a placeholder, switch to a different layout, or delete the existing content from the Content place-holder so that the Clip Art icon is available in it.

2. Click the Clip Art icon to open the Clip Art task pane, which you can see on the right side of Figure 15-6.

3. In the Search For box, type a word that describes the art-work you want; then click the Go button. Samples of the available clips appear. See Figure 15-6. If your Internet connection is active, PowerPoint includes clips from the Internet in the search results.

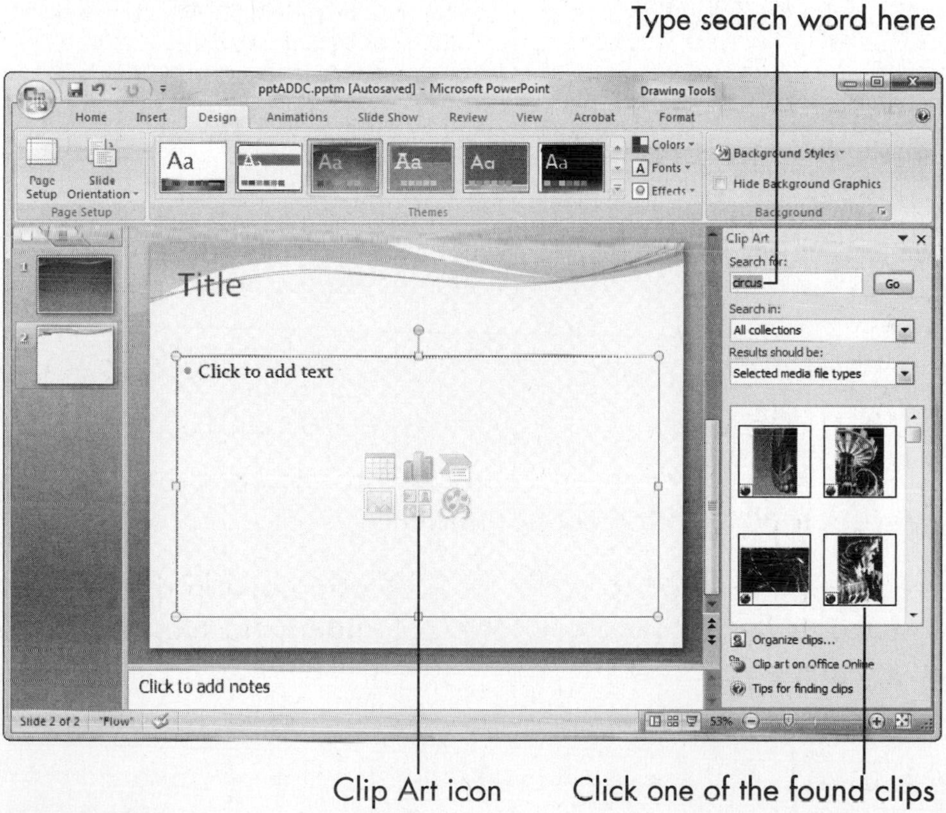

Type search word here

Clip Art icon   Click one of the found clips

Figure 15-6

4. Click the clip you want. It's inserted in the placeholder.

5. (Optional) Move or resize the image as desired.

- *To move the image:* Drag it by its center.

- *To resize the image:* Drag a selection handle around the edge.

 You can also insert clip art as independent objects on slides, separate from the layout placeholders. To do that, do not select a placeholder on the slide. Instead, just display the slide and then choose Insert➪Clip Art to open the Clip Art task pane, and go from there.

Insert Pictures from Files

One of the most common uses for PowerPoint is to display digital photos. There are a couple of ways to do that.

➡ **Insert individual photos into presentations.** I show you how to do it in this section.

➡ **Create a special Photo Album presentation.** I explain this in the next section.

First, look at how to put an individual photo on an individual slide:

1. To insert the picture into a layout placeholder, click the Picture icon on the placeholder. See Figure 15-7.

 If you want the picture to be independent of any placeholder, choose Insert➪Picture when no place-holder is selected.

2. In the Insert Picture dialog box that appears, select the picture you want to insert. Change the location if needed.

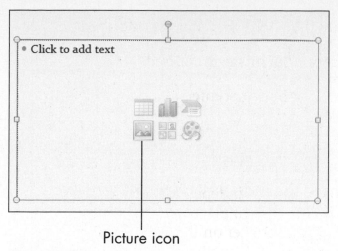

Picture icon

Figure 15-7

3. Click Insert. The picture appears on the slide.

4. (Optional) Move or resize the image as desired.

- *To move the image:* Drag it by its center.

- *To resize the image:* Drag a selection handle around
  the edge.

Create a Photo Album Presentation

If you want to create a presentation that is primarily (or exclusively)
photos, there's a special feature just for you! The Photo Album feature
makes it easy to create photo-centric presentations with special features
such as picture edging, framing, and captions.

 Before you get started, find your photos. Know where
on your computer they are stored. (Check the
Pictures folder! That's where many digital camera
management programs put them by default.)

Follow these steps to create a photo album:

1. Choose Insert⇨Photo Album. The Photo Album dialog box opens. See upcoming Figure 15-8.

2. Click the File/Disk button. The Insert New Pictures dialog box opens.

3. Select the pictures you want to include.

To select more than one picture at a time, hold down the Ctrl key while you click each one.

4. Click Insert. The pictures you select appear in the Pictures in Album list of the Photo Album dialog box. See Figure 15-8.

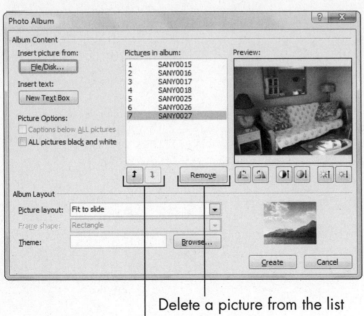

Delete a picture from the list

Reorder the pictures on the list

Figure 15-8

5. (Optional) Reorder the pictures.

    a. Select the picture that's not in the right place in the order.

    b. Click the up-arrow or down-arrow button below the list to reposition it.

6. (Optional) Rotate a picture or adjust its brightness or contrast.

    a. Select the picture's name.

    b. Use the buttons under the Preview pane to adjust the picture's appearance as needed. See Figure 15-9.

Decrease Brightness
Rotate Left

Increase Brightness
Decrease Contrast
Increase Contrast
Rotate Right

Figure 15-9

7. In the Album Layout section of the dialog box, select the following options:

- *Picture Layout:* Choose how many pictures you want per slide.

- *Frame Shape:* Choose a frame shape/style for each photo.

- *Theme (optional):* Click the Browse button and then select a presentation theme to apply to the photo album.

You don't have to choose the theme now; you can apply a theme change to the presentation after its creation (Design⇨Themes).

8. Click the Create button. A new presentation is created using your photos.

The resulting presentation is like any other presentation, except for one small extra: Because it is a photo album, you can return to the Photo Album dialog box at any time to manage the photos and effects. To do so, on the Insert tab, click the down arrow below the Photo Album button, and then choose Edit Photo Album from the menu that appears.

Adding Movement and Sound

Remember slide projectors? Maybe you still even have one in the back of your closet. They show one slide after another on a screen, with a *ker-chunk* sound as the next slide pushes the previous one out the chute. Not very glamorous or exciting.

In PowerPoint, though, because your slides are electronic, a presentation can have much more exciting animation. You can assign any sounds or music you want, and you can create interesting animations when one slide replaces another or when content appears on a slide. A bulleted list can appear one line at a time, a graphic can "fly" in separately from the text, or a trumpet sound can announce an important slide's appearance.

In this chapter, I show you how to create animation and transition effects on slides. I also show you how to add a musical soundtrack from an audio CD to a presentation.

Chapter 16

Get ready to . . .

➡ Animate Objects
   on a Slide 300

➡ Add Slide Transition Effects ... 305

➡ Set Slides to Automatically
   Advance 306

➡ Add a Musical Soundtrack . 307

Animate Objects on a Slide

By default, all the objects on a slide appear at once. Say you have a title, some text, and perhaps a graphic on a slide: They all show up together.

To add more visual interest to the presentation or to reveal bits of information at a time, you can use animation in PowerPoint. For example, you can pose a question in the title of the slide and then provide the answer in the body. Or, you can have each item in a bulleted list appear one at a time.

You can control when the delayed content shows up by setting

➡ A **time delay:** The additional content appears after a certain number of seconds. This technique is good for autonomous presentations (without human interaction).

➡ A **mouse click delay:** Additional content appears only when you click the mouse or press a key on the keyboard. This technique is good for presentations with a live speaker because if someone asks a question or you get off-schedule, the animation won't occur at the wrong time — you control its timing.

For simple animation, pick an animation style from the Animation tab. Follow these steps:

1. Select the object to be animated. For example, if you want to animate a bulleted list on a slide, select the text box that contains those bullets. Or if you want to animate a graphic, select the graphic.

2. Choose Animations➪Animate. A drop-down list opens. The three effects available are

- *Fade:* The object gradually fades into view.

- *Wipe:* The object is painted onto the screen in a wiping motion.

- *Fly In:* The object flies onto the slide.

If the object you chose is a text box, those three effects appear as category headings, as in Figure 16-1. The choices underneath each category are

- *All at Once:* The text appears when you click the mouse, all paragraphs at once.

- *By 1st Level Paragraphs:* The first paragraph of the text appears when you click the mouse, and then next paragraph when you click again, and so on.

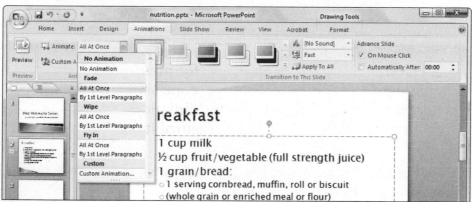

Figure 16-1

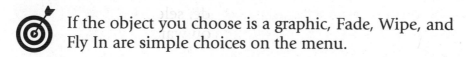 If the object you choose is a graphic, Fade, Wipe, and Fly In are simple choices on the menu.

3. Choose the option you want for the animation.

4. (Optional) To see a preview of the animation you chose, choose Animations↪Preview.

If you want animation other than one of these defaults, you must use the Custom Animation task pane. To do this

1. Choose Animations⇨Custom Animation.

2. In the Custom Animation task pane (on the right), any animations you created via the presets already appear. See Figure 16-2.

The most common custom animation is to set the animation to occur automatically on a time delay rather than having it execute on mouse click. To make this change, do the following:

1. Select the animation in the Custom Animation task pane.

2. In the task pane, open the Start drop-down list and choose After Previous.

3. Right-click the animation in the task pane and choose Timing. A dialog box appears for the effect with the Timing tab displayed. See Figure 16-2.

Figure 16-2

Instead of performing Step 2, you can wait until you open the dialog box (in Step 3) and then set the Start value to After Previous there in the dialog box.

4. Enter a number of seconds of delay in the Delay field.

5. Click OK.

Another common change you might want to make is to change how text is animated (all at once, or paragraph by paragraph). To do that

1. Double-click the animation in the task pane. A dialog box for the effect appears.

2. Click the Text Animation tab.

3. Open the Group Text drop-down list and choose the grouping for the animation (All at Once, By 1st Level Paragraphs, or some other choice.)

4. Click OK.

You can also set up your own custom animation effects from scratch. This is where the real power of custom animation comes into play!

Follow these steps to create your own custom animation for an object:

1. Select the object.

2. Open the Custom Animation task pane if it's not already open (choose Animations⇨Custom Animation).

3. Click Add Effect. A fly-out menu appears.

4. Point to Entrance on the fly-out menu. Several common entrance effects appear.

5. Click More Effects. The Add Entrance Effect dialog box opens. See Figure 16-3.

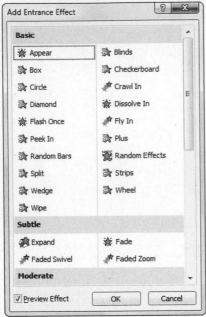

Figure 16-3

6. Click the effect you want.

 Notice that the effects are grouped according to the intensity of the effect. The ones categorized as Basic or Subtle are not too showy; the Moderate and Exciting ones will make your audience smile! (Beware, though, that if the audience is too involved with the style of the presentation, it could distract them from its content.)

7. Click OK.

After creating the effect, you can edit it the same as other effects. From the task pane, click the effect and then use these drop-down lists above it:

➡ **Start:** Choose to start on a mouse click, or with or after the previous animation effect.

➡ **Property:** This choice isn't always available. It is available if the animation effect you choose has options, such as flying in from a particular direction. The options available here vary.

➡ **Speed:** This choice controls the speed of the animation effect.

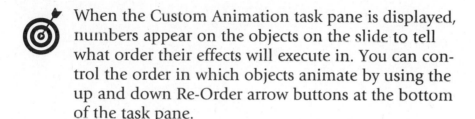 When the Custom Animation task pane is displayed, numbers appear on the objects on the slide to tell what order their effects will execute in. You can control the order in which objects animate by using the up and down Re-Order arrow buttons at the bottom of the task pane.

Add Slide Transition Effects

Transition effects are much like animations except that they apply to entire slides. A *transition effect* is the flourish that occurs when you transition between one slide and another. The default transition effect is No Transition, which means one slide simply goes away and another appears, with no flourish at all.

Some of the transition effects you can use include fades, cuts, dissolves, and wipes. It's difficult to explain each of these effects, but if you see them, you'll immediately understand them, so try them out:

1. Click the Animations tab.

2. In the Transition to This Slide group, point at one of the transition effects (see Figure 16-4). Its name appears in a ScreenTip, and a preview of it appears on the active slide.

Point to a transition to see a preview of it

Click here for more choices

Apply same transition to every slide in the presentation

Figure 16-4

For more choices, click the More button (the down arrow with a line across its top) to open a palette of more transition effects.

3. When you're ready to select a transition for a slide, click the transition you want (rather than just pointing at it). It's immediately applied to the active slide.

 Use the Speed and Sound drop-down list boxes to the right of the transitions to customize the speed at which the transition occurs and the sound that plays when the transition occurs (if any). Be wary of assigning sounds to transitions, though; in a long presentation, audiences might find them annoying.

Set Slides to Automatically Advance

By default, slides transition from one to another on mouse click, not automatically. If you want the slide show to progress automatically, with a certain amount of pause between slides, choose Animations⇨ Automatically After, and then enter a number of seconds. See Figure 16-4.

That setting applies only to the active slide, but you can easily apply it to all slides by doing the following:

1. Click in the Slides/Outline pane in Normal view, or switch to Slide Sorter view.

 Read about views in Chapter 14.

2. Press Ctrl+A to select all slides.

3. Choose Animations⇨Automatically After and enter the number of seconds. The change will apply to all slides.

 At any time, you can test your presentation by going into Slide Show view (choose View⇨Slide Show). Press Esc to return to Normal view.

Add a Musical Soundtrack

As your presentation plays, you might want to have music in the background. PowerPoint enables you to load an audio CD on the PC that's being used to show the presentation and play the CD in synchronization with the presentation.

 Musical soundtracks work best for *self-running presentations:* that is, those presentations where the slides are set to advance automatically after a certain number of seconds. In a presentation with a live speaker manually advancing the slides, that live speaker is probably also speaking to the audience, and the speech can interfere with the music (and vice versa).

To set up an audio CD track, follow these steps:

1. Select the first slide in the presentation, or the slide on which the music should start playing.

2. Insert the audio CD in your computer's CD drive.

3. On the Insert tab, click the down arrow below the Sound button, displaying a menu.

4. Click Play CD Audio Track. The Insert CD Audio dialog box opens.

5. Enter track numbers in the Start at Track and End at Track list boxes. See Figure 16-5.

Figure 16-5

6. (Optional) To have the chosen song(s) repeat if the presentation runs longer than the song, select the Loop Until Stopped check box.

7. Select the Hide Sound Icon During Slide Show check box.

8. Click OK. A prompt asks whether you want the music to play automatically or when clicked.

9. Click Automatically.

 At this point, the music is attached to the first slide in the presentation. The rest of the steps here are necessary to make the music continue to play after you move past the first slide.

10. Display the Custom Animation task pane (choose
Animations⇨Custom Animation).

11. Double-click the CD Audio animation in the task pane.
The Play Audio CD dialog box opens. See Figure 16-6.

Figure 16-6

12. In the Stop Playing Clip section, select the After *xx* Slides
radio button and then type **999** in the field.

13. Click OK.

14. Check your work by viewing the presentation in Slide
Show view (View⇨Slide Show).

 The music you pick isn't stored with the presentation:
the music is linked to it. If you show this presentation
on some other PC, you must have the same audio CD
available on that PC, or the music won't play.

Presenting the Show

Chapter 17

*P*resenting . . . *your show!*

The whole point of a PowerPoint presentation is to deliver a show to an audience. That audience might be in the same room with you or a thousand miles away. Folks might watch it simultaneously or pull it up on their own PCs at their convenience.

This chapter explains how to display a presentation on your own computer screen. That's useful if you're going to be there in-person when the audience views the show, like during a club meeting or religious service. I also show you how to pack a presentation to move it to a different PC as well as how to make printouts for yourself and your audience.

You also discover here how to make a self-running CD that you can send to people so they can view the presentation on their own computers. Finally, I show you how to distribute a presentation over the Internet.

Chapter 7

Get ready to . . .

➡ Display a Slide Show Onscreen 312

➡ Use the Slide Show Tools 313

➡ Print Copies of a Presentation 315

➡ Package a Presentation on a CD 317

➡ Save a Web Version of a Presentation 319

Display a Slide Show Onscreen

Slide Show view is the view that you use when showing the presentation to others. (Read more about PowerPoint views in Chapter 14.) One slide appears onscreen at a time, completely filling the screen. You might have used this view already — to check your work — while you were creating the presentation.

You can start Slide Show view from the first slide or from the current slide. Table 17-1 summarizes the methods of doing each.

Table 17-1	Methods of Entering Slide Show View	
	From First Slide	**From Current Slide**
Shortcut key(s)	Press F5	Press Shift+F5
View tab	View⇨From Beginning	View⇨From Current Slide
View buttons (bottom right of screen)	n/a	Slide Show View button

Then, after you're in Slide Show view, you can show your presentation. Here's how:

➡ **Move to the next slide** (in any of these ways):

- Click the mouse.

- Press any key on the keyboard (except Backspace or the left arrow).

- Right-click to display a shortcut menu and then choose Next.

➡ **Move to the previous slide** (in any of these ways):

- Press Backspace or the left arrow on the keyboard.

- Right-click to display a shortcut menu and choose Previous.

➠ **Jump to a specific slide:**

   a. *Right-click to display a shortcut menu.*

   b. *Point to Go to Slide.*

   c. *Click the slide you want to display. See Figure 17-1.*

Figure 17-1

➠ **End the show** (in any of these ways):

   • Click through to the end of the slide show (black screen) and then click one more time.

   • Press the Esc key.

   • Right-click to display a shortcut menu and then choose End Show.

Use the Slide Show Tools

In Slide Show view, a faint set of buttons appears in the lower-right corner. When you roll your mouse over these buttons, they brighten up. Figure 17-2 shows the buttons on this toolbar.

Previous Navigation
Pen Next

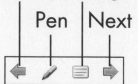

Figure 17-2

I enhanced Figure 17-2 to show all four buttons in their "bright" mode at once, so you can see them better. In reality, a button lights up only when you point at it, and you can point at only one at a time.

The buttons are

➡ **Previous:** A left-pointing arrow. Use this to go to the previous slide.

➡ **Pen:** Opens the Pen menu, which you can use to control a mouse-controlled "pen" that draws on the slides.

From the Pen menu, you can annotate a slide by drawing on it. You can use this tool to underline or circle important content, for example. Click the Pen button and then click one of the pen styles (such as Felt Tip). Then hold down the mouse and drag across the slide to "draw" on it. You can also change the ink color from the Pen menu. Give it a try!

➡ **Navigation:** Opens a navigation menu, which is identical to the shortcut menu from Figure 17-1.

➡ **Next:** A right-pointing arrow. Use this to go to the next slide.

PowerPoint allows you to lock down or disable certain navigation methods in Slide Show view so that people interacting with your presentation at an unattended computer won't inadvertently (or purposely) disable or damage the presentation. When one method is disabled, you might need to rely on another method.

Print Copies of a Presentation

There are many uses for printouts of a presentation. You might want to print the slides themselves, for example (one big slide per page), to use as a kind of low-tech delivery system. If you don't have a computer or projector available, you can just hold up each slide, one by one!

When you print in PowerPoint, you're given a choice of the type of printout you want. Here are the choices available:

➡ **Slides:** A full-page copy of one slide per sheet.

➡ **Handouts:** Multiple slides per page (2 to 9, depending on your choice of settings), suitable for giving to the audience to take home.

➡ **Notes Pages:** One slide per page, but with the slide occupying only the top half of the page. The bottom half is devoted to any speaker notes you typed into PowerPoint.

➡ **Outline View:** A text-only version of the presentation, structured as an outline, with the slide titles as the top-level outline items.

To print any of these types of printouts, follow these steps:

1. Choose Office➪Print. The Print dialog box opens.

2. Open the Print What drop-down list and choose what you want to print (handouts, slides, and so on).

3. Set any other print options desired:

- *Name:* Choose the printer you want to use (if you have more than one).

- *Print Range:* The default is All.

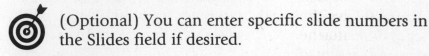 (Optional) You can enter specific slide numbers in the Slides field if desired.

- *Number of Copies:* The default is 1; enter another number here if desired.

- *Handouts:* If you choose Handouts in Step 2, choose the number of slides per page. See Figure 17-3.

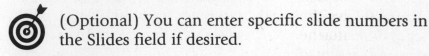 Different numbers of slides per page have different layouts. For example, if you choose 3 slides per page, the layout has lines next to each slide for the audience to take notes on.

4. Click OK. The slides print.

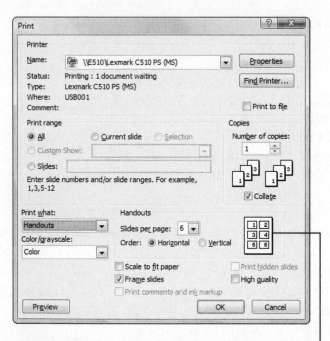

Preview the layout for chosen number of slides

Figure 17-3

Package a Presentation on a CD

The PC you play your presentation on might not always be the one you create it on. For example, if you're traveling to different clubs or organizations to give the same speech, each one might have its own computer system attached to its projector. If you have a laptop, you can bring your presentation with you, but you might find it easier to simply bring the presentation on a flash drive or a CD.

If your presentation consists only of text and pictures, it's self-contained in a single PowerPoint file (with a .pptx or .ppt extension), so you can just copy that file to your flash drive — or e-mail it to yourself as an e-mail attachment, or use some other method to carry it with you.

However, if you have multimedia content, such as video clips, those are not embedded in the PowerPoint file: They are *linked*. They are not stored in the main data file, but rather a link is created from their file to the data file, so that when the presentation plays, the content from the linked file is accessed. That means if you copy the PowerPoint file, you won't automatically copy the linked content. If you didn't know that in advance, you could run into a situation where you arrive at the site where you're going to give your speech only to find out that you didn't have all the presentation available!

There are other little gotchas as well about showing a presentation on a PC other than the one it was created on. For example, any fonts that the presentation uses must be available on the PC on which you're showing it. If those fonts aren't available, PowerPoint will try to substitute a similar font, but its definition of "similar" and yours might not be the same!

You can get around these problems by allowing PowerPoint to "pack" and copy the presentation file to another location. When it does so, it automatically also copies all the fonts, linked files, and other associated content needed to ensure a trouble-free show. You can package it to a folder on your hard drive and then copy that folder anywhere you like, or you can burn the package directly to a CD.

Here's how to pack a presentation to a CD:

1. Choose Office➪Publish➪Package for CD. The Package for CD dialog box opens. See Figure 17-4.

2. In the Name the CD field, type the label you want to assign to the CD.

3. Insert a blank, writeable CD into your PC's CD drive.

4. Click the Copy to CD button. If a warning appears about linked files, click Yes.

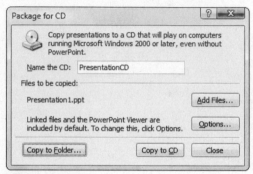

Figure 17-4

5. Wait for PowerPoint to copy the presentation to the CD.

6. A message appears asking whether you want to copy the same files to another CD. If so, insert another CD and click Yes. Otherwise, click No.

7. Click Close to close the Package for CD dialog box.

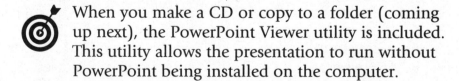 When you make a CD or copy to a folder (coming up next), the PowerPoint Viewer utility is included. This utility allows the presentation to run without PowerPoint being installed on the computer.

Here's how to pack a PowerPoint presentation if you want to copy the files to a folder, rather than to a CD:

1. Choose Office➪Publish➪Package for CD. The Package for CD dialog box opens. Refer to Figure 17-4.

2. Click the Copy to Folder button. The Copy to Folder dialog box opens.

3. In the Folder Name field, type the name of the folder you want to create.

4. In the Location field, type the path to the location where you want to store the new folder.

⊚ Click Browse to select a location by browsing if you prefer.

5. Click OK to accept the location. The files are copied to that location.

6. Click Close to close the Package for CD dialog box.

Save a Web Version of a Presentation

One way to distribute your presentation to other people remotely is to copy it to a CD or folder (as I describe in the preceding section) and then share that with other people. However, the person receiving the presentation must either have PowerPoint or the PowerPoint Viewer utility in order to see the show. (Read about this utility earlier in this chapter.)

An alternative is to publish the presentation in Web format so that anyone can see it in an ordinary Web browser such as Internet Explorer or Firefox, the same way they view Web sites on the Internet.

Some of the more complex features of PowerPoint don't work exactly the same in a browser as they do in PowerPoint. In most cases, though, the differences are very minor, and you won't notice them.

To create a Web-usable version of the presentation, follow these steps:

1. Choose Office➪Save As. The Save As dialog box opens.

2. Open the Save as Type drop-down list and choose Web Page.

3. Change the save location if needed.

4. In the File Name field, type the name you want to use for the presentation's main file. See Figure 17-5.

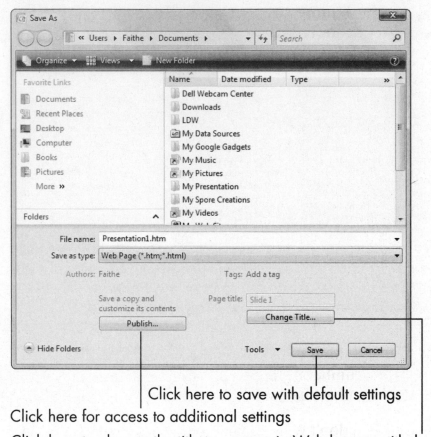

Click here to save with default settings

Click here for access to additional settings

Click here to change the title to appear in Web browser title bar

Figure 17-5

5. Click the Change Title button. The Set Page Title dialog box appears. Type a title that you want to appear in the Web browser title bar when the presentation runs, and then click OK.

6. Click Save to finish saving with the default settings, and skip the rest of these steps.

OR

Click the Publish button. The Publish as Web Page dialog box opens. See Figure 17-6.

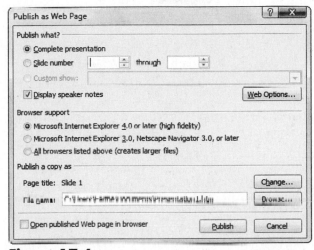

Figure 17-6

7. (Optional) If you don't want to include all the slides, select the Slide Number radio button and then enter a range of slide numbers in the fields there.

8. (Optional) If you don't want the audience to see your speaker notes, clear the Display Speaker Notes check box.

9. (Optional) If you want compatibility with much older Web browsers, choose one of the following:

- *Microsoft Internet Explorer 3.0, Netscape Navigator 3.0, or Later:* This saves the presentation in a more basic, backward-compatible format. It's not an issue for those of us using a modern version of Windows (XP or Vista), but if you will show the presentation to people with much older computers, it might help.

- *All Browsers Listed Above:* This saves the presentation in a hybrid Web format that supports both older and newer browsers. With a newer browser, the presentation uses all the available features; with an older one, the presentation's more basic. The file size will be larger than normal, though, because there are two different versions of the presentation stored in the same file.

10. (Optional) If you want to see the presentation in your default browser (to check how it looks), mark the Open Published Web Page in Browser check box.

11. Click the Publish button.

The files are "published" to whatever location you specified in Steps 3-4. You can then transfer them to an Internet location (enlist the help of a techie friend if needed) or put the files on a flash drive or CD and share them with others.

Customizing Office Applications

Appendix

People have different ideas about what constitutes the "best" way for a program to operate. For every feature that one person finds ideal, someone else might find that same feature very annoying. That's why Microsoft Office 2007 has a variety of options that you can customize to make the applications work more like you want.

In this appendix, I show you how to customize the Quick Access toolbar and the status bar in all the Office applications. (It works basically the same in all of them.) Then I go through some of the most common program options in each application.

Get ready to . . .

➥ Customize the Quick Access Toolbar 324

➥ Customize the Status Bar ... 326

➥ Set Word, Excel, and PowerPoint Options 327

➥ Set Outlook Options 329

Customize the Quick Access Toolbar

The *Quick Access toolbar* is the small toolbar immediately to the right of the Office button in each of the Office applications (except Outlook). See Figure A-1. By default, the Quick Access toolbar contains only a few buttons:

➡ **Button name:** What it does

➡ **Button name:** What it does

➡ **Button name:** What it does

One of the handiest things about the Quick Access toolbar is that it's available no matter which tab you're on.

 If you find yourself using a button frequently (other than one of the default buttons), consider placing it on the Quick Access toolbar so you don't have to switch tabs all the time.

Here's how to add a command to the Quick Access toolbar:

1. Right-click the button or other control. A shortcut menu opens.

2. Choose Add to Quick Access Toolbar.

Another use for the Quick Access toolbar is to add buttons for commands that don't appear on any of the tabs. (Yes, there are many such commands. Most of them are carryovers from previous versions of the software, but some are new 2007 features that are rather obscure.)

To browse the available commands and add any to the Quick Access toolbar (including commands not already on the Ribbon), follow these steps:

1. Choose Office⇨*application* Options where *application* is the program. For example, in Word, you choose Word Options. A dialog box appears.

2. Click Customize in the bar at the left. Two columns of commands appear in the middle of the window. The left column holds the commands you can add, and the right column holds the commands already on the Quick Access toolbar. See Figure A-1.

choose commands to display

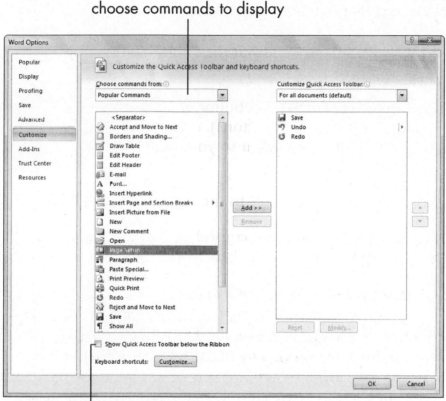

Relocate the Quick Access Toolbar below the Ribbon if desired

Figure A-1

3. At the top of the left list, open the drop-down menu and choose what commands you want to see on the list:

- *Popular Commands:* A selection of the most commonly used commands.

- *Commands Not in the Ribbon:* Commands that have no equivalent on any tab.

   Many of these are shortcuts to commands that were in previous versions of the application but are no longer featured in the 2007 version.

- *All Commands:* A list of all available commands.

- *Macros:* Any *macros* (recorded scripts) that have been stored in the active file or template.

4. Click a command in the left list and then click the Add button in the middle to move it to the list on the right. Repeat as desired to add more commands.

5. When finished, click OK.

To remove buttons from the Quick Access toolbar, return to the Customize lists (refer to Figure A-1), click a button's name in the right column, and then click the Remove button in the middle. Or, take the easy way. Just right-click the button on the Quick Access toolbar and then choose Remove from Quick Access Toolbar from the menu that appears.

Customize the Status Bar

The *status bar* is the thin bar along the bottom of the application window. It contains *View buttons* (for switching between views), the Zoom slider, and perhaps a few other items, depending on the settings.

Just like the Quick Access toolbar, you can customize the status bar:

1. Right-click the status bar. On the shortcut menu that appears is a list of all the items that the status bar can contain. The ones with check marks next to them are already displayed.

2. Click an item to toggle it on or off. See Figure A-2.

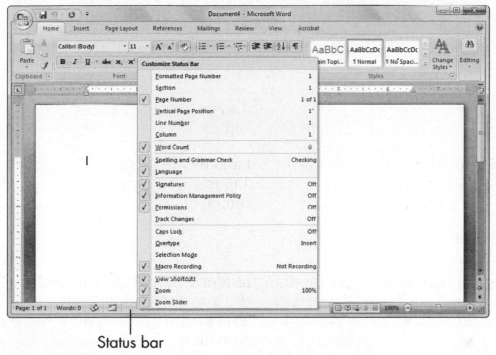

Status bar

Figure A-2

Set Word, Excel, and PowerPoint Options

So many options are available in each application that it would take a much larger book to cover them all. In this appendix, I review a few of my favorite options in Word, Excel, and PowerPoint. (I cover Outlook options separately because they are so different.)

For each application, access the options by clicking the Office button and then click the *application* Options command, where application is the name of the app. For example, in PowerPoint, it's PowerPoint Options. Then click a category at the left to display a page of options. See Figure A-3.

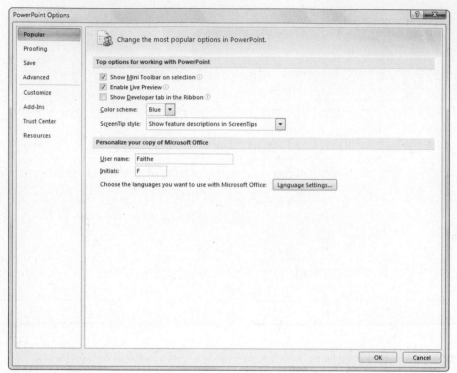

Figure A-3

Use Table A-1 as a handy guide to customize Word, Excel, and PowerPoint. Note that options are listed on the different tabs at the left. For example, maybe what you're looking for is on the Popular tab, or perhaps it's on the Proofing tab. Open each tab to explore what they hold.

Table A-1 Common Word, Excel, and PowerPoint Options

If You Want To . . .	Choose This . . .
Prevent the mini toolbar from popping up when you select text.	Popular⇨Show Mini Toolbar On Selection
Change the color of the application window.	Popular⇨Color Scheme. Then choose a color from the drop-down list.
Turn off wavy red underlines of misspelled words.	Proofing⇨Check Spelling as You Type
Save files in an earlier version of the application rather than in 2007 format.	Save⇨Save Files in This Format
Set the default file save location (determines the folder that appears by default in the Save As dialog box).	Save⇨Default File Location
Clear the Recent Documents list on the Office menu.	Advanced⇨Show This Number of Recent Documents; then set the number to 0.
Turn on the Developer tab, which contains extra commands, such as those for templates.	Popular⇨Show Developer Tab in Ribbon
Change the default user name and initials.	Popular⇨User Name and Popular⇨Initials
Set spelling options.	Proofing tab

Set Outlook Options

The options in Outlook work a little differently than in the other Office applications. To find them, choose Tools⇨Options. Then, in the Options dialog box that opens, click a tab and select options on that tab.

Table A-2 lists some of the most common options you can set in Outlook.

Table A-2	Common Options in Outlook
If You Want To . . .	**Choose This . . .**
Turn off the envelope icon that pops up by the clock in Windows when mail is being sent and received.	Tools⇨Options⇨Preferences tab⇨E-mail Options⇨Advanced E-Mail Options. Then select these check boxes: Show an Envelope Icon in the Notification Area; Display a New Mail Desktop Alert.
Choose whether to save copies of messages you send to the Sent Items folder.	Tools⇨Options⇨Preferences tab⇨E-mail Options⇨Save Copies of Messages in Sent Items Folder
Adjust the aggressiveness level of your junk mail–filtering feature.	Tools⇨Options⇨Preferences tab⇨Junk E-Mail
Adjust how frequently automatic sending/receiving occurs.	Tools⇨Options⇨Mail Setup tab⇨Send/Receive
Set the default text formatting for new e-mails.	Tools⇨Options⇨Mail Format tab⇨Compose in This Message Format
Empty the Deleted Items folder each time you exit Outlook.	Tools⇨Options⇨Other tab⇨Empty the Deleted Items Folder Upon Exiting
Bypass the confirmation prompt that appears when you permanently delete items (by pressing Shift+Delete).	Tools⇨Options⇨Other tab⇨Advanced Options⇨Warn Before Permanently Deleting Items
Choose which panes appear in Outlook.	Tools⇨Options⇨Other tab⇨Outlook Panes section

Index

• A •

ABS function (Excel), 165
accounts, e-mail
  setting up, 212–213
  troubleshooting, 214–216
Address bar, 53
Adobe Reader, 60
adware, 227
aligning
  paragraphs (Word), 78–79
  text in cells (Excel), 177–179
animation (PowerPoint)
  animation styles for, 300–301
  automatic slide advance, 306–307
  creating effects, 303–305
  custom, 302–305
  editing effects, 305
  entrance effects, 304
  mouse click delay for, 300, 302–303
  previewing, 301
  slide transition effects, 305–306
  text effects, 301, 303
  time delay for, 300
antivirus programs, 228
applications. *See also* specific
    applications
  exiting using Office menu, 14
  Options buttons for, 14
  starting, 8–9
  tabs for, 9–10
  third-party (non-Microsoft), 10

artwork. *See* Clip Art feature (Word);
    graphics; pictures
attachments to e-mail
  attaching files, 56–57, 225–226
  types not to open, 228
  viewing, 220–221
attributes, applying to text
  in Excel, 177–178
  in Office documents, 36
AutoFit feature (PowerPoint),
    276–278, 281–282
automatic slide advance (PowerPoint),
    306–307
AutoRecover feature, 65–66
AVERAGE function (Excel), 164

• B •

background colors (Word), 105–107
background images (Excel), 180
bold format
  applying in Excel, 139–140, 177–178
  applying in Office documents, 36
  in this book, 1
borders
  cell (Excel), 173–175
  chart (Excel), 187
  page (Word), 102–104
building blocks (Word)
  cover pages, 119–121
  headers and footers, 116–119
  page numbers, 114–116
  viewing all available, 121

bulleted lists
  PowerPoint, 290
  Word, 85–86
buttons
  for database fields (Excel), 194–195
  for font colors, 34–35
  Quick Access toolbar, 12, 324–326
  with resized, narrower window, 12
  for resizing fonts, 33
  on Ribbon tabs, using, 10–12
  Slide Show view (PowerPoint),
    312–313
  for text attributes, 36
  for views, 23

• C •

calculations in worksheets. *See*
    formulas (Excel); functions (Excel)
Calendar (Outlook)
  categorizing events, 261–262
  creating events, 255–257
  default view, 253–254
  deleting events, 257
  first day of week setting, 255
  holidays, adding, 261
  notes for events, 256
  printing, 263–264
  recurring events setup, 257–259
  reminders for events, 259–260
  removing recurrence, 259
  removing reminders, 260
  renaming categories, 262
  viewing, 253
  views, changing, 254
calling back sent e-mail, 225
categorizing (Outlook)
  events, 261–262
  notes, 243–245

CDs
  presentations on, 317–318
  as soundtracks (PowerPoint),
    307–309
cells (Excel)
  absolute references, 159
  active, changing, 138–139
  active, indicator for, 137, 138
  address for, 138
  borders, 173–175
  clearing contents, 144
  clearing formatting, 145
  copying content between, 157–159
  defined, 137
  deleting, 144, 149–150
  editing contents, 26–27, 143
  fill color for, 175–177
  formatting text in, 177–179
  inserting functions in, 161–163
  inserting new cells, 150–151
  moving content between, 157–159
  range, defined, 138
  range, selecting, 139–142
  referencing in formulas, 156–157,
    159–160
  referencing in functions, 160
  relative references, 159
  removing borders, 174
  removing fill color, 176
  selecting, 20–21
  text overflow in, 170
  text wrap in, 171–172
  typing text in, 15–16, 137, 143
center alignment (Word), 78
charts (Excel)
  changing data for, 183
  creating, 182
  formatting, 185–189
  moving, 183

overview, 181–182
placing on tab, 183
resizing, 182
styles for, 185
terminology for parts, 184–185
tools on Ribbon for, 184
clearing (Excel). *See also* deleting or
    removing
  cell contents, 144
  cell formatting, 145
  cutting versus, 144–145
  deleting versus, 144, 149
  filtering, 199, 201
clearing Recent Documents list, 329
Clip Art feature (PowerPoint),
    292–294
Clip Art feature (Word)
  defined, 96
  inserting in documents, 96–98
  library of clip art, 96
  media types supported, 96
  moving images in document, 100
  online database of clip art, 96
  resizing, 98–99
  rotating, 100
Clipboard
  commands for, 30–31
  cut-and-paste in Excel, 144–145
  described, 25
  moving or copying using, 28, 29–31
closing applications, 14
colors
  for application window, 329
  applying to text, 34–35
  background for page (Word), 105–107
  cell borders (Excel), 174–175
  for charts (Excel), 185, 187
  color themes, 41
  for events categories, 261–262
  fill, for cells (Excel), 175–177

for notes categories, 243–245
page borders (Word), 103
for presentations, 288–289
printing background colors, 105
red wavy underlines, 42–43, 329
for selected text, 20
for text in cells (Excel), 177–178
for worksheet tabs (Excel), 154
columns (Excel). *See* rows or columns
    (Excel)
columns (Word), 107. *See also* tables
    (Word)
Computers For Seniors For Dummies, 2
concatenating columns (Excel),
    203–206
contacts (Outlook)
  alphabetization, changing, 234
  deleting, 236–237
  editing, 236
  locating by filtering, 238
  mail merge using, 125, 126–127
  multiple items of information, 235
  phone dialing using, 240
  restoring, if accidentally deleted, 236
  storing information, 232–235
  tips for entering, 234–235
  views, changing, 237–238
Contacts folder, 232, 239–240
copy and paste. *See* Clipboard
Copy command, 30–31
copying
  between cells (Excel), 157–159
  Clipboard for, 28, 29–31
  by dragging and dropping, 28–29
  graphics, 21
COUNT function (Excel), 164
COUNTA function (Excel), 164
COUNTBLANK function (Excel), 164
cover pages (Word), 119–121
crashes, recovering work after, 65–66

customizing Office applications
  common options, 327–330
  Quick Access toolbar, 12–13,
    324–326
  status bar, 326–327
cut and paste. *See* Clipboard
Cut command, 30–31

• D •

data files, 47
database (Excel). *See also* tables (Excel)
  benefits of, 194
  converting cell ranges into tables,
    193–194
  defined, 191
  drop-down arrow buttons, 194–195
  filtering table data, 197–201
  mail merge using, 192–193
  merging columns, 203–206
  Paste Values feature, 204, 205–206
  removing filtering, 199, 201
  sorting, 195–197
  splitting columns, 201–202
  terminology, 191–192
date
  functions (Excel), 163–164
  inserting in Word, 129–131
Day view (Calendar), 254
Deleted Items folder (Outlook), 330
deleting or removing
  AutoFit (PowerPoint), 276–278
  borders around cells (Excel), 174
  Calendar events (Outlook), 257
  cells (Excel), 144, 149–150
  clearing cell contents (Excel), 144
  clearing Recent Documents list, 329
  columns (Excel), 205–206
  contacts (Outlook), 236–237
  e-mail, 330

fill color for cells (Excel), 176
filtering out (Excel), 199, 201
graphics, 21
notes (Outlook), 243
page numbers (Word), 116
recurrence for events (Calendar), 259
reminders (Calendar), 260
rows or columns (Excel), 148
table row or column (Word), 109
tasks (Outlook), 249
text, 26
worksheets (Excel), 152–153
Developer tab, 329
documents
  creating, 15
  file extensions for, 47
  inserting pictures in, 16–18
  moving around in, 18–20
  recently used, 13, 53, 270, 329
  typing text in, 15–17
  zooming, 21–22
Documents folder (Vista), 48, 50
double spacing. *See* line spacing
    (Word)
down-saving (Excel), 146
Draft view (Word), 23, 75, 77
dragging and dropping, 28–29

• E •

eBay, e-mail from, 229
effect themes, 41
effects. *See* animation (PowerPoint)
e-mail. *See also* Outlook
  accounts setup, 212–213
  addressing from Contacts list, 239
  attaching files to, 56–57, 225–226
  avoiding frauds, scams, and viruses,
    226–229
  calling back sent messages, 225
  composing, 223–224, 330

copying data into messages, 58
Deleted Items folder, 330
deleting, 330
flagging for follow-up, 246
junk-mail filtering feature, 330
Mail feature overview, 217–218
multiple addresses for contacts, 235
receiving and reading, 218–220, 330
replying to, 221–222
sending, 56–58, 224–225, 330
Sent Items folder, 330
starting from Contacts folder,
  239–240
troubleshooting setup for, 214–216
turning off envelope icon for, 330
viewing attachments, 220–221
Web-based providers, 213, 214
e-mail servers, 213, 214–215
entrance effects (PowerPoint), 304
envelope icon for e-mail, 330
envelopes, printing in Word, 122–123
erasing. *See* deleting or removing
EVEN function (Excel), 165
events. *See* Calendar (Outlook)
Excel. *See also* Microsoft Office,
  common features; specific features
 applying themes, 38–39, 40–41
 AutoRecover feature, 65–66
 borders around cells, 173–175
 charts, 181–189
 clearing cell contents, 144
 clearing cell formatting, 145
 clearing versus deleting or cutting,
  144–145, 149
 colors for worksheet tabs, 154
 copying data between cells, 157–159
 as database, 192–206
 default location for files, 53, 329
 deleting cells, 144
 deleting rows or columns, 148
 deleting worksheets, 152–153

down-saving your file, 146
editing text in cells, 26–27, 143
features unique to, 136–137
file extension for documents, 47
fill color for cells, 175–177
formatting text in cells, 177–179
formatting worksheets, 180–181
formulas, 137, 155–160
functions, 160–168
gridlines, 172
Grow Font button, 33
inserting cells, 150–151
inserting rows or columns, 147–148
mail merge using, 124, 126, 192–193
moving data between cells, 157–159
moving the cell cursor, 138–139
options, setting, 327–329
Page Layout options, 180–181
range, defined, 138
renaming worksheets, 153
resizing rows and columns, 170–171
saving your work, 48–53, 145–146
selecting cells in, 20–21
selecting entire sheet, 142
selecting ranges in, 139–142
Shrink Font button, 33
spreadsheet structure, 138
structure of worksheets, 138
switching between worksheets, 152
tab scroll to view worksheets, 152
terminology, 136–138
text overflow in, 170
text wrap in cells, 171–172
titles, 180, 193
typing text in cells, 15–16, 137, 143
uses for, 135
views, changing, 23
views available, 23
zooming, 22
exiting applications, 14
exploits, e-mail, 227

• F •

Favorite Links list, 52
field codes (Word)
  for date and time, 130–131
  for mail merge, 127–128
fields (Excel), 192
file extensions for documents
  compatible with earlier versions, 50
  default Office format, 47, 49
  macro-enabled files, 49–50
  PowerPoint presentations, 317
  Rich Text Format, 58
file paths, 50–51
fill color
  for background (Word), 106–107
  for cells (Excel), 175–177
filtering contacts (Outlook), 238
filtering table data (Excel), 197–201
financial functions (Excel), 165–168
first-line indent (Word), 82
folders
  default, for saved files, 48, 50, 329
  list in Save As dialog box, 52
  moving between, 52–53
Font Color button, 34–35
fonts and font sizes
  applying attributes, 36
  applying colors, 34–35
  choosing, 32–33
  font, defined, 31
  font size, defined, 31
  font themes, 41
  Grow Font button, 33
  modifying for all new documents, 33
  Shrink Font button, 33
  for Slide Masters (PowerPoint), 290
  specifying custom size, 33–34

for text in cells (Excel), 177–178
  Theme Fonts, 40–41
footers (Word)
  defined, 114
  different for first page, 119
  numbering pages in, 114–115, 119
  for odd and even pages, 119
  overview, 116
  putting content in, 117–119
  space allotted to, 119
formatting
  charts (Excel), 185–189
  clearing from cells (Excel), 145
  tables (Word), 110–111
  text in cells (Excel), 177–179
  text in Office documents, 34–36
  worksheets (Excel), 180–181
formulas (Excel). *See also* functions
    (Excel)
  absolute references in, 159
  copying between cells, 157–159
  defined, 137, 155
  differences from text, 155–156
  formula bar for, 137
  moving between cells, 157–159
  order of precedence in, 156
  referencing cells in another sheet, 160
  referencing cells in same sheet,
    156–157, 159
  relative references in, 159
frauds, e-mail, avoiding, 226–229
Full Screen Reading view (Word),
    23, 76
functions (Excel). *See also* formulas
    (Excel)
  arguments for, 161, 162–163
  for changing numbers, 165
  date and time, 163–164

defined, 160
financial, 165–168
inserting in cells, 161–163
with no argument, 163–164
referencing ranges in, 160
simple, with one argument, 164
syntax for, 161–162
typing in cells, 163
FV function (Excel), 166, 167, 168

• G •

grammar checker, 45
graphics. *See also* Clip Art feature
    (Word); pictures
  artwork for page borders (Word), 104
  Clip Art feature (PowerPoint),
    292–294
  selecting, 21
  types of, 18
gridlines (Excel), 172
Grow Font button, 33

• H •

Handout Master view (PowerPoint),
    273
handouts, printing (PowerPoint),
    315–316
hanging indent (Word), 82
headers (Word)
  different for first page, 119
  numbering pages in, 116
  for odd and even pages, 119
  overview, 116
  putting content in, 117–119
  space allotted to, 119
Help, Ribbon button for, 11

hiding paragraph markers (Word), 77
holidays, adding in Calendar, 261
HTTP e-mail servers, 213

• I •

I-beam pointer, 26
images. *See* Clip Art feature (Word);
    graphics; pictures
IMAP e-mail servers, 213
indenting paragraphs (Word), 79–82
insertion point, 26–27
italic format, applying
  in Excel, 177–178
  in Office documents, 36

• J •

junk-mail filtering feature, 330
justified alignment (Word), 78–79

• K •

keyboard shortcuts
  for moving around, 20, 139, 282–283
  for printing, 62
  for selecting text, 21, 283
  for undoing last action, 101

• L •

Landscape orientation, 72–73, 180
launching. *See* opening
line drawings. *See* Clip Art feature
    (Word)
line spacing (Word)
  changing, 84–85
  default settings, 83–84
  described, 82
  settings available, 83

• M •

macro-enabled files, saving, 49–50
Mail Merge utility (Word)
  data source for, 124–125, 126–127,
    192–193
  described, 70, 123–124
  field codes for, 127–128
  main document setup, 125–128
  previewing before printing, 128
  printing the letters, 128–129
  steps for, 124
margins
  in Word, 73–74, 116
  for worksheets (Excel), 180
MAX function (Excel), 164
McAfee VirusScan, 228
merging columns (Excel), 203–206
Microsoft Excel. *See* Excel
Microsoft Office, common features. *See
  also* specific applications
  attaching files to e-mail, 56–57
  changing the file listing view, 55
  creating documents, 15
  Developer tab, 329
  editing text, 26–27
  e-mailing from applications, 55–58
  fonts and font sizes, 31–34
  formatting text, 34–36
  grammar checker, 45
  inserting pictures in documents,
    16–18
  mini toolbar, 36–37, 329
  moving around in documents, 18–20
  opening saved files, 53–55
  Print Preview, 62, 63–64
  printing your work, 62–63
  Quick Access toolbar, 12–13,
    324–326
  recovering lost work, 65–66

Ribbon, 9–12
saving your work, 48–53
selecting content, 20–21
setting program options, 327–330
sharing work in other formats, 58–61
spell checker, 25, 42–44
starting applications, 8–9
status bar, customizing, 326–327
typing text in documents, 15–16, 17
viewers for documents, 58
views, changing, 22–24
in Vista versus XP, 2, 8
zooming, 21–22
Microsoft Outlook. *See* Outlook
Microsoft PowerPoint. *See* PowerPoint
Microsoft Word. *See* Word
MIN function (Excel), 164
mini toolbar, 36–37, 329
Month view (Calendar), 254
mouse click delay for animation
  (PowerPoint), 300, 302–303
movies, Clip Art feature for (Word), 96
moving around
  changing location for saving, 50–53
  in Excel, 138–139
  between folders, 52–53
  in Office documents, 18–20
  in Slide Show view (PowerPoint),
    312–313
  in Word, 71
moving items
  aligning paragraphs (Word), 78–79
  between cells (Excel), 157–159
  charts (Excel), 183
  clip art (PowerPoint), 294
  clip art (Word), 100
  Clipboard for, 28, 29–31
  by dragging and dropping, 28–29
  graphics, 21
  indenting paragraphs (Word), 79–82

merging columns (Excel), 203–206
notes (Outlook), 242
placeholder boxes (PowerPoint), 280, 291
rotating clip art (Word), 100
splitting columns (Excel), 201–202
windows, 28
musical soundtracks (PowerPoint), 307–309
My Documents folder (XP), 48

• *N* •

navigating. *See* moving around
newspaper style columns (Word), 107
non-modal dialog boxes, 188–189
Normal style (Word), 90
Normal view, 23, 272
Norton Antivirus, 228
notes (Outlook)
  categorizing, 243–245
  creating, 241–242
  deleting, 243
  described, 240–241
  moving, 242
  reopening, 242
  resizing, 243
  restoring after deleting, 243
Notes Master view (PowerPoint), 273
Notes Page view (PowerPoint), 24, 272
Notes Pages, printing (PowerPoint), 315–316
NOW function (Excel), 163–164
NPER function (Excel), 166, 167
numbered lists (Word), 85, 86–88
numbering pages (Word), 114–116

• *O* •

ODD function (Excel), 165
Office. *See* Microsoft Office, common features

Office button, 1, 13
Office menu
  overview, 13–14
  Print command, 62
  Recent Documents list, 13, 53, 270, 329
opening
  file listing view for, changing, 55
  notes (Outlook), 242
  Office applications, 8–9
  Office menu, 13
  presentations, 270–271
  saved files, 53–55
  tasks (Outlook), 248
order of precedence in formulas, 156
orientation
  of printed page, 72–73, 180
  of text in cells (Excel), 179
Outline view (Word), 23, 76
Outlook. *See also* e-mail; Microsoft Office, common features; specific features
  attaching files to e-mail, 56–57, 225–226
  avoiding frauds, scams, and viruses, 226–229
  Calendar feature, 253–264
  calling back sent e-mail, 225
  choosing panes for, 330
  composing e-mail, 223–224, 330
  Contacts feature, 232–240
  data file for, 47
  deleting e-mail, 330
  dial-up connection, 211–212, 240
  envelope icon for e-mail, 330
  first-time setup, 209–212
  flagging e-mail for follow-up, 246
  junk-mail filtering feature, 330
  Mail feature overview, 217–218
  mail merge data from, 125, 126–127
  Notes feature, 240–245

Outlook (*continued*)
  options, setting, 329–330
  personal folders files, 47
  Privacy Options, 211–212
  receiving and reading e-mail, 218–220, 330
  replying to e-mail, 221–222
  sending e-mail, 224–225, 330
  setting up e-mail accounts, 212–213
  Tasks feature, 245–251
  To-Do List feature, 246–247
  troubleshooting e-mail setup, 214–216
  viewing e-mail attachments, 220–221
  Web-based e-mail providers with, 213, 214

● *P* ●

packing presentations (PowerPoint), 318–319
page borders (Word)
  artwork for, 104
  choosing, 102–104
  uses for, 102
page description languages, 59–61
Page Layout view (Excel), 23
page numbers (Word), 114–116
pages (PowerPoint), 268
paper size
  setting in Excel, 180
  setting in Word, 71, 72
paragraphs (Word)
  aligning, 78–79
  indenting, 79–82
  showing/hiding markers for, 77
  styles, 90–95
Paste command, 30–31
Paste Values feature (Excel), 204, 205–206

paths for files, 50–51
PayPal, e-mail from, 229
PDF format, 60–61
phishing, 227
Photo Album feature (PowerPoint), 295–298
pictures. *See also* Clip Art feature (Word); graphics
  attaching files to e-mail, 56–57, 225–226
  attachments to e-mail, viewing, 220–221
  Format tab options (Word), 101
  graphics other than, 18
  inserting in documents, 16–18, 100–101, 294–295
  Photo Album feature (PowerPoint), 295–298
  rotating (PowerPoint), 297
  text wrap setting for (Word), 101–102
placeholders for slides (PowerPoint)
  creating, 274–275
  editing Slide Masters, 291
  moving, 280, 291
  resizing, 279–280, 291
  Shape Styles for, 291–292
PMT function (Excel), 166–167
point (pt), defined, 32
POP3 e-mail servers, 213
Portrait orientation, 72, 73, 180
PowerPoint. *See also* Microsoft Office, common features
  animating objects, 300–305
  applying themes, 40–41
  AutoFit feature, 276–278, 281–282
  automatic slide advance, 306–307
  AutoRecover feature, 65–66
  Clip Art feature, 292–294
  colors for presentations, 288–289
  creating placeholders, 274–275

creating slides, 273–274
default location for files, 53, 329
disabling navigation methods, 315
displaying presentations onscreen, 312–313
editing Slide Masters, 289–291
ending slide shows, 313
entering Slide Show view, 312
file extension for documents, 47
Grow Font button, 33
handouts, 315–316
inserting pictures in slides, 16–18, 294–295
manual text boxes, 280–282
moving between slides, 312–313
moving placeholder boxes, 280, 291
musical soundtracks, 307–309
navigation shortcuts, 282–283
opening existing files, 270–271
options, setting, 327–329
overview, 268–269
packing presentations, 318–319
Photo Album feature, 295–298
printing presentations, 315–316
publishing presentations on CD, 317–318
resizing placeholder boxes, 279–280, 291
saving presentations, 269
selecting text in, 20
self-running presentations, 306–307
Shape Styles, 291–292
Shrink Font button, 33
slide layouts, changing, 278–279
slide layouts, defined, 274
slide show tools, 313–314
slide transition effects, 305–306
terminology, 268
text selection shortcuts, 283
themes, 286–287, 291

typing text in slides, 16, 17
uses for, 267
views, changing, 23, 271
views available, 23–24, 271–273
Web versions of presentations, 319–322
zooming, 22
presentations. *See* PowerPoint
previewing
    animation (PowerPoint), 301
    mail merge results, 128
    before printing, 62, 63–64, 76
    themes, 40
Print Layout view (Word), 23, 75–76
Print Preview
    described, 62
    using, 63–64
    in Word, 76
printing. *See also* Mail Merge utility (Word)
    background colors, 105
    calendar (Outlook), 263–264
    envelopes (Word), 122–123
    options in Excel for, 180
    options in Office for, 62–63
    in PowerPoint, 315–316
    previewing before, 62, 63–64, 76
    Quick Print command, 62, 63
pt (point), defined, 32
publishing presentations (PowerPoint)
    on CD, 317–318
    in Web format, 319–322
PV function (Excel), 166

• *Q* •

Quick Access toolbar
    adding buttons to, 12–13, 324–326
    adding Quick Print command, 63
    default buttons on, 324

Quick Print command, 62, 63
Quick Styles Gallery (Word), 91–92
quitting applications, 14

• R •

range of cells (Excel)
  converting into table, 193–194
  defined, 138
  referencing in functions, 160
  selecting before issuing commands,
    139–140
  selecting entire worksheet, 142
  selecting noncontiguous cells, 141
  selecting rows or columns, 141–142
  selecting with keyboard and mouse,
    140
  selecting with keyboard shortcuts,
    141
  selecting with mouse, 140
RATE function (Excel), 166, 167
receiving and reading e-mail,
    218–220, 330
Recent Documents list, 13, 53, 270,
    329
records (Excel), 192
recovering lost work, 65–66
recurring events (Calendar), 257–259
red wavy underlines, 42–43, 329
reminders (Outlook)
  for Calendar events, 259–260
  for tasks, 250–251
removing. *See* deleting or removing
renaming
  categories (Calendar), 262
  user name and initials, 329
  worksheets (Excel), 153
reopening. *See* opening
replying to e-mail, 221–222

resizing
  charts (Excel), 182
  clip art (PowerPoint), 294
  clip art (Word), 98–99
  fonts, 33–34
  graphics, 21
  notes (Outlook), 243
  pictures (Word), 101
  placeholder boxes (PowerPoint),
    279–280, 291
  rows or columns (Excel), 170–171
  windows, 28
  worksheets for printing (Excel), 181
restoring deleted items (Outlook)
  contacts, 236
  notes, 243
Ribbon
  buttons and controls on tabs, 10–12
  described, 9
  Help (question mark) button on, 11
  with resized, narrower window, 12
  tabs on, 9–11
Rich Text Format (RTF), 58–59
right alignment (Word), 78
rotating
  clip art (Word), 100
  pictures (PowerPoint), 297
  3-D charts (Excel), 189
ROUND function (Excel), 165
rows or columns (Excel)
  adjusting height or width, 170–171
  deleting, 148
  inserting, 147–148
  merging columns, 203–206
  selecting, 141–142
  splitting columns, 201–202
RTF (Rich Text Format), 58–59
running. *See* opening

• S •

saving your work
  changing the file listing view, 55
  changing the file type, 49–50
  changing the location, 50–53, 329
  for compatibility with earlier versions, 50, 146, 329
  copies of sent e-mail, 330
  default location for files, 48, 53, 329
  in default Office format, 49
  down-saving (Excel), 146
  in Excel, 145–146
  macro-enabled files, 49–50
  methods of, 48
  in PDF format, 60–61
  in PowerPoint, 269
  presentations for Web, 319–322
  in XPS format, 60–61
scams, e-mail, avoiding, 226–229
ScreenTips for buttons, 11
scrolling
  in Office documents, 18–19
  tab scroll in Excel, 152
search toolbars, unwanted, 227, 229
security, e-mail, 226–229
selecting
  cell in Excel, 20–21
  graphics, 21
  range in Excel, 139–142
  text in PowerPoint, 20, 283
  text in Word, 20, 71
self-running presentations (PowerPoint)
  automatic slide advance for, 306–307
  musical soundtracks for, 307–309
Sent Items folder (Outlook), 330
shading for cells (Excel), 175–177
Shape Styles (PowerPoint), 291–292

sheets. *See* Excel
showing paragraph markers (Word), 77
Shrink Font button, 33
single spacing. *See* line spacing (Word)
Slide Master view (PowerPoint), 273
Slide Masters (PowerPoint), 289–291
Slide Show view (PowerPoint)
  buttons in lower-right corner, 312–313
  described, 24, 272, 312
  disabling navigation methods, 315
  methods of entering, 312
  moving between slides, 312–313
Slide Sorter view (PowerPoint), 23, 272
slides (PowerPoint). *See also* PowerPoint
  animating objects on, 300–305
  automatically advancing, 306–307
  clip art for, 292–294
  creating, 273–274
  creating placeholders for, 274–275
  defined, 268
  inserting pictures, 16–18, 294–295
  layouts, changing, 278–279
  layouts, defined, 274
  manual text boxes on, 280–282
  moving placeholder boxes, 280, 291
  printing, 315–316
  resizing placeholder boxes, 279–280, 291
  Shape Styles for, 291–292
  transition effects, 305–306
  typing text in, 16, 17
sorting Excel tables, 195–197
sounds
  Clip Art feature (Word) for, 96
  soundtracks (PowerPoint), 307–309

spell checker
described, 25
for entire document, 43–44
for individual mistakes, 42–43
options, 329
red wavy underlines, 42–43, 329
splitting a column (Excel), 201–202
spoofing, 227
spreadsheets. *See* Excel
spyware, 227
Start menu, 8–9
starting. *See* opening
status bar, customizing, 326–327
styles (Excel)
for borders, 174–175
for charts, 185
styles (Word)
advantages of, 90
defined, 90
Normal, 90
paragraph, applying, 91–92
paragraph, defined, 90
Quick Styles Gallery, 91–92
style sets, changing, 92–95
themes versus, 70
Word 2003 style set, 94
SUM function (Excel), 164
switching between worksheets (Excel),
152
Symantec (Norton) Antivirus, 228

● *T* ●

tables (Excel). *See also* database (Excel)
converting cell ranges into, 193–194
defined, 191
filtering data, 197–201
merging columns, 203–206
removing filtering, 199, 201
sorting, 195–197

splitting columns, 201–202
Word tables versus, 193
tables (Word)
applying styles to, 110–111
changing cell height, 109
changing column width, 110
defined, 107
deleting row or column, 109
entering text in, 108
Excel tables versus, 193
formatting, 110–111
inserting in document, 107–108
inserting row or column in, 109
mail merge using, 124, 126
Table Tools commands for, 108–109
tabs on Ribbon, 9–12
tasks (Outlook)
creating, 247–248
deleting, 249
described, 245
reminders for, 250–251
reopening, 248
To-Do List versus, 246–247
updating status of, 249
viewing the Tasks area, 245–246
templates (Word), 71–72
text. *See also* fonts and font sizes
animation effects (PowerPoint), 301,
303
applying attributes, 36
applying colors, 34–35
AutoFit (PowerPoint), 276–278,
281–282
composing e-mail, 223–224, 330
deleting, 26
editing contact information
(Outlook), 236
editing in cells (Excel), 26–27, 143
editing in Office documents, 26–27
entering in tables (Word), 108

formatting in cells (Excel), 177–179
formatting in Office documents,
    34–36
formula differences from (Excel),
    155–156
manual text boxes on slides
    (PowerPoint), 280–282
mini toolbar commands for, 36–37
Notes feature (Outlook), 240–245
overflow in Excel, 170
selecting, 20
selection shortcuts (PowerPoint), 283
typing in documents, 15–16
text file for mail merge, 124–125
text wrap
    in cells (Excel), 171–172
    setting for pictures (Word), 101–102
themes
    applying colors to text, 35
    applying in PowerPoint, 40
    applying in Word or Excel, 38–39,
        40–41
    for chart colors (Excel), 185
    color themes, 41
    effect themes, 41
    for fill color for cells (Excel), 176, 177
    font themes, 41
    further information, 41
    no effect when applied, fixing, 40–41
    overview, 37–38
    for presentations, 286–287, 291
    previewing, 40
    Theme Fonts, 40–41
    uses for, 25, 38
    Word styles versus, 70
    for workbooks (Excel), 177
time
    delay for animation (PowerPoint), 300
    function for current (Excel), 163–164
    inserting in Word, 129–131

titles (Excel)
    avoiding for mail merge, 193
    printing, 180
TODAY function (Excel), 163–164
To-Do List (Outlook), 246–247
transition effects for slides
    (PowerPoint), 305–306
troubleshooting e-mail setup, 214–216

• U •

uninstalling search toolbars, 229
updating task status (Outlook), 249

• V •

viewers for Office documents, 58
views
    buttons for, 23
    Calendar (Outlook), 254
    for contacts (Outlook), 237–238
    described, 22
    Excel, 23
    file listing in Save As and Open
        dialog boxes, 55
    performance in Word affected by, 77
    PowerPoint, 23–24, 271–273
    Print Preview, 62, 63–64, 76
    Word, 23, 74–77
viruses, with e-mail, avoiding,
    226–229

• W •

Web Layout view (Word), 23, 76
Web versions of presentations
    (PowerPoint), 319–322
Web-based e-mail providers, 213, 214
Week view (Calendar), 254
Windows Vista or XP
    default location for saved files, 48, 50
    Office 2007 differences, 2, 8

Word. *See also* Microsoft Office,
  common features; specific features
aligning paragraphs, 78–79
applying themes, 38–39, 40–41
AutoRecover feature, 65–66
background color for page, 105–107
building blocks, 114–121
bulleted lists, 85–86
Clip Art feature, 96–100
cover pages, 119–121
default font and font size, 32
default location for files, 53, 329
envelopes, printing, 122–123
features, 70
file extension for documents, 47
Fill Effects, 106–107
first-line indent, 82
footers, 114–115, 116–119
Grow Font button, 33
hanging indent, 82
headers, 116–119
indenting paragraphs, 79–82
inserting date and time, 129–131
inserting pictures, 16–18, 100–101
line spacing settings, 82–85
Mail Merge utility, 70, 123–129
margin settings, 73–74
moving around in, 71
moving insertion point beyond end
  of document, 27
newspaper style columns, 107
numbered lists, 85, 86–88
numbering pages, 114–116
options, setting, 327–329
page borders, 102–104

page orientation, 72–73
paper size, 71, 72
printing your work, 62–63
selecting text in, 20, 71
showing/hiding paragraph markers, 77
Shrink Font button, 33
styles, 70, 90–95
tables, creating, 107–110
tables, formatting, 110–111
templates, 71–72
text wrap for pictures, 101–102
Type New List feature, 125, 126, 127
typing text in documents, 15
uses for, 69
views, changing, 23, 76–77
views, performance affected by, 77
views, uses for, 74, 76–77
views available, 23, 75–76
Word 2003 style set, 94
zooming, 22
workbooks (Excel). *See also* Excel
  default worksheets contained in, 151
  defined, 137
  switching between worksheets, 152
  tab scroll to view worksheets, 152
  themes for, 177
worksheets. *See* Excel
worms, 227

• *X* •

XPS format, 60–61

• *Z* •

zooming, 21–22